The Candlestick Trading Profit Formula

Complete Trading Manual for Expert Market Analysis, Strategic Trade Execution and Building a Profitable Trading System

David L. Carter

© 2024 David L. Carter - The Candlestick Trading Profit Formula - All rights reserved.

This document is intended exclusively for informational purposes in connection with The Candlestick Trading Profit Formula.' Any unauthorized copying, sharing, or distribution of this book, either in full or in part, is strictly forbidden. The publisher accepts no liability for any harm or loss that may arise from the application or misapplication of the information presented in this book. The content is provided 'as is,' without any guarantees or warranties, whether express or implied. All trademarks and brand names referenced herein are the property of their respective owners.

Table of Content

PART 1: FOUNDATIONS OF CANDLESTICK TRADING 7

CHAPTER 1: THE ORIGIN AND EVOLUTION OF CANDLESTICK TRADING 8
- 1.1 The Japanese Origins of Candlestick Charts 8
- 1.2 Historical Development and Modern Adoption 9
- 1.3 Why Candlesticks Have Endured in Modern Trading 10

CHAPTER 2: UNDERSTANDING CANDLESTICK ANATOMY 12
- 2.1 Basic Structure of a Candlestick 12
- 2.2 The Significance of Open, High, Low, and Close 14
- 2.3 Understanding Price Movement Through Body Size 16
- 2.4 Reading and Interpreting Shadow Length 18
- 2.5 Color Coding and Its Meaning 21

CHAPTER 3: ESSENTIAL TRADING TERMINOLOGY 22
- 3.1 Key Technical Analysis Terms 22
- 3.2 Market Structure Terminology 25
- 3.3 Order Types and Trading Mechanics 27

CHAPTER 4: CHART ANALYSIS FUNDAMENTALS 30
- 4.1 Different Types of Charts Compared 30
- 4.2 Advantages of Candlestick Charts 34
- 4.3 Time Frames and Their Impact 37
- 4.4 Reading Price Action Effectively 41
- 4.5 Identifying Market Context 43

PART 2: MASTERING CANDLESTICK PATTERNS 45

AUTOMATIC CANDLESTICK DETECTION TOOL 46

CHAPTER 5: SINGLE CANDLESTICK PATTERNS 48

- 5.1 Marubozu Patterns 48
  - Complete Marubozu 48
  - Opening and Closing Marubozu 49
- 5.2 Doji Patterns 51
  - Standard Doji 51
  - Long-Legged Doji 52
  - Dragonfly Doji 52
  - Gravestone Doji 52
- 5.3 Hammer Family 54
  - Hammer 54
  - Inverted Hammer 54
  - Hanging Man 55
  - Shooting Star 56
- 5.4 Spinning Tops and Their Significance ... 57

CHAPTER 6: DUAL CANDLESTICK PATTERNS 60
- 6.1 Engulfing Patterns 60
  - Bullish Engulfing 61
  - Bearish Engulfing 61
- 6.2 Harami Patterns 62
  - Bullish Harami 63
  - Bearish Harami 63
  - Harami Cross 64
- 6.3 Piercing Patterns 65
  - Piercing Line 65
  - Dark Cloud Cover 66
- 6.4 Tweezer Formations 67
  - Tweezer Tops 68
  - Tweezer Bottoms 68

CHAPTER 7: TRIPLE CANDLESTICK PATTERNS 70
- 7.1 Star Formations 70
  - Morning Star 70
  - Evening Star 71
  - Doji Star Variations 71
- 7.2 Soldier Patterns 72
  - Three White Soldiers 72
  - Three Black Crows 73
- 7.3 Three Methods Patterns 74
  - Rising Three Methods 74
  - Falling Three Methods 75

7.4 Abandoned Baby Patterns 76
   Bullish Abandoned Baby 76
   Bearish Abandoned Baby 77

CHAPTER 8: COMPLEX PATTERN RECOGNITION 80
8.1 Multiple Timeframe Pattern Analysis 80
8.2 Pattern Confluence 84
8.3 Pattern Failure Analysis 86
8.4 Contextual Pattern Strength 89
8.5 Volume Confirmation in Patterns 91

PART 3: CHART PATTERN ANALYSIS 93
AUTOMATED TECHNICAL ANALYSIS TOOL 94
CHAPTER 9: FUNDAMENTALS OF CHART PATTERNS 96
9.1 Introduction to Chart Patterns 96
9.2 Chart Patterns vs. Candlestick Patterns 98
9.3 The Psychology Behind Chart Patterns 100

CHAPTER 10: REVERSAL CHART PATTERNS 102
10.1 Understanding Pattern Reversals 102
10.2 Double Top and Double Bottom Patterns 104
10.3 Head and Shoulders Patterns 106
   Classic Head and Shoulders 106
   Inverse Head and Shoulders 108
10.4 Wedge Patterns 109
   Rising Wedge 109
   Falling Wedge 110
10.5 Complex Reversal Patterns 113

CHAPTER 11: CONTINUATION CHART PATTERNS 118
11.1 The Nature of Continuation Patterns . 118
11.2 Rectangle Patterns 120
   Bullish Rectangle 120
   Bearish Rectangle 121
11.3 Flag and Pennant Patterns 123
   Bullish and Bearish Flags 123
   Bullish and Bearish Pennants 124
11.4 Measuring Moves and Price Targets . 125
11.5 Failed Continuation Patterns 127

CHAPTER 12: BILATERAL CHART PATTERNS 130
12.1 Understanding Bilateral Patterns 130
12.2 Triangle Patterns 132
   Ascending Triangles 132
   Descending Triangles 133
   Symmetrical Triangles 134
12.3 Volume Analysis in Triangle Patterns . 135
12.4 Trading Triangle Breakouts 137
12.5 Managing Triangle Pattern Failures ... 140

PART 4: TECHNICAL INDICATORS AND INTEGRATION 143
CHAPTER 13: UNDERSTANDING TECHNICAL INDICATORS 144
13.1 Types of Technical Indicators 144
13.2 Leading vs. Lagging Indicators 145
13.3 Avoiding Indicator Redundancy 149
13.4 Building an Indicator Framework 151

CHAPTER 14: TREND-FOLLOWING INDICATORS 154
14.1 Moving Averages and Their Variations 154
14.2 MACD Analysis and Trading 157
14.3 ADX and Trend Strength 160
14.4 Ichimoku Cloud Analysis 162

CHAPTER 15: MOMENTUM INDICATORS . 166
15.1 Relative Strength Index (RSI) 166
15.2 Stochastic Oscillator 168

CHAPTER 16: VOLUME-BASED INDICATORS 172
16.1 On-Balance Volume (OBV) 172
16.2 Volume Price Analysis (VPA) 174
16.3 Accumulation/Distribution Line 177
16.4 Money Flow Index 179

PART 5: BUILDING YOUR TRADING SYSTEM 183
CHAPTER 17: STRATEGY DEVELOPMENT 184
17.1 Defining Your Trading Style 184
17.2 Creating Entry Rules 187

17.3 Establishing Exit Criteria.................... 190
17.4 Position Sizing Methodology 193

CHAPTER 18: RISK MANAGEMENT FRAMEWORK 196
18.1 Risk per Trade Calculation 196
18.2 Portfolio Risk Management 198
18.3 Drawdown Management.................... 201
18.4 Risk Adjustment in Volatile Markets .. 203
18.5 Position Scaling Techniques 207

CHAPTER 19: TRADE EXECUTION.......... 210
19.1 Entry Techniques.............................. 210
19.2 Exit Management............................. 212
19.3 Partial Profit Taking 214
19.4 Stop Loss Placement........................ 217
19.5 Order Types and Usage 219

PART 6: TRADING PSYCHOLOGY........... 223

CHAPTER 20: PSYCHOLOGICAL FOUNDATIONS.. 224
20.1 Understanding Trading Psychology... 224
20.2 Common Psychological Challenges .. 225
20.3 Developing Mental Resilience 227
20.4 Building Trading Confidence 229

CHAPTER 21: EMOTIONAL MANAGEMENT 233
21.1 Dealing with Fear................................233
21.2 Controlling Greed 234
21.3 Managing Trading Stress 235
21.4 Maintaining Discipline.........................236
21.5 Recovery from Losses.......................238

PART 7: PRACTICAL APPLICATION 240

CHAPTER 22: CASE STUDIES 241
22.1 Successful Trade Analysis 241
22.2 Failed Trade Analysis.........................242
22.3 Market Condition Analysis..................244
22.4 Pattern Recognition in Practice 247
22.5 Risk Management Examples..............248

CONCLUSION: THE PATH TO TRADING MASTERY... 251
Summary of Key Concepts.........................251
Creating Your Trading Plan........................252
Final Thoughts and Recommendations......255

Disclaimer

This book is intended for educational purposes only and should not be construed as financial or investment advice. Trading in financial markets carries a high level of risk and may not be suitable for all investors. The strategies, techniques, and concepts outlined in this book are based on the author's personal experiences and research, but no guarantee of profitability or success can be made.

Readers are strongly advised to conduct their own research, seek professional financial advice, and thoroughly understand the risks involved before engaging in any trading activities. Past performance is not indicative of future results, and market conditions can change rapidly.

The author and publisher disclaim any liability for losses or damages, including but not limited to monetary losses, that may arise directly or indirectly from the application of the information presented in this book. By reading this book, you agree to take full responsibility for your trading decisions and outcomes.

If you are unsure about any aspect of trading or financial markets, please consult with a qualified financial advisor or professional.

PART 1:
Foundations of Candlestick Trading

Chapter 1: The Origin and Evolution of Candlestick Trading

1.1 THE JAPANESE ORIGINS OF CANDLESTICK CHARTS

The roots of candlestick charting trace back to the 18th century, originating in Japan during the Edo period, a time of flourishing trade and commerce. These charts were first developed by a rice merchant named Munehisa Homma, who sought a systematic way to analyze the fluctuating rice prices in the markets of Sakata. Homma's innovation was more than a financial tool—it was a groundbreaking approach to understanding the psychology of buyers and sellers, a concept that remains central to modern trading.

Homma's candlestick system went beyond simple price records. It captured the **emotions of the market**—fear, greed, and indecision—through a visual representation of price movements. Each candlestick conveyed a story: the balance of power between bulls and bears and the resulting momentum in either direction. By studying these patterns, Homma could predict price trends with remarkable accuracy, giving him a competitive edge over his peers.

Imagine being able to decipher the sentiment of an entire market from a single candlestick. This is the brilliance of the system Homma developed—a technique so effective that it was adopted by Japanese traders for centuries before making its way to the Western world in the 20th century.

Today, candlestick charts are an indispensable tool for traders across all markets, from stocks to commodities and forex. But the fundamental principles remain rooted in Homma's original philosophy: understanding **price action as a reflection of human behavior**. As you delve deeper into the world of candlestick trading, you'll see how these timeless patterns can provide you with insights that go beyond numbers, giving you the clarity to make confident trading decisions.

1.2 Historical Development and Modern Adoption

After its inception in Japan, candlestick charting remained a closely guarded secret of Japanese traders for centuries. It wasn't until the late 20th century that the Western world discovered this powerful technique, thanks to the efforts of market analyst Steve Nison, who introduced candlestick charting to a global audience through his groundbreaking books and seminars. Nison's work unveiled a system that, while deeply rooted in Japanese traditions, proved universally applicable across modern financial markets.

The historical development of candlestick charting reflects its adaptability and effectiveness. Initially used to trade rice in the local markets of Sakata, the system evolved alongside Japan's growing economy, transitioning from agricultural commodities to stocks and bonds. Japanese traders refined these patterns, creating a structured methodology that could be applied to any asset class.

As global markets expanded and technology advanced, candlestick charts found their way into trading platforms worldwide. Today, they are a staple in modern charting software, seamlessly integrated into tools like MetaTrader, ThinkorSwim, and TradingView. This widespread adoption is not merely a result of their aesthetic appeal; it's their unmatched ability to provide a clear, visual representation of market sentiment that sets them apart.

In modern trading, candlestick charts serve as a universal language for interpreting price action. Whether you're analyzing a bullish engulfing pattern on a forex chart or identifying a hammer in a stock's daily timeframe, the principles remain the same. The integration of candlestick techniques with other tools like RSI, MACD, and moving averages has further enhanced their utility, allowing traders to develop strategies that are both precise and adaptive.

What makes candlestick charts enduringly relevant? They combine simplicity with depth, offering insights into market psychology that other charting methods often overlook. This blend of historical richness and modern functionality has solidified candlestick charting as an essential skill for traders of all levels.

Chapter 1:
The Origin and Evolution of Candlestick Trading

As you continue to explore the nuances of candlestick patterns, remember that you're not just learning a tool—you're mastering a system that has stood the test of time and continues to empower traders in today's fast-paced markets.

1.3 WHY CANDLESTICKS HAVE ENDURED IN MODERN TRADING

Candlestick charts have stood the test of time because they offer something unique: a concise yet detailed snapshot of market sentiment. Unlike other charting methods that focus solely on price movements, candlesticks provide a visual narrative of the ongoing battle between buyers and sellers, making it easier to interpret market psychology. This ability to blend technical precision with human behavior is why they remain indispensable for modern traders.

One of the most compelling reasons for their enduring popularity is their **clarity and versatility**. A single candlestick conveys a wealth of information, including the opening price, closing price, highs, lows, and overall price direction—all at a glance. This makes them an invaluable tool for both short-term traders seeking to capture quick profits and long-term investors analyzing broader market trends.

Candlestick patterns are also highly adaptable to various asset classes and markets. Whether you're trading equities, forex, commodities, or cryptocurrencies, the principles of candlestick analysis apply universally. This cross-market applicability has cemented their status as a go-to tool for traders worldwide.

Another factor in their lasting relevance is their compatibility with modern technical analysis. Candlestick patterns integrate seamlessly with indicators like RSI, MACD, and Bollinger Bands, enabling traders to confirm signals and build comprehensive strategies. For instance, pairing a bullish engulfing pattern with a positive RSI divergence can significantly enhance the accuracy of your trades.

Moreover, candlestick charts excel at highlighting **context**. They help traders identify not just price movements, but the emotional undercurrents driving those movements. For example:

- A **long shadow** on a candlestick might indicate indecision, warning traders to proceed cautiously.
- A **strong-bodied candle** could signal decisive momentum, offering a clear entry or exit point.

Their intuitive design and adaptability to both manual and algorithmic trading also ensure their place in modern financial markets. Even with the rise of AI-driven trading systems, candlestick patterns remain a cornerstone of algorithmic strategies, highlighting their continued relevance in a rapidly evolving industry.

Ultimately, candlesticks endure because they simplify complexity. They take the chaos of market data and transform it into actionable insights, empowering traders to make informed decisions with confidence. As you integrate candlestick patterns into your own trading, you'll discover their unparalleled ability to provide clarity, precision, and an edge in any market condition.

Chapter 2: Understanding Candlestick Anatomy

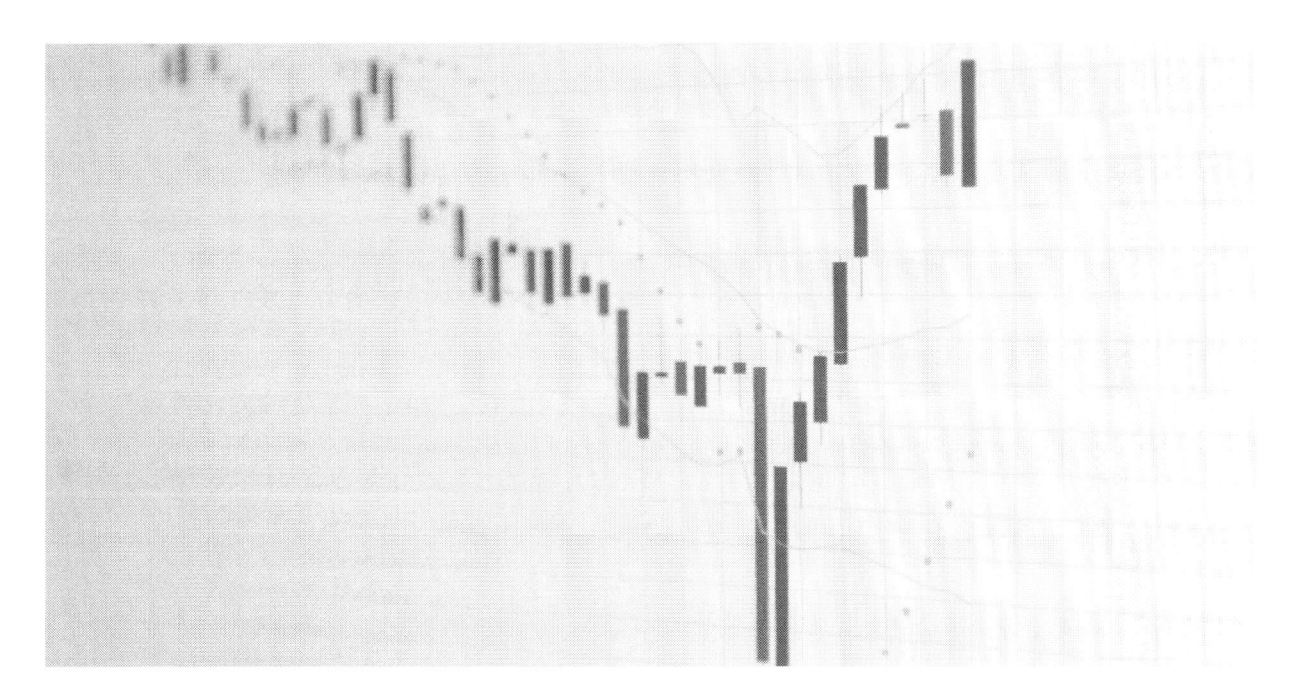

2.1 Basic Structure of a Candlestick

At its core, a candlestick is a simple yet powerful tool that visually represents the price movements of an asset over a specific period. Unlike other charting methods, such as line or bar charts, candlesticks provide a richer and more detailed perspective of market behavior, offering insights that are both intuitive and actionable.

Each candlestick is composed of three key elements:

1. **The Body:** The rectangular area between the opening and closing prices.
2. **The Upper Shadow:** A thin vertical line extending from the top of the body to the highest price reached during the time frame.

3. **The Lower Shadow:** A similar line that stretches from the bottom of the body to the lowest price during the same period.

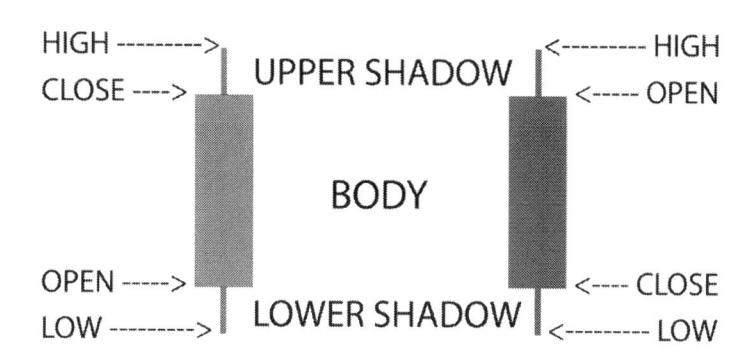

```
HIGH --------->          <--------- HIGH
                UPPER SHADOW
CLOSE ---->  ▓           ▓  <----- OPEN
             ▓           ▓
             ▓   BODY    ▓
             ▓           ▓
OPEN ----->  ▓           ▓  <---- CLOSE
                LOWER SHADOW
LOW --------->           <--------- LOW
```

These elements come together to form a complete picture of market activity. For instance, a **long body** indicates strong momentum, while **short shadows** suggest minimal price fluctuation outside the open and close. Conversely, a candlestick with a small body and long shadows might signal indecision or market hesitation.

The structure of a candlestick also helps traders quickly distinguish between bullish and bearish market conditions.

- **Bullish Candlestick:** Indicates that the closing price is higher than the opening price, signaling buying strength.

- **Bearish Candlestick:** Occurs when the closing price is lower than the opening price, reflecting selling pressure.

By analyzing the body and shadows, traders can determine who held control during a specific period—the buyers or the sellers—and how decisively. For example, a candlestick with a **long upper shadow** but a small body suggests that buyers initially pushed the price higher, only to be overwhelmed by selling pressure before the close. This insight is invaluable for identifying potential reversals or continuations in price trends.

The elegance of the candlestick lies in its ability to convey so much information in a single, compact shape. Mastering its basic structure is the first step toward unlocking its full potential as a tool for understanding price action and market sentiment.

Chapter 2:
Understanding Candlestick Anatomy

2.2 THE SIGNIFICANCE OF OPEN, HIGH, LOW, AND CLOSE

The four critical data points in a candlestick—**Open**, **High**, **Low**, and **Close**—are the foundation of candlestick analysis. Together, these values encapsulate a complete story of market behavior for a specific time frame, whether it's a minute, an hour, a day, or longer. Understanding the role of each data point is crucial to interpreting candlestick patterns and identifying trading opportunities.

1. Open: Setting the Stage

The **opening price** represents where trading began for the chosen period. It sets the initial sentiment:

- A high opening price suggests bullish enthusiasm as buyers dominate early on.
- A low opening price indicates bearish sentiment, with sellers controlling the narrative at the outset.

The opening price serves as a benchmark for comparing subsequent price movements, helping traders gauge whether the market has maintained or reversed its initial direction.

2. High: Testing Resistance

The **highest price** reached during the time frame reveals the upper boundary of price action, often reflecting market exuberance or resistance.

- A long upper shadow indicates that buyers pushed prices upward but failed to sustain those levels, signaling potential selling pressure or resistance at higher levels.
- A high without a significant upper shadow may suggest strong bullish momentum.

Identifying the high is especially useful for placing **stop-loss levels** above resistance or confirming bullish breakouts when the high surpasses a key level.

3. Low: Testing Support

The **lowest price** during the period marks the level of maximum downward pressure, often driven by aggressive selling or bearish sentiment.

- A long lower shadow can signal that sellers attempted to push prices lower but were countered by strong buying interest.
- A low price without significant recovery may indicate sustained bearish pressure.

This data point is instrumental in identifying **support levels** where buying interest could emerge or in setting **stop-loss orders** below key support levels.

4. Close: The Final Word

The **closing price** is arguably the most critical component of a candlestick because it reflects the final sentiment and momentum as the time frame concludes.

- A close above the opening price creates a bullish candlestick, signifying that buyers maintained control.

- A close below the opening price forms a bearish candlestick, suggesting that sellers prevailed.

The close often determines the overall strength of the candlestick pattern. For example:
- A close near the high signals robust buying momentum.
- A close near the low indicates strong selling pressure.

Why These Values Matter

The interplay of these four data points defines the candlestick's body and shadows, providing traders with actionable insights:

- **Large Price Ranges:** A wide gap between the high and low suggests volatility, often presenting trading opportunities or risks.
- **Small Price Ranges:** A narrow range indicates consolidation or indecision, which may precede a breakout.
- **Relative Closeness of Open and Close:** Determines the strength of the candlestick (e.g., long-bodied candles show decisiveness, while small-bodied candles like doji indicate indecision).

Practical Application

By analyzing the open, high, low, and close together, you can:

- Identify key **support and resistance levels**.
- Determine the **strength of market participants** (buyers or sellers).
- Confirm trends or anticipate **potential reversals**.

For instance, a candlestick with a low close near its low suggests bearish dominance, possibly signaling a continuation of a downtrend. Conversely, a candlestick with a high close near its high after a long lower shadow indicates strong bullish recovery, potentially marking the start of an uptrend.

Mastering these data points allows traders to interpret the nuances of market behavior, empowering them to make informed and confident decisions.

Chapter 2:
Understanding Candlestick Anatomy

2.3 UNDERSTANDING PRICE MOVEMENT THROUGH BODY SIZE

The size of a candlestick's body—the area between its opening and closing prices—offers vital clues about market sentiment and the strength of price movements. By interpreting the body size, traders can gauge the level of control exerted by buyers or sellers during a specific period, providing a foundation for informed decision-making.

The Role of Body Size in Candlestick Analysis

1. **Long Bodies: Decisive Momentum**

   A long candlestick body indicates that there was a significant price movement between the open and close, reflecting strong momentum in one direction.

   o **Bullish Long Body:** A large green (or white) body signifies that buyers dominated, driving the price up decisively. This often suggests strong bullish sentiment and the potential for continued upward momentum.

   o **Bearish Long Body:** A large red (or black) body reveals that sellers had control, pushing the price down sharply. This can indicate strong bearish sentiment and may foreshadow further downward movement.

Bullish   Bearish

Example: In an uptrend, a bullish long body near resistance might signal a breakout. Conversely, in a downtrend, a bearish long body can confirm the continuation of selling pressure.

2. **Small Bodies: Indecision or Consolidation**

   A small body occurs when the opening and closing prices are close together, indicating minimal price movement and a balance between buyers and sellers.

   o   This is often a sign of **market indecision** and can precede a significant price move in either direction.

   o   When paired with long shadows, small-bodied candlesticks (like doji) can signal potential reversals, especially near key support or resistance levels.

Example: A small body following a series of long bullish bodies may indicate that the uptrend is losing momentum and that a reversal or consolidation is possible.

How to Interpret Body Size in Context

The significance of a candlestick's body size is amplified when considered in the context of the broader market trend and the surrounding candlesticks:

- **In an Uptrend:** Long bullish bodies confirm the strength of the trend, while small bodies may indicate slowing momentum or a pause.
- **In a Downtrend:** Long bearish bodies reinforce the continuation of the trend, while small bodies can suggest hesitation or potential support.
- **In Consolidation Zones:** A series of small bodies indicates a tight trading range, which may lead to a breakout once momentum picks up.

Practical Implications for Traders

Understanding body size helps traders identify opportunities and manage risks:

- **Entering Trades:** A long bullish body breaking above a resistance level can signal a strong buy opportunity. Conversely, a long bearish body breaking below support might indicate a sell signal.
- **Exiting Trades:** Small-bodied candles following a long trend suggest a potential reversal, signaling traders to lock in profits or tighten stop-loss levels.
- **Avoiding False Signals:** Candlesticks with small bodies in volatile conditions may lead to choppy price action, so it's critical to confirm signals with other indicators or candlestick patterns.

Combining Body Size with Shadows

The relationship between the candlestick's body and its shadows can provide even deeper insights into market sentiment.

- **Long Body, Short Shadows:** Indicates decisive control by either buyers or sellers, with little opposition.
- **Short Body, Long Shadows:** Reflects significant pushback or indecision, with both buyers and sellers attempting to assert control.

By mastering the nuances of candlestick body size, you'll be better equipped to decode market sentiment and make precise trading decisions.

Chapter 2:
Understanding Candlestick Anatomy

2.4 READING AND INTERPRETING SHADOW LENGTH

The shadows, or "wicks," of a candlestick represent the highest and lowest prices reached during a specific time frame. While the body of the candlestick conveys the opening and closing prices, the shadows provide essential context about price volatility, market sentiment, and potential reversals. Interpreting shadow length is a critical skill for understanding the dynamics of buyer and seller interaction.

The Role of Shadows in Candlestick Analysis

1. **The Upper Shadow: Indicating Resistance or Exhaustion**

    The upper shadow extends from the top of the candlestick body to the highest price reached during the session.

    - A **long upper shadow** often suggests that buyers pushed prices higher but were eventually overwhelmed by selling pressure, causing the price to retreat before the close. This can indicate resistance or weakening bullish momentum.
    - A **short upper shadow** implies that buyers maintained control throughout the session, signaling strong bullish sentiment.

Example:

- In an uptrend, a candlestick with a long upper shadow near a resistance level may signal that the upward momentum is fading.
- During consolidation, a long upper shadow might hint at failed breakout attempts.

2. **The Lower Shadow: Indicating Support or Rejection**

    The lower shadow stretches from the bottom of the body to the lowest price reached during the session.

    - A **long lower shadow** suggests that sellers drove the price down but were met with strong buying interest, causing the price to recover before the close. This can indicate support or rejection of lower prices.
    - A **short lower shadow** indicates that sellers had little impact during the session, reflecting strong bearish control.

Example:

- In a downtrend, a long lower shadow near a support level may signal a potential reversal as buyers defend the price.
- After a significant sell-off, a long lower shadow can suggest that selling pressure is weakening.

Key Shadow Patterns and Their Implications

1. **Long Upper Shadow + Short Lower Shadow:**

    This configuration often indicates bearish pressure and potential resistance.

    - **Practical Use:** Look for confirmation of reversal patterns or resistance zones before taking action.

2. **Long Lower Shadow + Short Upper Shadow:**

    Suggests bullish rejection of lower prices and potential support.

    - **Practical Use:** Use these signals near support levels to anticipate a rebound or reversal.

3. **Long Shadows on Both Ends:**

    Reflects significant indecision and volatility, with buyers and sellers struggling for control. Often appears in doji patterns.

    - **Practical Use:** Avoid trading based on these candlesticks alone; wait for confirmation from subsequent candles.

4. **Short Shadows on Both Ends:**

    Indicates decisive momentum with minimal price fluctuation outside the open and close.

    - **Practical Use:** These candlesticks confirm strong trends and may signal continuation.

Shadow Length in Context

The significance of shadow length varies depending on its placement in the market structure:

- **In an Uptrend:**
    - Long upper shadows may signal resistance and caution for continued buying.
    - Long lower shadows suggest strong buying interest and potential continuation.
- **In a Downtrend:**
    - Long lower shadows may indicate support and a possible reversal.
    - Long upper shadows confirm continued selling pressure.

By observing shadows alongside candlestick bodies, you can better interpret the interplay of market forces, gaining a clearer understanding of whether buyers or sellers have the upper hand.

Chapter 2:
Understanding Candlestick Anatomy

Practical Applications for Traders

1. **Spotting Reversals:**
    - A long upper shadow after a series of bullish candlesticks may signal a reversal to the downside.
    - A long lower shadow after a bearish trend can indicate a bullish reversal.

2. **Confirming Support and Resistance:**
    - Long shadows at key levels often confirm their significance as areas of strong support or resistance.

3. **Avoiding False Breakouts:**
    - Candlesticks with long shadows but small bodies near breakout levels may suggest fake moves and signal caution.

2.5 COLOR CODING AND ITS MEANING

Color coding is one of the most intuitive and impactful features of candlestick charts. By using distinct colors to differentiate between bullish and bearish movements, candlestick charts provide a quick visual representation of market sentiment. This color distinction helps traders immediately grasp whether the price moved up or down within a specific time frame.

Bullish vs. Bearish Candlesticks

- **Bullish Candlesticks:** Typically represented by a green or white body, a bullish candlestick shows that the closing price is higher than the opening price. This indicates buying momentum and is often associated with rising markets or potential upward trends.

- **Bearish Candlesticks:** Usually displayed with a red or black body, a bearish candlestick reveals that the closing price is lower than the opening price. This suggests selling pressure and is commonly linked to declining markets or downward momentum.

The contrast between bullish and bearish colors provides immediate context. For example, a series of consecutive green candlesticks signals a strong uptrend, while a cluster of red candlesticks indicates sustained selling pressure.

Color Intensity and Its Implications

Some charting platforms offer variations in color intensity to represent changes in volume or momentum. For instance:

- **Lighter Green or Red Candles:** May indicate lower trading volume or weaker price momentum during the period.

- **Darker Green or Red Candles:** Suggest stronger volume or higher conviction behind the price movement.

These subtle visual cues can help traders assess the strength of a trend without needing additional indicators.

Color Coding for Shadows

While the body of the candlestick is the primary focus, shadows may also reflect the candlestick's color on certain platforms. For example:

- **Green Shadow:** Suggests bullish activity during the period, even if the candlestick itself closes bearish.

- **Red Shadow:** Reflects bearish activity, even if the candlestick closes bullish.

These details offer deeper insights into intraperiod price behavior, helping traders understand market dynamics more comprehensively.

Chapter 3: Essential Trading Terminology

3.1 KEY TECHNICAL ANALYSIS TERMS

Technical analysis is the backbone of effective trading, providing traders with the tools to interpret market data and predict potential price movements. Understanding key technical analysis terms is essential for navigating charts, identifying opportunities, and making informed decisions. In this section, we'll break down some of the most important concepts, ensuring you have the foundation to apply them confidently in your trading.

Support and Resistance

Support refers to a price level where demand is strong enough to prevent the price from falling further. Resistance, on the other hand, is a level where selling pressure prevents the price from rising. These levels act as psychological barriers, often reflecting the collective sentiment of buyers and sellers.

- *Example:* If a stock repeatedly bounces off $100, that price is considered support. Conversely, if it struggles to break above $120, that level is resistance.
- *Application:* Use support and resistance levels to set entry and exit points, manage risk, and identify breakout opportunities.

Trend

A trend represents the overall direction in which a market or asset is moving. Trends are categorized as:

- **Uptrend:** Higher highs and higher lows, indicating bullish momentum.
- **Downtrend:** Lower highs and lower lows, reflecting bearish sentiment.
- **Sideways (or Range-bound):** Price oscillates within a defined range, signaling market indecision.
- *Application:* Recognizing trends helps you align your trades with market momentum, a strategy often summarized as "trade with the trend."

Breakout

A breakout occurs when the price moves beyond a significant support, resistance, or trendline level, often accompanied by increased volume. This signals a potential shift in market sentiment.

- *Example:* A stock breaking above a resistance level of $120 with high volume may indicate the start of a strong upward trend.
- *Application:* Use breakouts to identify high-probability entry points for trend-following strategies.

Volume

Volume measures the number of shares or contracts traded during a specific period. It acts as a confirmation tool, validating price movements.

- *High Volume:* Indicates strong market interest and often confirms the strength of a price move.
- *Low Volume:* Suggests weaker interest and may lead to false signals.
- *Application:* Pair volume analysis with candlestick patterns or chart breakouts to increase the reliability of your trades.

Moving Average

A moving average smooths out price data to identify trends by calculating the average price over a set number of periods.

- **Simple Moving Average (SMA):** A straightforward average of closing prices over a specific period.
- **Exponential Moving Average (EMA):** Places greater weight on recent prices, making it more responsive to new data.
- *Application:* Use moving averages to identify trend direction or as dynamic support and resistance levels.

Chapter 3:
Essential Trading Terminology

Relative Strength Index (RSI)

RSI is a momentum oscillator that measures the speed and change of price movements on a scale of 0 to 100.

- **Overbought Levels (70+):** Indicates that the asset may be overvalued and due for a pullback.
- **Oversold Levels (30 or below):** Suggests that the asset may be undervalued and ready for a rebound.
- *Application:* Combine RSI signals with candlestick patterns to refine entry and exit points.

Fibonacci Retracement

Fibonacci retracement levels are horizontal lines that indicate potential support and resistance levels based on key Fibonacci ratios (e.g., 38.2%, 50%, 61.8%).

- *Application:* Use these levels to identify where price corrections might reverse during trending markets.

Candlestick Patterns

Candlestick patterns, such as hammers, engulfing patterns, and doji, are visual representations of market psychology and price action. These patterns offer clues about potential reversals, continuations, or indecision in the market.

- *Example:* A hammer at a support level often signals a bullish reversal.
- *Application:* Combine candlestick patterns with other technical tools like RSI or moving averages for a well-rounded analysis.

Consolidation

Consolidation occurs when the price moves within a narrow range, indicating a pause in the prevailing trend. It often precedes a breakout.

- *Application:* Watch for consolidation near support or resistance levels to anticipate potential breakouts or reversals.

Divergence

Divergence happens when the price of an asset moves in the opposite direction of an indicator, such as RSI or MACD.

- **Bullish Divergence:** Price makes lower lows, but the indicator makes higher lows, suggesting a potential upward reversal.
- **Bearish Divergence:** Price makes higher highs, but the indicator makes lower highs, indicating a potential downward reversal.
- *Application:* Use divergence to spot weakening trends and prepare for potential reversals.

By mastering these key technical analysis terms, you'll build a strong foundation for interpreting market data and crafting effective trading strategies. As you explore charts and patterns, remember that each of these concepts works best when used in combination with others, creating a holistic view of the market. Start applying these terms to your analysis today and watch your confidence as a trader grow exponentially.

3.2 MARKET STRUCTURE TERMINOLOGY

Understanding market structure is fundamental to successful trading. It provides the framework for interpreting price movements and identifying opportunities. By familiarizing yourself with key market structure terminology, you'll gain the tools to navigate trends, reversals, and consolidations effectively. This section will define the essential terms you need to decode market behavior and align your trades with the broader context.

Trend

A trend refers to the general direction in which the market or a specific asset is moving.

- **Uptrend:** Characterized by higher highs and higher lows, signaling bullish momentum.
- **Downtrend:** Defined by lower highs and lower lows, reflecting bearish momentum.
- **Sideways Trend (Range):** The price oscillates between consistent support and resistance levels without a clear directional bias.
- *Practical Use:* Identifying the trend helps you align your trades with market momentum, often summarized as "the trend is your friend."

Support and Resistance

These are foundational concepts that represent levels where the price historically reverses or pauses.

- **Support:** A level where buying interest is strong enough to prevent the price from falling further.
- **Resistance:** A level where selling pressure prevents the price from rising.
- *Practical Use:* Use support and resistance levels to determine entry and exit points or anticipate breakouts.

Breakout

A breakout occurs when the price moves beyond a key support, resistance, or trendline level, often accompanied by increased volume.

- **Upward Breakout:** Indicates bullish momentum and potential trend continuation.
- **Downward Breakout:** Signals bearish momentum or a potential downtrend.
- *Practical Use:* Monitor breakouts to identify high-probability trading opportunities, especially when confirmed by volume.

Chapter 3:
Essential Trading Terminology

Pullback and Retracement

These terms describe temporary reversals against the prevailing trend.

- **Pullback:** A short-term price movement counter to the primary trend, often offering opportunities to enter at a better price.
- **Retracement:** A deeper correction within the trend, typically measured using Fibonacci levels (e.g., 38.2%, 50%, 61.8%).
- *Practical Use:* Use pullbacks to buy during uptrends or sell during downtrends while staying aligned with the overall trend.

Swing High and Swing Low

- **Swing High:** The highest point reached before the price starts to decline.
- **Swing Low:** The lowest point reached before the price starts to rise.
- *Practical Use:* Swing highs and lows are critical for identifying trends and setting support/resistance levels.

Range and Consolidation

Range-bound markets occur when the price moves sideways between defined support and resistance levels. Consolidation refers to a temporary pause in price movement, often preceding a breakout.

- *Practical Use:* Recognize ranges to anticipate breakouts or to trade within the defined boundaries.

Trendlines

Trendlines are diagonal lines drawn on a chart to connect consecutive highs or lows, indicating the direction of the trend.

- **Uptrend Line:** Drawn by connecting higher lows, acting as dynamic support.
- **Downtrend Line:** Drawn by connecting lower highs, serving as dynamic resistance.
- *Practical Use:* Trendlines help identify potential reversal or continuation points and provide visual confirmation of the trend.

Channels

Channels are formed by parallel trendlines that encapsulate price movement.

- **Ascending Channel:** A bullish structure with higher highs and higher lows.
- **Descending Channel:** A bearish structure with lower highs and lower lows.
- **Horizontal Channel:** A neutral structure, indicating range-bound trading.
- *Practical Use:* Use channels to trade within the bounds or anticipate a breakout.

Market Cycles

Markets move through distinct phases that repeat over time. These include:

- **Accumulation:** Price consolidates at a low level as buyers gradually enter the market.
- **Advancement (Markup):** The price rises as buying pressure increases.
- **Distribution:** The price consolidates at a high level as sellers prepare to exit.
- **Decline (Markdown):** The price falls as selling pressure dominates.
- *Practical Use:* Identifying the current market phase helps you align your strategy with the dominant forces.

Gap

A gap occurs when the price opens significantly higher or lower than the previous closing price, creating a space on the chart.

- **Breakaway Gap:** Signals the start of a new trend.
- **Continuation Gap:** Occurs within a trend, confirming its strength.
- **Exhaustion Gap:** Appears near the end of a trend, signaling potential reversal.
- *Practical Use:* Gaps often act as support or resistance levels and can indicate strong market sentiment.

Order Flow

Order flow refers to the activity of buyers and sellers in the market, as reflected in bid/ask prices and volume.

- *Practical Use:* Monitoring order flow can help you identify where institutional traders are placing their orders, providing an edge in timing your trades.

By mastering market structure terminology, you'll gain a deeper understanding of price action and be better equipped to anticipate market movements. Each of these terms offers unique insights into the market's behavior, and applying them in combination with candlestick patterns will elevate your trading to a new level.

3.3 ORDER TYPES AND TRADING MECHANICS

Understanding order types and how they function is a critical step in mastering the mechanics of trading. Order types dictate how and when your trades are executed, allowing you to implement strategies effectively while managing risk. Whether you're entering a position, locking in profits, or mitigating losses, selecting the appropriate order type is essential for executing your trading plan with precision.

Chapter 3:
Essential Trading Terminology

Market Order

A market order executes your trade immediately at the best available price.

- **Advantages:** Fast execution ensures you enter or exit the trade without delay, making it ideal in fast-moving markets.
- **Drawbacks:** Price slippage may occur in volatile conditions, meaning you could pay more or sell for less than anticipated.
- *Practical Use:* Use market orders when speed is more important than price, such as during breakouts or to exit a losing position quickly.

Limit Order

A limit order allows you to specify the exact price at which you're willing to buy or sell.

- **Buy Limit:** Sets a maximum price for buying, ensuring you don't pay more than your target price.
- **Sell Limit:** Sets a minimum price for selling, ensuring you don't sell below your target price.
- *Practical Use:* Use limit orders to buy at support levels or sell at resistance, ensuring better control over execution price.

Stop Order (Stop-Loss Order)

A stop order becomes a market order once a specified price (the stop price) is reached.

- **Buy Stop:** Triggers a purchase above the current market price, often used to enter positions in momentum-driven markets.
- **Sell Stop:** Triggers a sale below the current market price, commonly used to minimize losses in a long position.
- *Practical Use:* Protect your trades by setting stop-loss orders to limit potential losses in volatile markets.

Stop-Limit Order

A stop-limit order combines the features of stop and limit orders. Once the stop price is reached, a limit order is triggered.

- **Advantages:** Provides control over both the activation price (stop) and execution price (limit).
- **Drawbacks:** If the price moves quickly past your limit, the order may not be executed, leaving your position unprotected.
- *Practical Use:* Use stop-limit orders when precision is required, such as during periods of high volatility.

Trailing Stop Order

A trailing stop dynamically adjusts the stop price as the market moves in your favor, locking in profits while allowing the position to remain open.

- **Advantages:** Automatically protects gains without requiring manual adjustment.
- **Drawbacks:** May close your position prematurely if the market experiences temporary pullbacks.
- *Practical Use:* Ideal for capturing profits in trending markets while safeguarding against sudden reversals.

Good-'Til-Canceled (GTC) vs. Day Orders

- **GTC Order:** Remains active until it's executed or manually canceled. Useful for trades requiring patience, such as those tied to long-term support or resistance levels.
- **Day Order:** Expires if not executed by the end of the trading day. Commonly used for short-term trades.
- *Practical Use:* Choose the appropriate order duration based on your trading time frame and strategy.

Filling and Partial Fills

- **Full Fill:** When your entire order is executed at the desired price or better.
- **Partial Fill:** When only part of your order is executed due to limited market liquidity.
- *Practical Use:* Monitor partial fills in low-volume assets, which can affect the timing and execution of your strategy.

Order Execution in Different Market Conditions

- **High-Volatility Markets:** Use stop orders or market orders for faster execution, but be prepared for slippage.
- **Low-Volatility Markets:** Limit orders are more effective for precision and avoiding slippage.
- *Practical Tip:* Always consider market conditions when selecting an order type to avoid unexpected outcomes.

How to Incorporate Order Types into Your Strategy

- Combine **limit orders** with technical analysis to place entries near support or resistance.
- Use **stop-loss orders** to define your risk level before entering a trade.
- Employ **trailing stops** in trending markets to maximize profits while minimizing the risk of losing gains.
- Adjust your order type based on the asset's liquidity and volatility to ensure smooth execution.

Chapter 4: Chart Analysis Fundamentals

4.1 Different Types of Charts Compared

Understanding the different types of charts available for market analysis is essential for making informed trading decisions. Each chart type offers unique perspectives on price movements, catering to various trading styles and strategies. By comparing their features, strengths, and limitations, you can determine which chart type aligns best with your objectives and trading approach.

1. Line Charts

Line charts are the simplest type of chart, connecting closing prices over a specified period with a continuous line. They provide a clear view of the overall trend without the distractions of intraday price fluctuations.

- **Strengths:** Ideal for identifying long-term trends and major price movements. Simple to interpret, making them suitable for beginners or when a high-level overview is required.

- **Limitations:** Lack of detail on opening, high, and low prices. This simplicity can obscure important market activity.

- *Practical Use:* Use line charts to gain a quick sense of the overall trend or compare performance across assets.

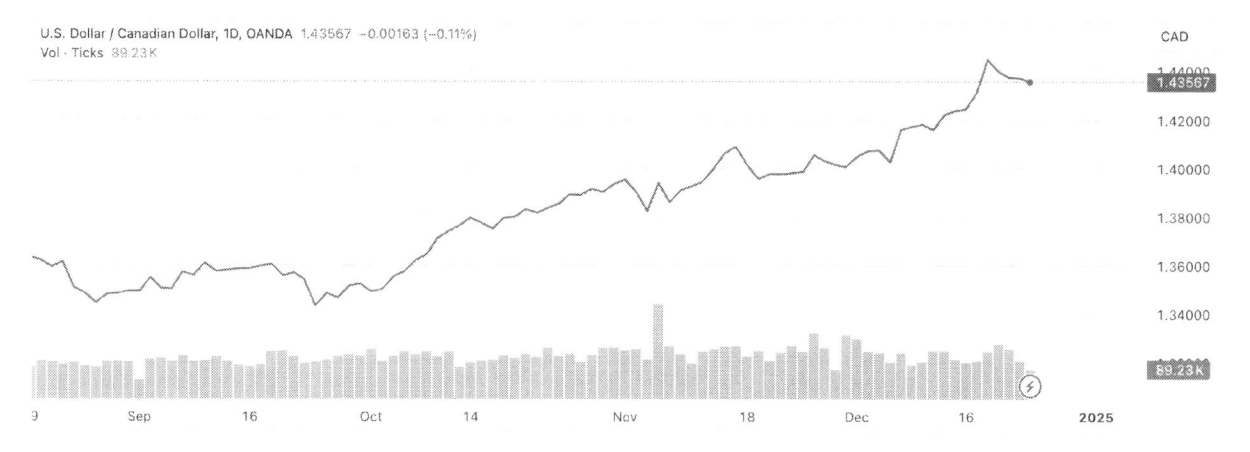

2. Bar Charts

Bar charts offer more information than line charts, displaying the open, high, low, and close (OHLC) for each period. A vertical line represents the price range, while horizontal ticks on the left and right sides mark the opening and closing prices, respectively.

- **Strengths:** Provides a more comprehensive view of price action within each period, allowing for better analysis of volatility and momentum.

- **Limitations:** Can be visually cluttered, especially when analyzing short time frames or multiple assets.

- *Practical Use:* Suitable for traders who need more detail on intraday price movements while maintaining a clear chart layout.

Chapter 4:
Chart Analysis Fundamentals

3. Candlestick Charts

Candlestick charts, as discussed throughout this book, are the most visually intuitive and widely used chart type. Each candlestick represents the open, high, low, and close prices for a given period, with the body and shadows providing additional insights into market sentiment.

- **Strengths:** Combines detailed information with visual clarity. The color-coded bodies and shadows make it easy to identify patterns, trends, and market psychology.
- **Limitations:** Requires familiarity with candlestick patterns and terminology to fully leverage its advantages.
- *Practical Use:* Ideal for traders seeking to interpret price action, identify patterns, and analyze market sentiment with precision.

4. Renko Charts

Renko charts focus exclusively on price movements, ignoring time and volume. They are composed of bricks, which change direction only when the price moves by a predetermined amount.

- **Strengths:** Removes noise caused by minor price fluctuations, making it easier to spot trends and reversals.
- **Limitations:** Ignores time, which can make it difficult to assess the pace of market activity. Not suitable for analyzing intraday price movements.
- *Practical Use:* Best for identifying long-term trends and significant price moves without distractions.

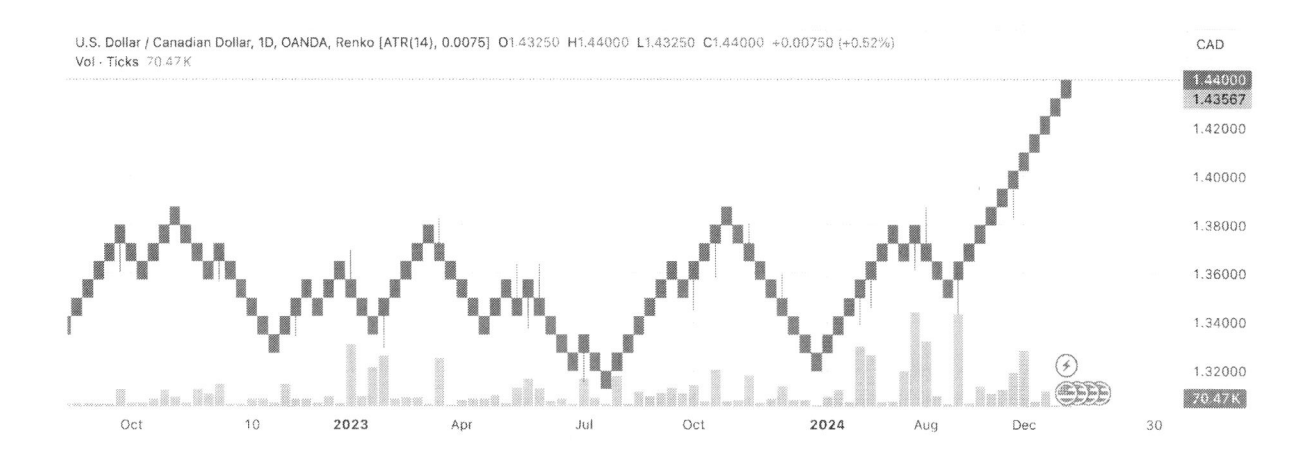

5. Heikin-Ashi Charts

Heikin-Ashi charts use modified candlesticks to smooth out price action, creating a clearer picture of trends by averaging data points.

- **Strengths:** Excellent for visualizing trends and reducing the impact of market noise. Helps identify when to stay in a trade or exit during trend reversals.
- **Limitations:** Lagging in nature due to its averaging formula, which can obscure precise entry and exit points.
- *Practical Use:* Perfect for swing traders and trend followers who prioritize clarity over granular details.

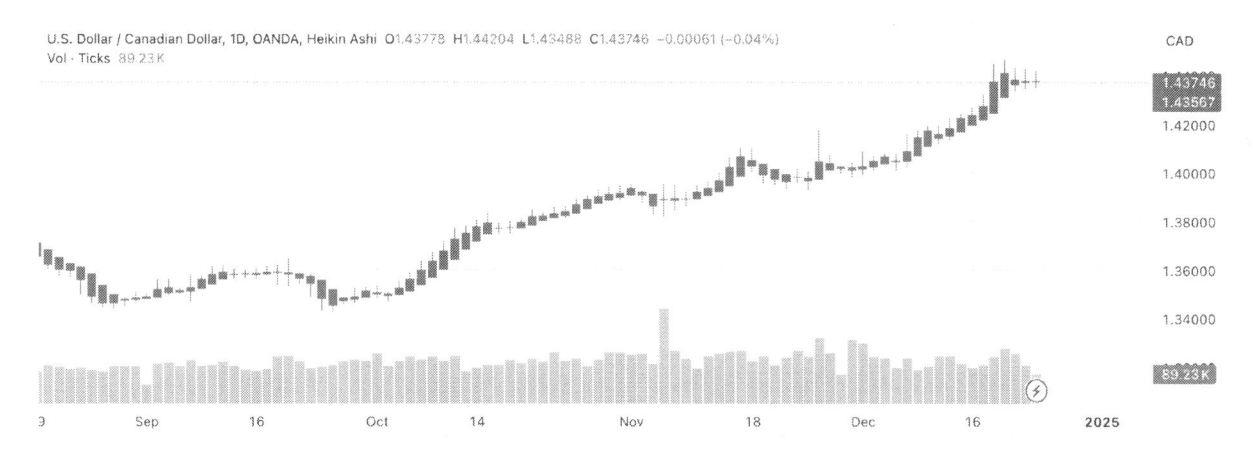

6. Point and Figure Charts

Point and figure charts focus on price changes without considering time, using columns of X's and O's to represent rising and falling prices, respectively.

- **Strengths:** Highlights significant price movements and filters out insignificant price action. Useful for identifying support and resistance levels.

Chapter 4:
Chart Analysis Fundamentals

- **Limitations:** Ignores time and volume, making it unsuitable for time-sensitive trading strategies.
- *Practical Use:* Use to identify breakouts, reversals, and long-term price targets.

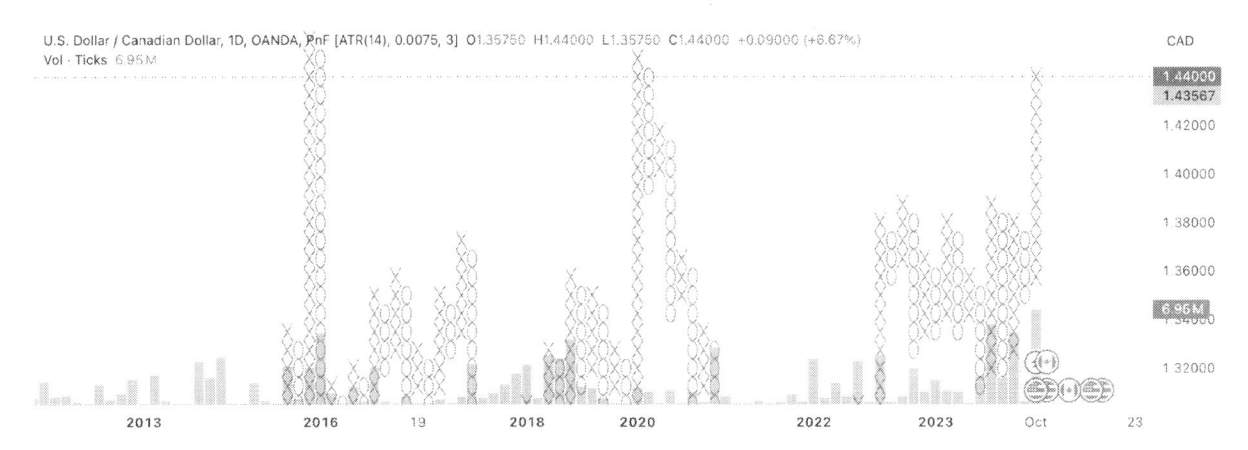

By comparing these chart types, it becomes clear that each serves a specific purpose depending on the trader's goals, time frame, and need for detail. While line charts provide a broad overview, candlestick charts excel in their ability to convey market sentiment and price action with unmatched clarity. As you continue to refine your trading strategies, you'll find that choosing the right chart type—or combining multiple types—can enhance your ability to interpret market data and make confident trading decisions. Candlestick charts, in particular, stand out for their versatility and depth, which is why they form the foundation of this book.

4.2 ADVANTAGES OF CANDLESTICK CHARTS

Candlestick charts are one of the most widely used tools in technical analysis, renowned for their ability to combine simplicity with depth. Their visual appeal and the wealth of information they convey make them indispensable for traders at all skill levels. Understanding the advantages of candlestick charts will help you appreciate why they are the foundation of effective market analysis.

1. Clarity and Visual Intuition

One of the greatest strengths of candlestick charts is their ability to present complex market data in a visually intuitive way. Each candlestick represents the open, high, low, and close prices for a specific period, all encapsulated in a single, easy-to-read shape. The color-coded bodies—typically green for bullish and red for bearish—make it simple to identify whether the market is trending upward or downward at a glance.

Example: A series of green candlesticks with long bodies and short shadows instantly signals strong bullish momentum without requiring further interpretation.

2. Insights into Market Psychology

Candlestick charts go beyond numbers to reveal the emotional dynamics of the market. The relationship between the candlestick's body and shadows tells a story of buyer and seller activity, enabling traders to gauge market sentiment.

- **Long Shadows:** Indicate indecision or rejection of price levels.
- **Strong Bodies:** Reflect decisive market action, signaling clear buyer or seller dominance.
  Example: A doji candlestick, where the open and close prices are nearly identical, highlights market indecision and often precedes significant price moves.

3. Versatility Across Markets and Time Frames

Candlestick charts are not limited to specific markets or time frames. They work equally well for analyzing stocks, forex, commodities, cryptocurrencies, and more. Whether you're trading on a 1-minute chart or a monthly time frame, the principles of candlestick analysis remain consistent, making them a universal tool for all traders.

Practical Application: Use short time frames for day trading and longer time frames for swing or position trading, all with the same candlestick techniques.

4. Early Identification of Trends and Reversals

Candlestick patterns are powerful tools for spotting the beginning of new trends or the reversal of existing ones. Patterns such as the **morning star** or **engulfing pattern** provide early warning signals of changing market dynamics, allowing traders to enter positions with confidence.
Example: A hammer candlestick at the bottom of a downtrend often indicates that selling pressure is waning, signaling a potential reversal to the upside.

5. Seamless Integration with Technical Indicators

Candlestick charts complement other technical analysis tools like moving averages, RSI, and MACD. Combining candlestick patterns with these indicators allows traders to confirm signals and improve the accuracy of their analysis.

Example: A bullish engulfing pattern confirmed by an oversold RSI provides a higher-probability buy signal than either tool used alone.

6. Applicability to All Trading Strategies

Candlestick charts support a wide range of trading strategies, from scalping to swing trading and long-term investing.

- **Scalpers:** Can use candlestick patterns on 1-minute or 5-minute charts to spot intraday reversals or breakouts.
- **Swing Traders:** Analyze daily or weekly candlestick patterns to identify key support and resistance levels.
- **Investors:** Use monthly candlestick charts to understand long-term trends and turning points.

Chapter 4:
Chart Analysis Fundamentals

7. Quick Identification of Key Market Levels

The structure of candlesticks makes it easy to identify crucial support and resistance levels, trendlines, and breakouts. The high and low points of candlesticks naturally align with key levels, simplifying the process of charting.

Example: A candlestick with a long lower shadow near a support zone suggests strong buying interest and reinforces the significance of that level.

8. Dynamic Analysis with Live Updates

Unlike static chart types, candlestick charts evolve dynamically as each new price tick arrives. This real-time adaptability allows traders to observe market behavior as it unfolds, making candlesticks particularly valuable for day trading and active strategies.

Practical Use: Monitor forming candlesticks during high-impact news events to capitalize on rapid market shifts.

Candlestick charts are more than just a way to visualize price action—they are a window into the market's psyche, a tool for predicting trends, and a guide for executing strategies with confidence. By mastering their advantages, you can elevate your trading skills and make more informed decisions, regardless of the market or time frame you're analyzing.

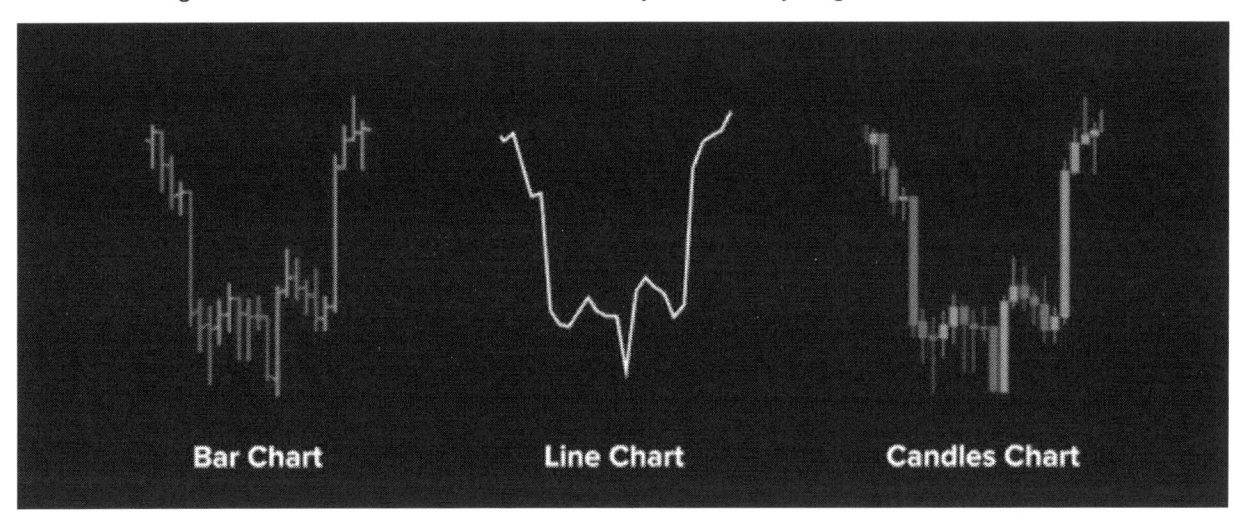

4.3 TIME FRAMES AND THEIR IMPACT

Time frames play a crucial role in trading, influencing how you interpret price action and make decisions. A candlestick's time frame defines the period it represents, whether it's a single minute, an hour, a day, or longer. Choosing the right time frame depends on your trading style, objectives, and the level of detail you need. Understanding the impact of time frames is essential for developing a trading strategy that aligns with your goals.

1. The Basics of Time Frames

Each candlestick reflects the price action within a specific period. For example:

- A **1-minute candlestick** shows the open, high, low, and close prices for one minute of trading.
- A **daily candlestick** aggregates an entire trading day into one candle.

Shorter time frames provide granular details, capturing the market's every move, while longer time frames filter out noise, focusing on broader trends.

2. Time Frames and Trading Styles

Different time frames cater to different trading styles:

- **Scalping:** Involves ultra-short time frames, such as 1-minute or 5-minute charts, to capitalize on small price movements.
- **Day Trading:** Relies on 15-minute or hourly charts to identify intraday opportunities without holding positions overnight.
- **Swing Trading:** Uses daily or weekly charts to capture multi-day price movements and broader trends.
- **Position Trading/Investing:** Analyzes weekly or monthly charts for long-term market direction.

Example: A scalper analyzing a 5-minute chart looks for quick reversals, while a swing trader focuses on daily charts to identify significant trends.

3. Shorter Time Frames: Pros and Cons

Shorter time frames offer detailed insights into price action but come with trade-offs:

- **Advantages:**
    - Provide precise entry and exit points.
    - Reveal market noise and volatility in real-time.
    - Useful for high-frequency trading and quick decision-making.
- **Disadvantages:**
    - Increased noise can lead to false signals.

Chapter 4:
Chart Analysis Fundamentals

- Require constant monitoring and faster reaction times.
- Higher susceptibility to emotional decision-making.

Practical Use: Short time frames are ideal for active traders who thrive in fast-paced environments but require robust discipline and focus.

4. Longer Time Frames: Pros and Cons

Longer time frames smooth out market noise, offering a clearer view of trends and market structure.

- **Advantages:**
    - Emphasize the bigger picture, reducing false signals.
    - Suitable for long-term strategies that require less frequent monitoring.
    - Allow for greater confidence in decisions based on well-established trends.
- **Disadvantages:**
    - May miss short-term opportunities.
    - Delayed signals can result in less precise entries and exits.

Practical Use: Longer time frames work well for swing traders and investors who prioritize trend-following over short-term fluctuations.

5. The Importance of Multi-Time Frame Analysis

Multi-time frame analysis involves using multiple time frames simultaneously to gain a more comprehensive understanding of the market.

- **Example:** A swing trader might use a weekly chart to identify the overall trend, a daily chart to find trade setups, and a 4-hour chart for precise entry points.
- **Benefits:**
    - Combines the strengths of different time frames.
    - Reduces the risk of misinterpreting signals.
    - Enhances confidence in decision-making by aligning trends across time frames.

6. Adapting Time Frames to Market Conditions

Market volatility and liquidity can influence the effectiveness of time frames:

- In highly volatile markets, shorter time frames help capture quick opportunities.
- In stable markets, longer time frames provide more reliable signals.

Practical Tip: Adjust your time frame based on the asset's behavior and the market conditions. For instance, use shorter time frames during news events but revert to longer ones in calmer periods.

7. Aligning Time Frames with Goals

Your time frame selection should align with your trading goals and personality:

- If you prefer fast-paced trading and can dedicate time to constant monitoring, shorter time frames are suitable.
- If you value patience and focus on major trends, longer time frames offer a better fit.

Time frames are more than just a choice—they are a critical component of how you view the market. By mastering their impact, you can tailor your analysis to match your strategy, optimize your entries and exits, and stay adaptable in ever-changing conditions.

1-minute time frame:

15-minute time frame:

Chapter 4:
Chart Analysis Fundamentals

Daily time frame:

4.4 READING PRICE ACTION EFFECTIVELY

Reading price action is one of the most valuable skills a trader can develop. It involves analyzing raw price movements on a chart to understand market behavior without relying heavily on technical indicators. By focusing on the interaction between buyers and sellers as reflected in candlestick formations, trends, and patterns, traders can gain insights into market sentiment, momentum, and potential reversals.

1. **Understanding the Flow of Price Action**
   Price action represents the ongoing battle between buyers (demand) and sellers (supply). Observing how prices react at key levels—support, resistance, or psychological thresholds—provides clues about the market's intentions.

   - **Bullish Price Action:** Characterized by higher highs and higher lows, showing that buyers are in control.

   - **Bearish Price Action:** Defined by lower highs and lower lows, signaling dominance by sellers.

   Example: In an uptrend, a series of bullish candlesticks with long bodies and minimal shadows suggests strong buying pressure.

2. **Key Components of Price Action**
   To read price action effectively, focus on these essential elements:

   - **Candlestick Patterns:** Look for patterns like hammers, doji, or engulfing patterns that reveal potential reversals or continuations.

   - **Trendlines:** Draw trendlines to identify the direction of the market and validate price movements within that direction.

   - **Support and Resistance:** Pay attention to how price behaves when approaching these levels. Strong rejections often indicate a continuation of the current trend, while breakouts suggest a shift in momentum.

   - **Volume:** Combine price action with volume analysis to confirm the strength of moves. High volume during a breakout, for instance, supports the validity of the move.

3. **Spotting Reversals and Continuations**
   Price action is especially effective for identifying reversals and continuations:

   - **Reversals:** Look for patterns such as double tops, double bottoms, or candlesticks like shooting stars and hammers at significant levels. These indicate a potential change in trend.

   - **Continuations:** Flags, pennants, or a series of small-bodied candles (indecision) within a trend often signal that the market is pausing before continuing in the same direction.
   Practical Tip: Combine these observations with larger market context to avoid mistaking temporary pullbacks for full reversals.

Chapter 4:
Chart Analysis Fundamentals

4. Recognizing Momentum Through Price Action

Momentum refers to the strength or speed of price movements. Candlestick characteristics can reveal momentum:

- **Strong Momentum:** Long-bodied candles with minimal shadows, especially in a series, indicate high momentum.

- **Weak Momentum:** Small-bodied candles with long shadows suggest indecision or reduced momentum.

  Example: A strong uptrend with consecutive large bullish candlesticks suggests robust buying interest, while smaller bodies and increased shadows may signal that the trend is weakening.

5. The Role of Context in Price Action

Price action should never be analyzed in isolation. Understanding the broader market context enhances its effectiveness:

- **Trend Context:** In an uptrend, focus on bullish price action signals; in a downtrend, prioritize bearish signals.

- **Market Conditions:** Adapt your analysis to match volatile or consolidating markets. Consolidation zones often precede breakouts, while volatile periods can lead to exaggerated price movements.

- **Key Levels:** Watch how price reacts at significant levels, such as Fibonacci retracements, pivot points, or psychological round numbers (e.g., $100, $1,000).

6. The Importance of Multi-Time Frame Analysis in Price Action

Analyzing price action across multiple time frames provides a clearer picture of market behavior:

- Use a higher time frame (e.g., daily or weekly) to identify the overall trend.

- Use a lower time frame (e.g., 15-minute or 1-hour) to fine-tune entries and exits. This approach ensures your trades align with the dominant trend while capitalizing on short-term opportunities.

7. Practical Steps to Master Price Action

- Start by observing candlestick formations and patterns on live charts.

- Practice drawing trendlines and identifying support and resistance levels.

- Use price action to validate your trades instead of relying solely on technical indicators.

- Monitor how price reacts to news events, as these often trigger decisive movements.
  Example: During a news release, a long candlestick with a large upper shadow may indicate an initial bullish reaction followed by bearish rejection.

Price action is a dynamic, real-time representation of market sentiment and decision-making. By mastering how to read and interpret these movements, you can gain an edge in anticipating market trends and executing trades with confidence. It's not about predicting the future but understanding the present, allowing you to act with clarity and precision.

4.5 IDENTIFYING MARKET CONTEXT

Identifying market context is a cornerstone of effective trading. Market context refers to the broader conditions and trends that influence price movements, providing a framework for interpreting price action and making informed decisions. By understanding the bigger picture, traders can align their strategies with prevailing market dynamics and avoid costly mistakes.

1. The Importance of Market Context

Market context helps you answer critical questions:

- Is the market trending or consolidating?
- Are we in a bullish, bearish, or neutral phase?
- How do external factors, such as economic data or geopolitical events, influence current price action?

Without this context, even the most well-executed technical analysis can result in poor trading outcomes. For example, trading against a strong trend often leads to frustration and losses.

2. Key Elements of Market Context

To effectively identify market context, focus on these critical elements:

- **Trend Analysis:** Determine whether the market is in an uptrend, downtrend, or sideways range. Use tools like trendlines, moving averages, and higher time frames to confirm the dominant trend.
- **Market Phases:** Markets typically move through accumulation, advancement, distribution, and decline. Recognizing these phases helps you adapt your strategy to the current conditions.
- **Support and Resistance Levels:** Identify key price levels where the market has historically reacted. These levels often define the boundaries of market context.
- **Volatility:** Assess current volatility levels to gauge the likelihood of sharp price movements or prolonged consolidations.

Example: In a high-volatility environment, a breakout is more likely to lead to sustained momentum. In low-volatility markets, breakouts are more prone to failure.

3. The Role of Time Frames in Context

Market context varies depending on the time frame you're analyzing. For example:

Chapter 4:
Chart Analysis Fundamentals

- On a **weekly chart,** the market may appear to be in a long-term uptrend.

- On a **daily chart,** the same market might show short-term consolidation or a pullback. Use multiple time frames to understand how short-term price action fits within the larger trend.
  Practical Tip: Align your trades with the dominant trend observed in higher time frames, while using lower time frames for precise entries and exits.

4. News and External Influences

Economic reports, central bank announcements, and geopolitical events can drastically shift market context. For example:

- A strong jobs report might reinforce a bullish context in equity markets.

- Rising geopolitical tensions could introduce uncertainty and increased volatility.
  Practical Use: Stay informed about upcoming news events and consider their potential impact on the markets you're trading.

5. Recognizing Market Cycles

Markets move through repeating cycles that provide valuable clues about context:

- **Accumulation:** A period of consolidation at low levels, often preceding an uptrend.

- **Advancement (Markup):** A sustained upward movement marked by higher highs and higher lows.

- **Distribution:** A consolidation phase at high levels, signaling potential reversals.

- **Decline (Markdown):** A sustained downward movement marked by lower highs and lower lows.

Understanding which cycle the market is in helps you position your trades strategically. *Example:* During an accumulation phase, focus on potential breakout opportunities. In a distribution phase, look for signs of exhaustion or reversal.

Market context is dynamic, and conditions can change rapidly. A strong uptrend might transition into a consolidation phase before resuming upward or reversing entirely. Stay flexible and adjust your strategy as new information emerges.

Practical Tip: Use alerts and regular chart reviews to stay updated on changing market conditions, ensuring your analysis remains relevant.

Understanding market context allows you to make decisions based on the broader picture rather than isolated signals. By aligning your trades with the prevailing conditions, you increase the likelihood of success and reduce unnecessary risks. This perspective not only enhances your trading results but also builds confidence in your ability to navigate complex markets.

PART 2:
Mastering Candlestick Patterns

Automatic
Candlestick Detection Tool

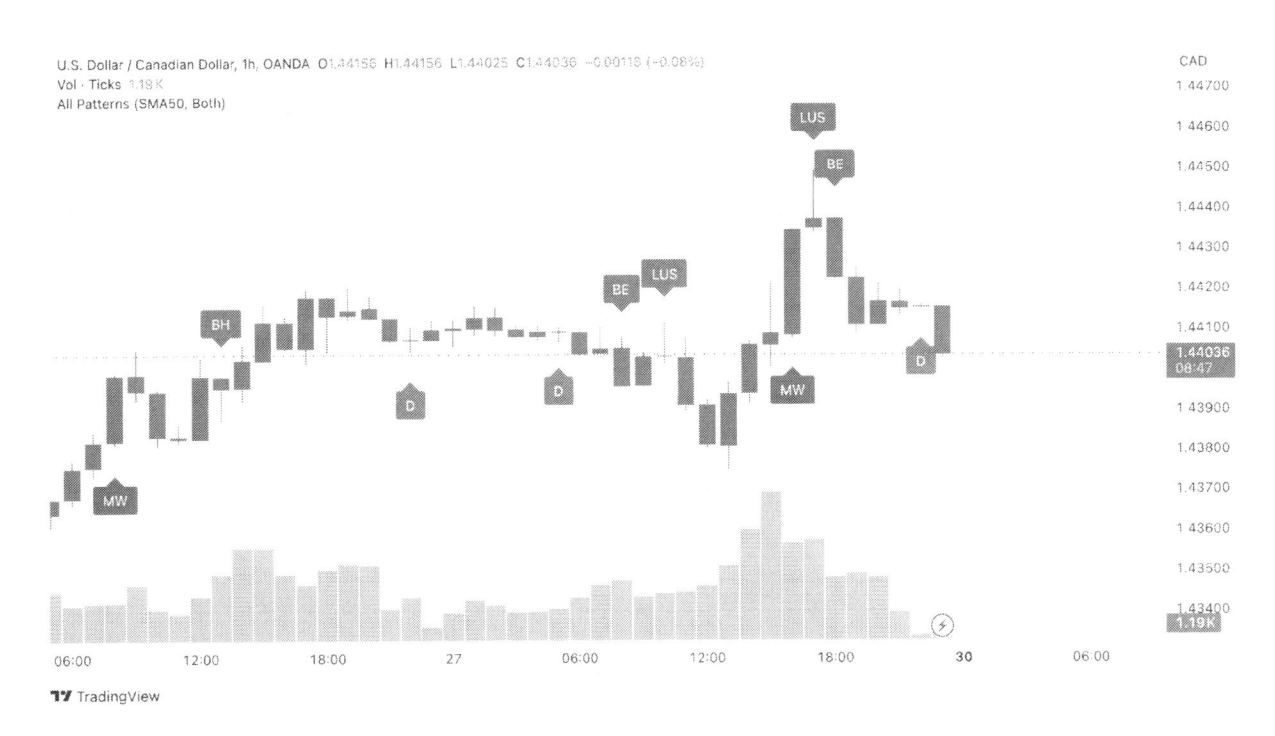

Understanding candlestick patterns is a cornerstone of technical analysis, and mastering them can provide a significant edge in trading. To complement the knowledge shared in this book, I'm excited to introduce the **Automatic Candlestick Detection** tool available on **TradingView**. This tool simplifies your trading experience by identifying candlestick patterns automatically, saving you time and ensuring accuracy in your analysis.

What Is the Automatic Candlestick Detection Tool?

The **Automatic Candlestick Detection** tool is a powerful indicator that identifies key candlestick patterns on your charts in real time. Whether you're analyzing **doji**, **engulfing**, **hammer**, or other patterns, this tool highlights them directly on the chart and provides detailed descriptions, allowing you to make informed trading decisions quickly.

Key Features:

- **Automatic Pattern Recognition**: Detects a wide range of candlestick patterns instantly.
- **Detailed Explanations**: Offers full descriptions for each detected pattern.
- **Customizable Settings**: Tailor the tool to fit your trading style and preferences.

- **Time-Saving**: Focus on strategy execution rather than manual pattern identification.

How to Use the Tool

Getting started with the **Automatic Candlestick Detection** tool is simple. Follow these steps:

1. **Scan the QR Code**: Use your smartphone or device to scan the QR code below.
2. **Watch the Video Guide**: Access the step-by-step tutorial on how to install and use the tool effectively.

Why This Tool Matters

By combining the theoretical knowledge from this book with the practical application of the **Automatic Candlestick Detection** tool, you can:

- **Bridge Theory and Practice**: Apply what you've learned in real-time trading scenarios.
- **Improve Accuracy**: Reduce errors and ensure consistent identification of patterns.
- **Enhance Decision-Making**: Gain insights faster and act on opportunities with confidence.

Scan to Access the Video Guide

Use the QR code below to watch the complete tutorial on setting up and using the **Automatic Candlestick Detection** tool:

Empower your trading journey with the **Automatic Candlestick Detection** tool. This exclusive addition ensures you're equipped with the best resources to stay ahead in the markets. Combine the depth of candlestick analysis with cutting-edge technology to take your trading to the next level.

Chapter 5:
Single Candlestick Patterns

Chapter 5:
Single Candlestick Patterns

―――――― SINGLE CANDLE PATTERNS ――――――

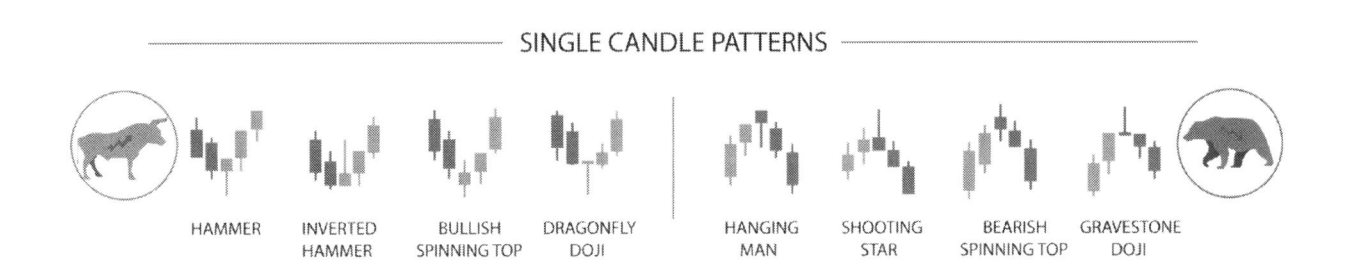

| HAMMER | INVERTED HAMMER | BULLISH SPINNING TOP | DRAGONFLY DOJI | HANGING MAN | SHOOTING STAR | BEARISH SPINNING TOP | GRAVESTONE DOJI |

5.1 MARUBOZU PATTERNS

Marubozu patterns are among the simplest and most impactful single candlestick patterns in technical analysis. Their name, derived from the Japanese word meaning "close-cropped," reflects their defining characteristic—candlesticks with no shadows. A Marubozu signifies decisive market sentiment, as the open and close prices represent the highest and lowest prices of the session, with no price movement beyond these levels. These patterns are powerful indicators of momentum and are commonly used to confirm the strength of trends or predict potential breakouts.

Complete Marubozu

A Complete Marubozu has no upper or lower shadows, meaning the open and close prices align precisely with the high and low of the session. This candlestick conveys absolute control by either buyers (bullish Marubozu) or sellers (bearish Marubozu).

The Candlestick Trading Profit Formula

- **Bullish Complete Marubozu:** The session opens at the lowest price and closes at the highest, indicating overwhelming buying pressure. This is often seen in strong uptrends or at the start of a bullish breakout.

- **Bearish Complete Marubozu:** The session opens at the highest price and closes at the lowest, signaling dominant selling pressure. This typically occurs in strong downtrends or during bearish breakouts.

- *Example:* Imagine a stock trading at $50. A bullish Complete Marubozu forms when the session opens at $50 (the low) and closes at $55 (the high) with no price movement beyond these levels.

Practical Application:

- Use Complete Marubozu patterns as confirmation signals. For example, a bullish Complete Marubozu breaking above a resistance level often indicates strong upward momentum.

- Pair them with volume analysis to validate the strength of the move. High volume accompanying a Complete Marubozu reinforces the reliability of the signal.

Opening and Closing Marubozu

Opening and Closing Marubozu patterns differ slightly from the Complete Marubozu, as they have shadows on one end of the candlestick. These shadows provide additional context about market behavior during the session.

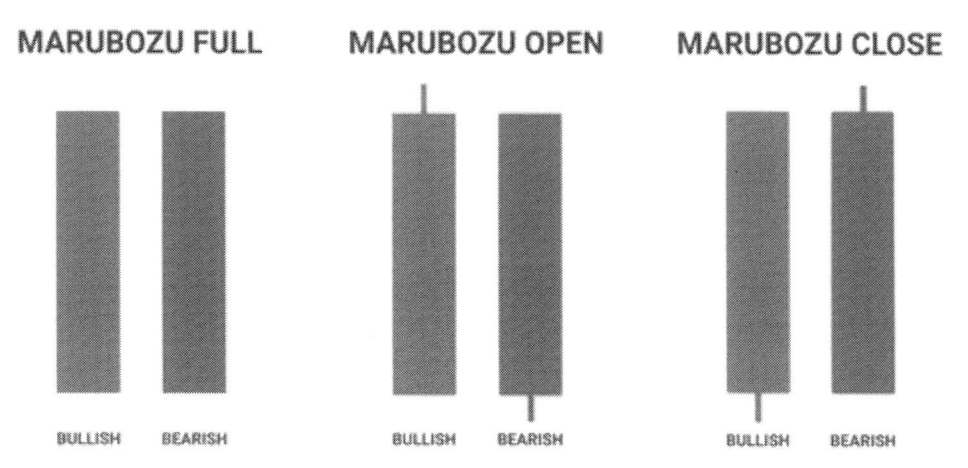

- **Opening Marubozu:** This candlestick has no shadow at the open but features a shadow at the close.

Chapter 5:
Single Candlestick Patterns

- - **Bullish Opening Marubozu:** The price opens at the low with no lower shadow, rises strongly, and then retracts slightly to form an upper shadow. This suggests robust buying with minor profit-taking at the session's end.
  - **Bearish Opening Marubozu:** The price opens at the high with no upper shadow, falls sharply, and then recovers slightly, leaving a lower shadow. This indicates strong selling with modest buying interest late in the session.
- **Closing Marubozu:** This candlestick has no shadow at the close but features a shadow at the open.
  - **Bullish Closing Marubozu:** The price opens, dips slightly to form a lower shadow, and then rallies to close at the high with no upper shadow. This pattern reflects increasing buying pressure as the session progresses.
  - **Bearish Closing Marubozu:** The price opens, climbs briefly to create an upper shadow, and then sells off to close at the low with no lower shadow. This highlights intensifying selling pressure as the session unfolds.
    Practical Application:
- Use Opening and Closing Marubozu patterns to gauge shifts in momentum. For example, a bearish Opening Marubozu near a resistance level may indicate that sellers are gaining control.
- Combine these patterns with trendlines or support/resistance levels to validate potential reversals or continuations.

Marubozu patterns are powerful indicators of market sentiment, providing clarity about buyer or seller dominance. By recognizing these patterns and interpreting their context, you can make informed decisions about the strength of trends and the likelihood of future price movements. Understanding the nuances between Complete, Opening, and Closing Marubozu patterns equips traders with a deeper appreciation of candlestick analysis and its predictive power.

5.2 DOJI PATTERNS

Doji patterns are unique candlesticks that represent indecision or equilibrium in the market. A Doji forms when the opening and closing prices are nearly identical, resulting in a small or nonexistent body. These patterns highlight a temporary balance between buyers and sellers, often serving as precursors to significant market moves. Depending on their shape and position within a trend, Doji candles can indicate potential reversals, continuation, or periods of consolidation.

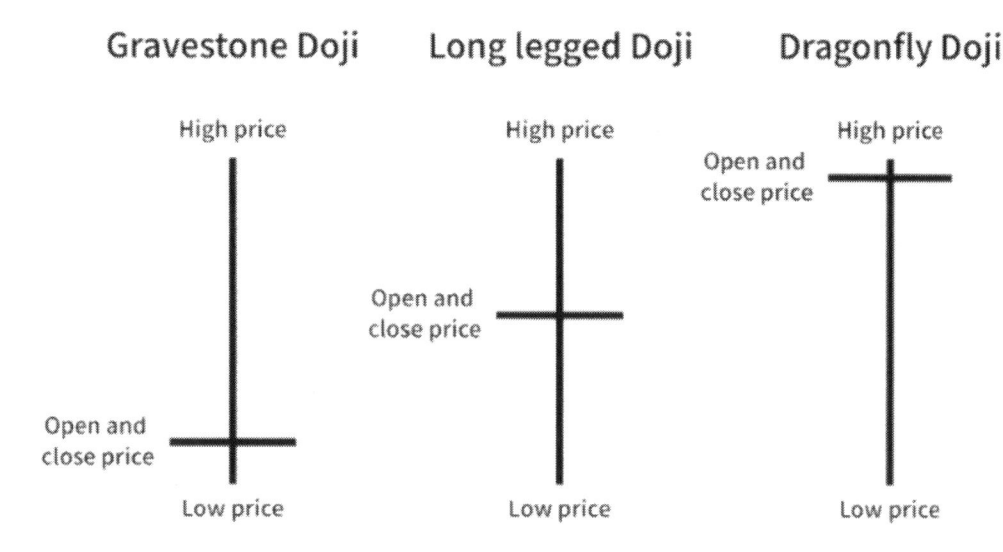

Standard Doji

The Standard Doji is the simplest form of this pattern, characterized by an almost invisible body with equal-length upper and lower shadows. It reflects complete indecision, where neither buyers nor sellers have a clear advantage.

- **Significance:** A Standard Doji in a strong trend often signals hesitation and may precede a reversal or consolidation.

- *Example:* During an uptrend, a Doji forming near resistance indicates that buying pressure is weakening, suggesting a potential reversal or temporary pause in the trend.
  Practical Application:

- Confirm Standard Doji patterns with subsequent candlesticks or indicators. For instance, a bearish candlestick following a Doji in an uptrend strengthens the case for a reversal.

- Use support and resistance levels to gauge the Doji's context. A Doji at support is often less concerning than one forming at resistance.

Chapter 5:
Single Candlestick Patterns

Long-Legged Doji

The Long-Legged Doji features extended upper and lower shadows, emphasizing heightened market volatility and indecision during the session. The long shadows indicate that both buyers and sellers tried to dominate but ultimately failed to establish control.

- **Significance:** This pattern often appears at key turning points in the market, signaling potential reversals or breakouts.

- *Example:* A Long-Legged Doji forming after a series of bullish candlesticks in an overbought market can indicate that buyers are losing momentum, paving the way for a bearish correction.

   Practical Application:

- Use Long-Legged Doji candles in combination with momentum indicators like RSI or MACD to confirm overbought or oversold conditions.

- Pay close attention to volume. High volume during a Long-Legged Doji suggests a stronger likelihood of a breakout or reversal.

Dragonfly Doji

The Dragonfly Doji has a long lower shadow with little to no upper shadow, and its open and close prices are at or near the session's high. This pattern reflects significant selling pressure early in the session, followed by a strong recovery driven by buyers.

- **Significance:** The Dragonfly Doji often appears at the end of a downtrend, signaling potential bullish reversals.

- *Example:* In a downtrend, a Dragonfly Doji forming near a support level indicates that sellers have failed to push prices lower, and buyers are gaining control.
   Practical Application:

- Look for confirmation from the next candlestick. A strong bullish candlestick following a Dragonfly Doji reinforces the likelihood of a reversal.

- Use trendlines or moving averages to validate the pattern's significance within the broader market structure.

Gravestone Doji

The Gravestone Doji is the inverse of the Dragonfly Doji, featuring a long upper shadow with little to no lower shadow. The open and close prices are at or near the session's low, indicating that buyers attempted to drive the price higher but were overpowered by sellers before the close.

- **Significance:** This pattern often appears at the end of an uptrend, signaling potential bearish reversals.
- *Example:* In an uptrend, a Gravestone Doji forming near resistance indicates that buying pressure has diminished, increasing the likelihood of a price decline.
Practical Application:
- Use the Gravestone Doji in conjunction with resistance levels or overbought indicators to confirm its bearish implications.
- A strong bearish candlestick following the Gravestone Doji provides additional confirmation of a potential downtrend.

Doji patterns are invaluable tools for identifying indecision, reversals, and consolidation points in the market. While they provide critical insights, Doji patterns are most effective when used in conjunction with other technical indicators, key levels, and market context. Recognizing the nuances among Standard, Long-Legged, Dragonfly, and Gravestone Doji candles equips traders with a versatile framework for interpreting price action and anticipating market movements.

Chapter 5:
Single Candlestick Patterns

5.3 Hammer Family

The Hammer family of candlestick patterns is a group of single-candlestick formations that provide crucial insights into potential market reversals. These patterns are characterized by their small real bodies and long shadows, which reflect significant shifts in market sentiment. Depending on their position within a trend and their specific shape, they can signal either bullish or bearish reversals. Recognizing and interpreting these patterns is a fundamental skill for any trader.

Hammer

The Hammer is a bullish reversal pattern that forms at the bottom of a downtrend. It is defined by a small real body near the upper end of the candlestick range and a long lower shadow that is at least twice the length of the body.

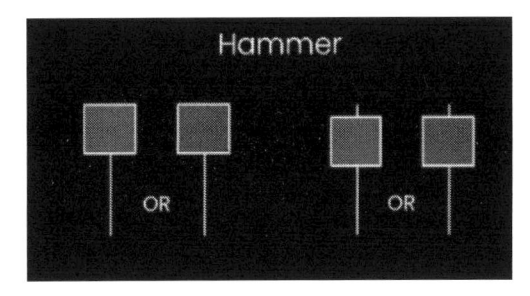

- **Significance:** The Hammer indicates that sellers initially drove prices lower during the session, but strong buying pressure allowed the price to close near its opening level.

- *Example:* In a declining market, a Hammer forming at a key support level often signals the start of a reversal to the upside.

Practical Application:

- Look for confirmation in the form of a bullish candlestick following the Hammer. This strengthens the likelihood of a trend reversal.

- Use volume analysis to validate the pattern. Higher volume during the Hammer increases its reliability.

Inverted Hammer

The Inverted Hammer is a bullish reversal pattern that also forms at the bottom of a downtrend. It features a small real body near the lower end of the candlestick range and a long upper shadow that is at least twice the length of the body.

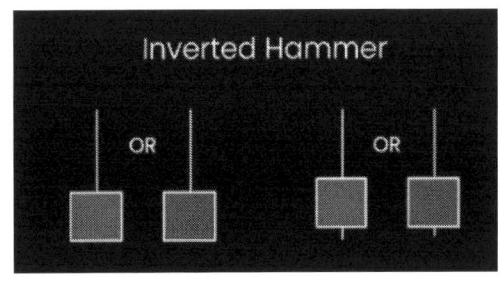

- **Significance:** The Inverted Hammer indicates that buyers attempted to push prices higher during the session, but selling pressure kept the price near its opening level. Despite the upper shadow, the pattern suggests weakening bearish momentum.

- *Example:* After a prolonged downtrend, an Inverted Hammer near a support level often precedes a reversal to the upside.

Practical Application:

- Wait for confirmation, such as a bullish candlestick closing above the Inverted Hammer's high, before entering a trade.

- Combine the pattern with trendlines or Fibonacci retracements to identify strong reversal zones.

Hanging Man

The Hanging Man is a bearish reversal pattern that forms at the top of an uptrend. It resembles the Hammer in structure but occurs in a different context. The pattern features a small real body near the top of the range and a long lower shadow.

- **Significance:** The Hanging Man suggests that selling pressure emerged during the session, pushing prices significantly lower before buyers regained control. This indicates potential weakness in the uptrend.

- *Example:* In a rising market, a Hanging Man forming near resistance may signal the start of a price decline.

Practical Application:

- Look for confirmation from the next candlestick. A strong bearish candlestick following the Hanging Man reinforces its bearish implications.

- Use additional indicators, such as RSI, to confirm overbought conditions when interpreting the pattern.

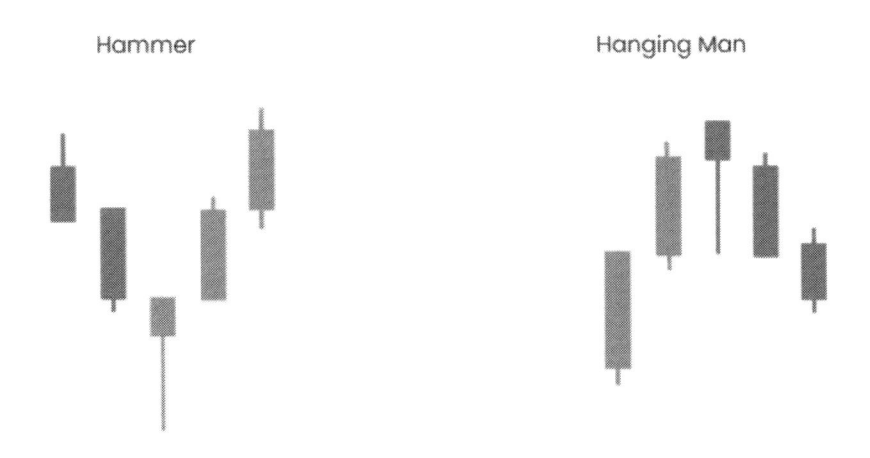

Chapter 5:
Single Candlestick Patterns

Shooting Star

The Shooting Star is a bearish reversal pattern that forms at the top of an uptrend. It is characterized by a small real body near the lower end of the candlestick range and a long upper shadow that is at least twice the length of the body.

- **Significance:** The Shooting Star indicates that buyers pushed prices higher during the session, but selling pressure overwhelmed them, causing the price to close near its opening level. This reflects a loss of bullish momentum.
- *Example:* In an uptrend, a Shooting Star forming near resistance often precedes a price decline.

Practical Application:

- Wait for a bearish candlestick closing below the Shooting Star's low to confirm the reversal.
- Combine the pattern with key resistance levels or overbought indicators to strengthen its predictive value.

The Hammer family provides invaluable signals for spotting potential reversals in both bullish and bearish markets. While these patterns are effective on their own, they are best used in conjunction with other technical tools, such as support and resistance levels, volume analysis, and trend confirmation, to enhance accuracy and reduce false signals. Mastering these patterns equips traders with a powerful framework for anticipating market turning points and capitalizing on trading opportunities.

5.4 SPINNING TOPS AND THEIR SIGNIFICANCE

Spinning Tops are candlestick patterns characterized by their small real bodies and relatively long upper and lower shadows. They represent indecision in the market, where neither buyers nor sellers have taken definitive control. Spinning Tops often appear during periods of consolidation, at the end of strong trends, or near key support and resistance levels, making them important patterns to watch for potential reversals or continuations.

Structure of a Spinning Top

- **Small Real Body:** Indicates that the opening and closing prices are very close to each other, reflecting a lack of momentum.

- **Long Shadows:** Show that there was significant price movement in both directions during the session, but neither buyers nor sellers could maintain control.

- **Neutral Appearance:** Spinning Tops are typically neutral, but their significance increases when they appear in certain market contexts.

Spinning Top

Bullish   **Bearish**

Close → / Open → (Bullish)

← Open / ← Close (Bearish)

Significance of Spinning Tops

1. **Indecision in the Market:** Spinning Tops reflect a balance between buyers and sellers. While price fluctuates significantly during the session, the close near the open indicates uncertainty about the next direction.

2. **Potential Reversal:** When a Spinning Top appears after a strong trend, it often signals that the trend is losing momentum and a reversal may be imminent.

    - In an uptrend, it may indicate that buyers are hesitant, suggesting a potential shift to bearish sentiment.

    - In a downtrend, it can signal weakening selling pressure, possibly leading to a bullish reversal.

3. **Continuation Signals:** In some cases, Spinning Tops appear within consolidation phases and precede a continuation of the prevailing trend.

Chapter 5:
Single Candlestick Patterns

Interpreting Spinning Tops in Context

Spinning Tops are most meaningful when analyzed in conjunction with the broader market structure and additional technical tools:

- **In an Uptrend:** A Spinning Top forming near resistance or after a series of strong bullish candlesticks suggests waning buying pressure and the possibility of a reversal.

- **In a Downtrend:** A Spinning Top near support or following a string of bearish candlesticks indicates that sellers may be losing momentum.

- **In Consolidation Zones:** When Spinning Tops appear in sideways markets, they often signify a lack of direction and the need for additional confirmation before acting.

Practical Applications of Spinning Tops

1. **Confirmation is Key:** Spinning Tops are not standalone patterns. Wait for confirmation from the next candlestick to determine the market's direction:
   - A strong bullish or bearish candlestick following a Spinning Top validates the reversal signal.
   - A continuation of small-bodied candlesticks may indicate ongoing indecision.

2. **Combine with Support and Resistance Levels:** Spinning Tops at key levels provide stronger signals. For example, a Spinning Top forming at a resistance level increases the likelihood of a bearish reversal.

3. **Volume Analysis:** Higher volume accompanying a Spinning Top enhances its significance, as it reflects strong market participation despite indecision.

Real-World Example

Imagine a stock in a strong uptrend approaching a resistance level at $100. A Spinning Top forms, showing a high of $102, a low of $98, and a close at $100. This pattern indicates that buyers attempted to push prices higher, but sellers countered strongly, causing the price to close near the open. The subsequent bearish candlestick breaking below $98 confirms the reversal, signaling a shorting opportunity.

Spinning Tops are versatile candlestick patterns that provide insights into market sentiment and potential reversals. While they do not guarantee directional changes, they are powerful signals when used alongside other technical tools, such as trendlines, moving averages, and volume analysis. Recognizing and interpreting Spinning Tops in the right market context allows traders to anticipate shifts and make more informed trading decisions.

TYPES OF CANDLESTICK PATTERNS

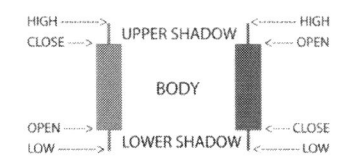

BASICS

HIGH → UPPER SHADOW ← HIGH
CLOSE → BODY ← OPEN
OPEN → LOWER SHADOW ← CLOSE
LOW → ← LOW

NEUTRAL CANDLESTICKS

DOJI | SPINNING TOP | MARUBOZU | STAR

SINGLE CANDLE PATTERNS

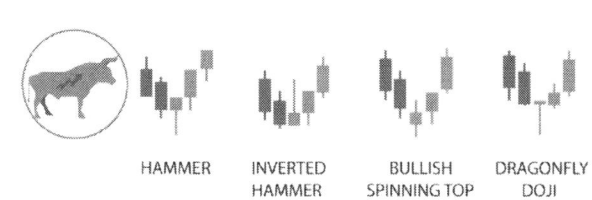

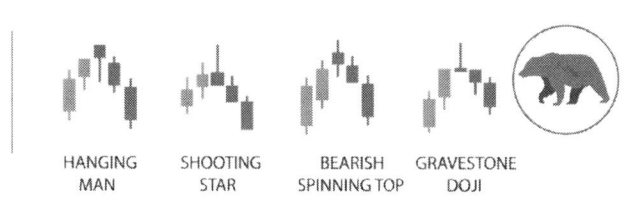

HAMMER | INVERTED HAMMER | BULLISH SPINNING TOP | DRAGONFLY DOJI | HANGING MAN | SHOOTING STAR | BEARISH SPINNING TOP | GRAVESTONE DOJI

Candlestick Patterns Cheat Sheet

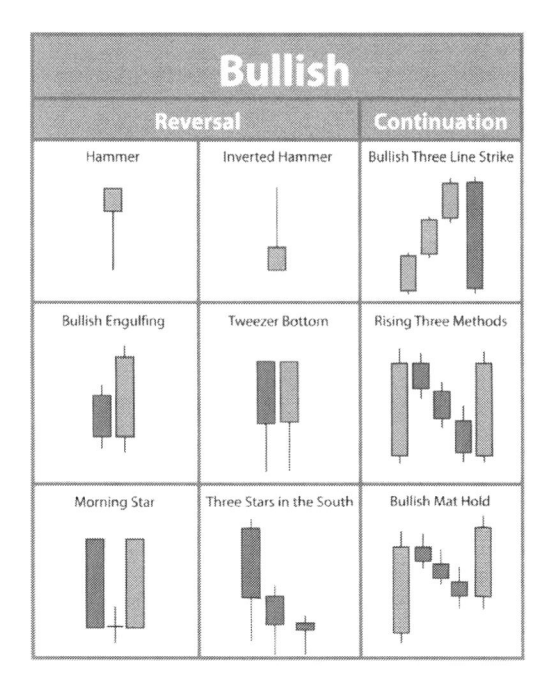

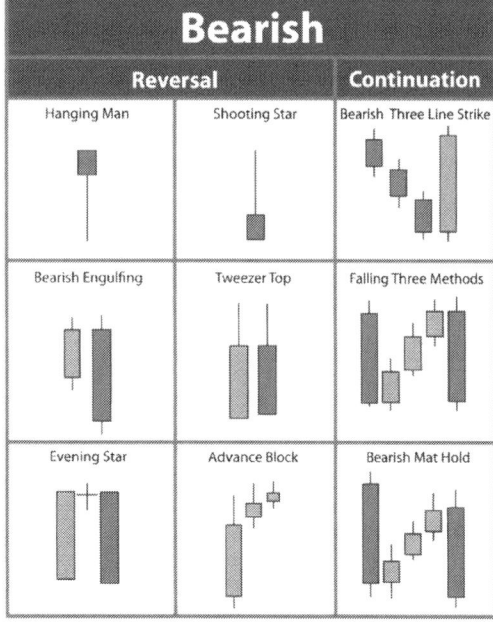

Bullish			Bearish			Neutral
Reversal		**Continuation**	**Reversal**		**Continuation**	
Hammer	Inverted Hammer	Bullish Three Line Strike	Hanging Man	Shooting Star	Bearish Three Line Strike	Doji
Bullish Engulfing	Tweezer Bottom	Rising Three Methods	Bearish Engulfing	Tweezer Top	Falling Three Methods	Gravestone Doji
Morning Star	Three Stars in the South	Bullish Mat Hold	Evening Star	Advance Block	Bearish Mat Hold	Dragonfly

Chapter 6:
Dual Candlestick Patterns

Chapter 6:
Dual Candlestick Patterns

―――――――― DOUBLE CANDLE PATTERNS ――――――――

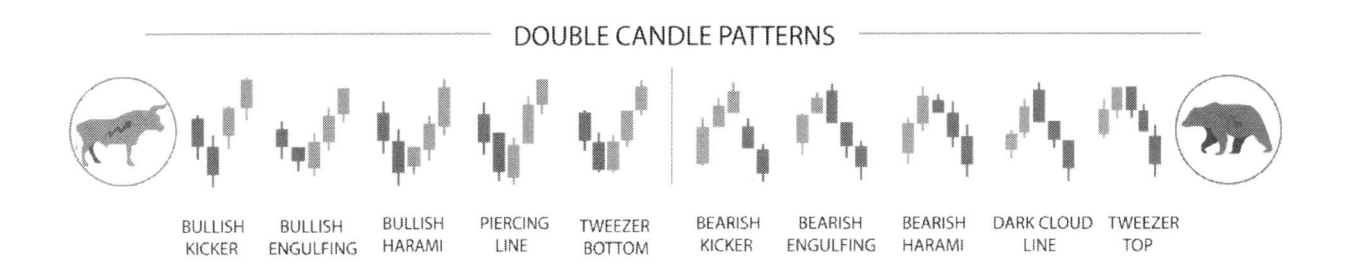

| BULLISH KICKER | BULLISH ENGULFING | BULLISH HARAMI | PIERCING LINE | TWEEZER BOTTOM | BEARISH KICKER | BEARISH ENGULFING | BEARISH HARAMI | DARK CLOUD LINE | TWEEZER TOP |

6.1 ENGULFING PATTERNS

Engulfing patterns are powerful dual-candlestick formations that signal a potential reversal in the market. These patterns occur when a smaller candlestick is followed by a larger candlestick that completely "engulfs" the previous candle's body. The engulfing candlestick represents a decisive shift in market sentiment, making these patterns highly reliable for identifying turning points. Depending on their context, engulfing patterns can signal either bullish or bearish reversals.

Bullish Engulfing

Bearish Engulfing

Bullish Engulfing

A Bullish Engulfing pattern forms in a downtrend and signals a potential reversal to the upside. It consists of a small bearish candlestick followed by a larger bullish candlestick that completely engulfs the body of the first candle.

- **Key Characteristics:**
    - The first candle is bearish, representing continued selling pressure.
    - The second candle is bullish, opening lower than the first candle's close and closing higher than its open, engulfing the body entirely.
    - Shadows (if present) are less significant than the body of the engulfing candle.
- **Significance:** The larger bullish candle indicates that buyers have decisively overpowered sellers, suggesting a shift in momentum. This pattern is most reliable when it forms at a key support level.
- **Example:** In a downtrend, a stock closes at $50 (first bearish candle), but the next session opens at $49 and closes at $52 (bullish engulfing candle), signaling a potential reversal.
Practical Application:
- Confirm the pattern by waiting for a subsequent bullish candlestick or increased trading volume.
- Use the high of the bullish engulfing candle as a potential breakout level for entry.
- Place stop-loss orders below the low of the pattern to manage risk.

Bearish Engulfing

A Bearish Engulfing pattern forms in an uptrend and signals a potential reversal to the downside. It consists of a small bullish candlestick followed by a larger bearish candlestick that completely engulfs the body of the first candle.

- **Key Characteristics:**
    - The first candle is bullish, representing continued buying pressure.
    - The second candle is bearish, opening higher than the first candle's close and closing lower than its open, engulfing the body entirely.
    - Shadows (if present) are less significant than the body of the engulfing candle.
- **Significance:** The larger bearish candle indicates that sellers have overwhelmed buyers, signaling a potential shift in momentum. This pattern is most reliable when it forms at a key resistance level.

Chapter 6:
Dual Candlestick Patterns

- **Example:** In an uptrend, a stock closes at $100 (first bullish candle), but the next session opens at $101 and closes at $97 (bearish engulfing candle), suggesting a reversal.
  Practical Application:
- Wait for confirmation in the form of a subsequent bearish candlestick or a break below a key support level.
- Use the low of the bearish engulfing candle as a potential breakout point for entry.
- Place stop-loss orders above the high of the pattern to protect against false signals.

Engulfing patterns are most effective when used in conjunction with other technical tools, such as support and resistance levels, trendlines, or oscillators like RSI to confirm overbought or oversold conditions. Their ability to highlight clear shifts in market sentiment makes them a valuable addition to any trader's toolkit.

6.2 Harami Patterns

Harami patterns are dual-candlestick formations that signify a potential reversal or pause in the prevailing trend. The word "harami" means "pregnant" in Japanese, reflecting the pattern's visual appearance: a small candlestick (the "baby") entirely contained within the body of the preceding larger candlestick (the "mother"). Harami patterns indicate a shift in momentum and are valuable tools for identifying reversals or consolidations.

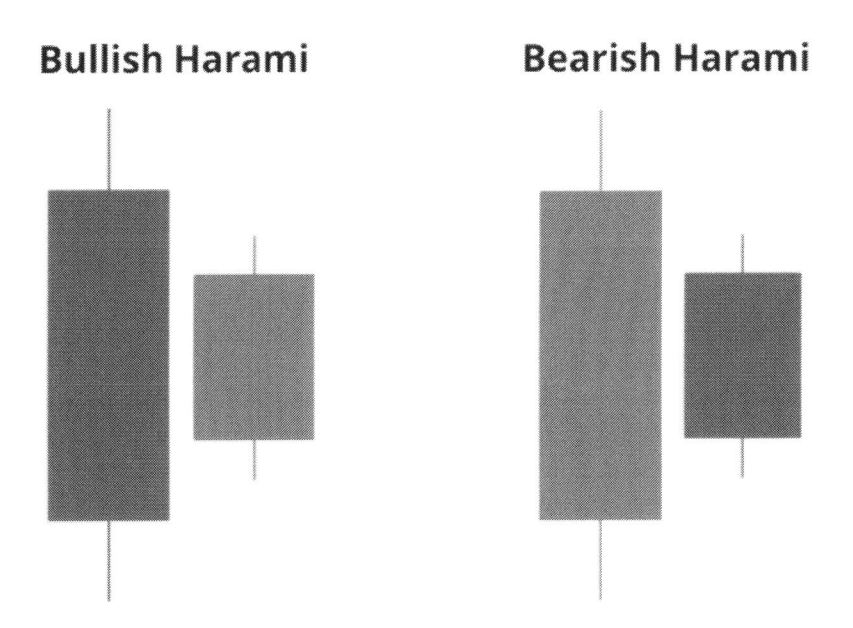

Bullish Harami   **Bearish Harami**

Bullish Harami

A Bullish Harami pattern forms during a downtrend and signals a potential reversal to the upside. It consists of a large bearish candlestick followed by a smaller bullish candlestick whose body is entirely contained within the body of the first candle.

- **Key Characteristics:**
    - The first candlestick is bearish, indicating strong selling pressure.
    - The second candlestick is bullish, opening and closing within the body of the first candle.
    - Shadows may extend outside the range of the first candle, but the body must remain fully contained.
- **Significance:** The Bullish Harami suggests that selling pressure is weakening, and buyers are beginning to regain control, potentially leading to an upward reversal.
- **Example:** A stock in a downtrend closes at $50 (first bearish candle). The next session opens at $49, closes at $51, and remains within the range of the previous candle, forming a Bullish Harami.
Practical Application:
- Look for confirmation from a subsequent bullish candlestick that closes above the high of the pattern.
- Combine with key support levels or oversold indicators like RSI to validate the pattern.
- Place stop-loss orders below the low of the first candlestick to manage risk.

Bearish Harami

A Bearish Harami pattern forms during an uptrend and signals a potential reversal to the downside. It consists of a large bullish candlestick followed by a smaller bearish candlestick whose body is entirely contained within the body of the first candle.

- **Key Characteristics:**
    - The first candlestick is bullish, reflecting strong buying pressure.
    - The second candlestick is bearish, opening and closing within the body of the first candle.
    - Shadows may extend beyond the first candle, but the body must stay fully contained.
- **Significance:** The Bearish Harami indicates that buying momentum is fading, and sellers may begin to take control, possibly leading to a downward reversal.

Chapter 6:
Dual Candlestick Patterns

- **Example:** A stock in an uptrend closes at $100 (first bullish candle). The next session opens at $101, closes at $99, and remains within the range of the previous candle, forming a Bearish Harami.
  Practical Application:
- Wait for confirmation from a bearish candlestick that closes below the low of the pattern.
- Use resistance levels or overbought indicators to strengthen the case for a reversal.
- Place stop-loss orders above the high of the first candlestick to limit potential losses.

Harami Cross

The Harami Cross is a variation of the Harami pattern where the second candlestick is a Doji, indicating even greater indecision in the market. A Doji forms when the open and close prices are nearly identical, resulting in a very small or nonexistent body.

- **Bullish Harami Cross:** Appears during a downtrend and signals potential bullish reversal. The small Doji highlights extreme hesitation among sellers, suggesting a possible shift in momentum.

- **Bearish Harami Cross:** Forms during an uptrend and signals potential bearish reversal. The Doji reflects indecision among buyers, indicating waning momentum.
  Significance: The Harami Cross is considered a stronger reversal signal than the standard Harami due to the presence of the Doji, which underscores market indecision.
  Practical Application:

- Look for confirmation in the form of a strong candlestick following the Harami Cross in the direction of the anticipated reversal.

- Combine the pattern with support/resistance levels and volume analysis to validate its significance.

- Place stop-loss orders below or above the range of the Harami Cross to protect against false signals.

Harami patterns are effective tools for identifying early signs of reversals or pauses in market trends. While they provide valuable insights, they are most reliable when confirmed by additional technical tools such as trendlines, support/resistance levels, and momentum indicators. Recognizing and utilizing Bullish Harami, Bearish Harami, and Harami Cross patterns allows traders to make more informed decisions and capitalize on market shifts.

6.3 Piercing Patterns

Piercing patterns are dual-candlestick formations that signal potential reversals in the market. They highlight a significant shift in sentiment, making them reliable indicators for spotting turning points. The Piercing Line and Dark Cloud Cover are two key patterns within this category, representing bullish and bearish reversals, respectively. Understanding their structure and context is crucial for effectively integrating these patterns into your trading strategy.

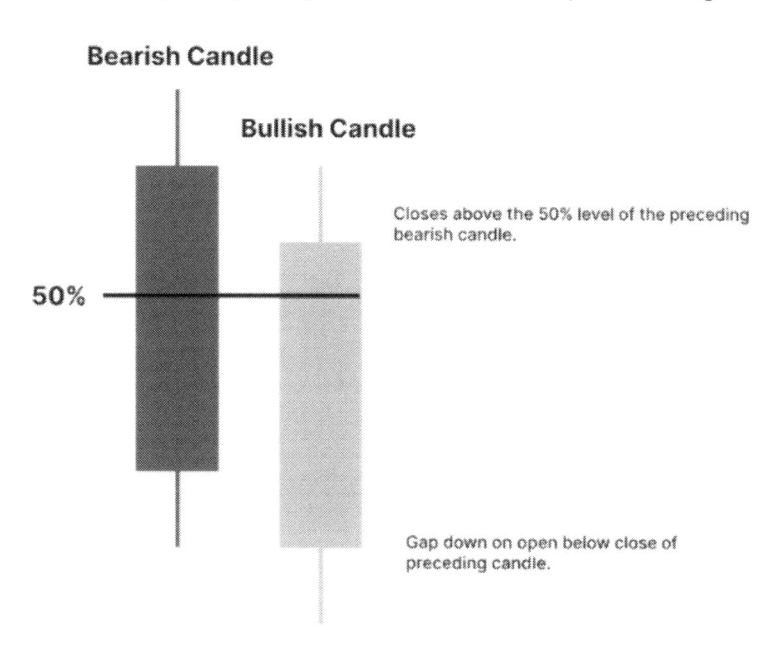

Piercing Line

The Piercing Line is a bullish reversal pattern that forms during a downtrend. It consists of a bearish candlestick followed by a bullish candlestick that "pierces" more than halfway into the body of the previous bearish candle.

- **Key Characteristics:**
    - The first candlestick is bearish, showing continued selling pressure.
    - The second candlestick is bullish, opening below the previous candle's close and closing above the midpoint of the first candle's body.
    - Shadows are less significant; the focus is on the bodies of the candles.
- **Significance:** The Piercing Line indicates that buyers are gaining control after a period of selling, suggesting a potential upward reversal. This pattern is more reliable when it appears at a key support level.

Chapter 6:
Dual Candlestick Patterns

- **Example:** During a downtrend, a stock closes at $50 (first bearish candle). The next session opens at $48, rises steadily, and closes at $52, piercing more than halfway into the previous candle's body.

    Practical Application:

- Confirm the pattern by waiting for a bullish candlestick or increased volume in the next session.
- Use the high of the bullish candlestick as a breakout point for entry.
- Place stop-loss orders below the low of the pattern to manage risk.

Dark Cloud Cover

The Dark Cloud Cover is a bearish reversal pattern that forms during an uptrend. It consists of a bullish candlestick followed by a bearish candlestick that "clouds" more than halfway into the body of the previous bullish candle.

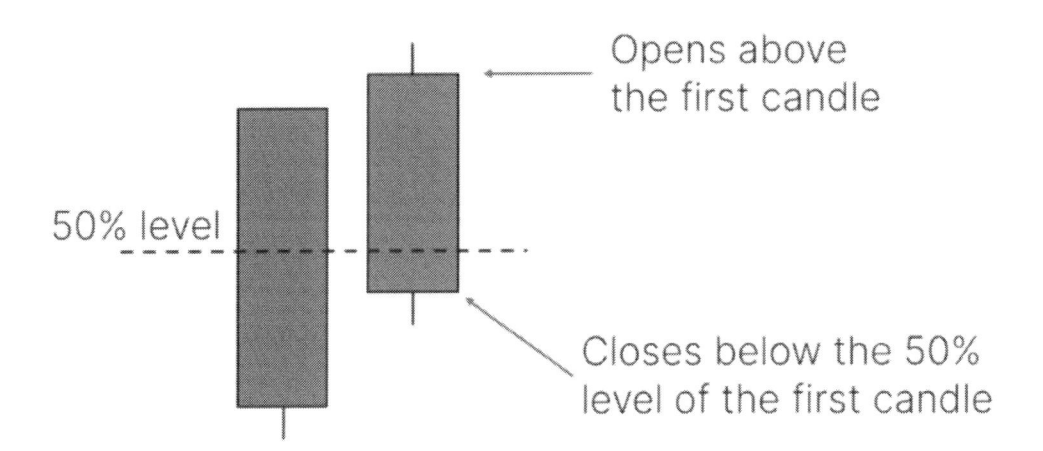

- **Key Characteristics:**
    - The first candlestick is bullish, reflecting strong buying momentum.
    - The second candlestick is bearish, opening above the previous candle's close and closing below the midpoint of the first candle's body.
    - Shadows are less important, but the bearish candle's body must close deeply into the bullish candle's body.

- **Significance:** The Dark Cloud Cover suggests that selling pressure is increasing, potentially reversing the prevailing uptrend. It is most effective when it forms near a resistance level or in overbought conditions.
- **Example:** In an uptrend, a stock closes at $100 (first bullish candle). The next session opens at $102, falls sharply, and closes at $98, penetrating more than halfway into the previous candle's body.

Practical Application:

- Wait for confirmation with a bearish candlestick that breaks below the low of the pattern or significant volume indicating seller dominance.
- Use the low of the bearish candlestick as a signal for entering a short position.
- Place stop-loss orders above the high of the pattern to limit risk.

Piercing patterns are highly effective for identifying reversals when used in the proper context. To maximize their reliability, combine them with key support and resistance levels, momentum indicators, or trendlines. These patterns are particularly powerful in volatile markets where sentiment shifts are more pronounced.

6.4 TWEEZER FORMATIONS

Tweezer formations are dual-candlestick patterns that indicate potential reversals in the market. These patterns derive their name from the resemblance of their shape to a pair of tweezers. Tweezer Tops and Tweezer Bottoms are key variations that signify bearish and bullish reversals, respectively. They are most reliable when they occur at significant support or resistance levels.

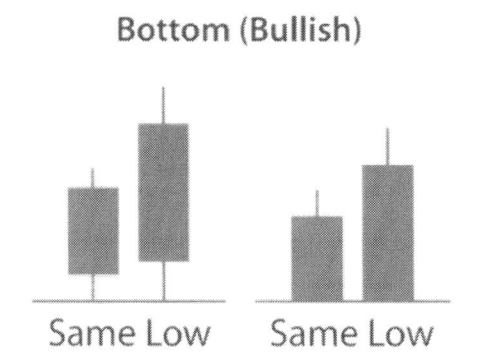

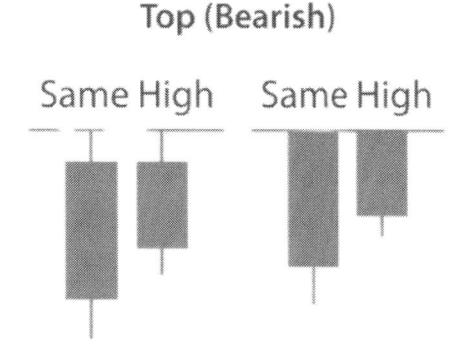

Chapter 6:
Dual Candlestick Patterns

Tweezer Tops

Tweezer Tops are bearish reversal patterns that form during an uptrend. This formation consists of two consecutive candlesticks with matching or nearly identical highs, signaling that buying momentum is weakening.

- **Key Characteristics:**
    - The first candlestick is bullish, indicating strong buying pressure.
    - The second candlestick is bearish, opening at or near the first candlestick's high and closing lower.
    - The identical or closely matching highs suggest resistance at that level.
- **Significance:** The matching highs highlight that buyers failed to push the price higher on the second attempt, paving the way for sellers to take control.
- **Example:** In an uptrend, a stock closes at $100 (first bullish candle). The next session opens at $101 but closes at $99 (second bearish candle), forming a Tweezer Top.
Practical Application:
- Confirm the pattern with a bearish candlestick following the Tweezer Top or a break below a key support level.
- Use the low of the second candlestick as a potential breakout point for entering a short position.
- Place stop-loss orders above the high of the pattern to manage risk.

Tweezer Bottoms

Tweezer Bottoms are bullish reversal patterns that form during a downtrend. This formation comprises two consecutive candlesticks with matching or nearly identical lows, signaling that selling pressure is diminishing.

- **Key Characteristics:**
    - The first candlestick is bearish, showing strong selling momentum.
    - The second candlestick is bullish, opening at or near the first candlestick's low and closing higher.
    - The identical or closely matching lows suggest support at that level.
- **Significance:** The matching lows indicate that sellers were unable to push the price lower on the second attempt, allowing buyers to regain control.
- **Example:** In a downtrend, a stock closes at $50 (first bearish candle). The next session opens at $49 but closes at $51 (second bullish candle), forming a Tweezer Bottom.
Practical Application:

- Look for confirmation with a bullish candlestick after the Tweezer Bottom or a break above a key resistance level.
- Use the high of the second candlestick as a signal for entering a long position.
- Place stop-loss orders below the low of the pattern to limit potential losses.

Context and Application of Tweezer Formations

Tweezer formations are most effective when they appear at significant support or resistance levels and are confirmed by additional technical indicators.

- **In an Uptrend:** Tweezer Tops near a resistance level can signal the end of the trend and the start of a bearish reversal.
- **In a Downtrend:** Tweezer Bottoms near a support level suggest the beginning of a bullish reversal.

These patterns often benefit from volume analysis. Higher volume on the second candlestick of the Tweezer formation increases the reliability of the signal.

Chapter 7:
Triple Candlestick Patterns

7.1 STAR FORMATIONS

Star formations are triple-candlestick patterns that signal potential reversals in the market. These patterns derive their name from the middle candlestick, which appears separated from the others, resembling a "star." Morning Star and Evening Star patterns indicate bullish and bearish reversals, respectively, while variations involving Doji candles add nuance to their interpretation. Recognizing these formations and understanding their context can help traders anticipate significant trend changes.

Morning Star

The Morning Star is a bullish reversal pattern that forms at the end of a downtrend. It consists of three distinct candlesticks:

1. **First Candle (Bearish):** A large bearish candlestick that reflects strong selling pressure, continuing the prevailing downtrend.

2. **Second Candle (Indecision or Small Body):** A small-bodied candlestick that gaps below the first candle, indicating hesitation or a balance between buyers and sellers. This "star" is the key component, reflecting a potential shift in sentiment.

3. **Third Candle (Bullish):** A strong bullish candlestick that closes well into the body of the first candlestick, confirming the reversal.

- **Significance:** The Morning Star highlights a transition from seller dominance to buyer control, signaling the potential start of an uptrend.

- **Example:** A stock in a downtrend closes at $50 (first bearish candle), gaps down to open at $48 and closes at $49 (second indecisive candle), and then opens at $49 and closes at $53 (third bullish candle).

Practical Application:

- Confirm the pattern by observing a bullish candlestick or higher volume in subsequent sessions.

- Use the high of the third candlestick as a potential breakout level for entry.
- Place stop-loss orders below the low of the pattern to manage risk.

Evening Star

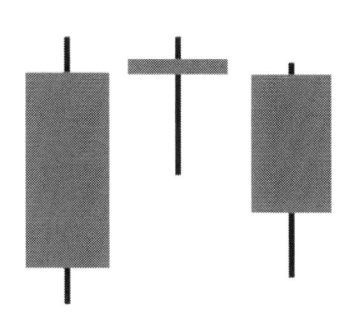

The Evening Star is a bearish reversal pattern that forms at the end of an uptrend. It is the opposite of the Morning Star and consists of three candlesticks:

1. **First Candle (Bullish):** A large bullish candlestick reflecting strong buying pressure, continuing the prevailing uptrend.

2. **Second Candle (Indecision or Small Body):** A small-bodied candlestick that gaps above the first candle, indicating hesitation or a balance between buyers and sellers. This "star" signifies waning bullish momentum.

3. **Third Candle (Bearish):** A strong bearish candlestick that closes well into the body of the first candlestick, confirming the reversal.

- **Significance:** The Evening Star highlights a transition from buyer dominance to seller control, signaling the potential start of a downtrend.

- **Example:** A stock in an uptrend closes at $100 (first bullish candle), gaps up to open at $102 and closes at $101 (second indecisive candle), and then opens at $101 and closes at $95 (third bearish candle).

  Practical Application:

- Wait for confirmation in the form of a bearish candlestick breaking below key support levels.
- Use the low of the third candlestick as a potential entry point for short positions.
- Place stop-loss orders above the high of the pattern to limit potential losses.

Doji Star Variations

Doji Star variations occur when the second candlestick in the Morning Star or Evening Star pattern is a Doji. A Doji forms when the open and close prices are nearly identical, resulting in a very small or nonexistent body.

- **Morning Doji Star:** A bullish reversal pattern that forms after a downtrend, where the middle Doji candle amplifies market indecision before the reversal.

Chapter 7:
Triple Candlestick Patterns

- **Evening Doji Star:** A bearish reversal pattern that forms after an uptrend, where the middle Doji candle intensifies the signal of waning momentum.
- **Significance:** The presence of a Doji increases the reliability of the pattern as it underscores the market's uncertainty and hesitation before the reversal.
Practical Application:
- Look for strong confirmation following a Doji Star variation, such as a large bullish or bearish candlestick accompanied by high volume.
- Combine these patterns with key support and resistance levels or trendlines to validate their significance.

Context and Use of Star Formations
- **In Downtrends:** Morning Stars and Morning Doji Stars signal that selling pressure is dissipating, offering opportunities to enter long positions.
- **In Uptrends:** Evening Stars and Evening Doji Stars highlight diminishing buying momentum, suggesting potential short-selling opportunities.
- **Support and Resistance:** The effectiveness of Star formations increases when they appear near major support or resistance levels.

7.2 SOLDIER PATTERNS

Soldier patterns are powerful triple-candlestick formations that indicate a strong continuation or reversal of a trend. The **Three White Soldiers** pattern signals a bullish continuation or reversal, while the **Three Black Crows** pattern suggests a bearish reversal or continuation. These patterns are particularly effective when they form after a prolonged trend or near key support and resistance levels, providing clear and reliable signals for traders.

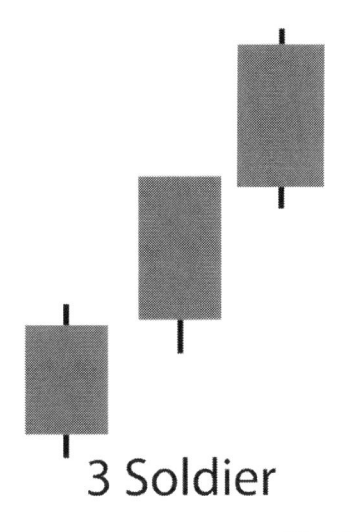

Three White Soldiers

The Three White Soldiers pattern is a bullish reversal or continuation formation that appears after a downtrend or a period of consolidation. It consists of three consecutive bullish candlesticks, each with progressively higher closes.

- **Key Characteristics:**
  ○ Each candlestick opens within or near the previous candlestick's body and closes above its high.
  ○ The candlesticks have long bodies, reflecting strong buying momentum.

3 Soldier

- o Shadows are typically short, indicating minimal resistance from sellers during the session.
- **Significance:** This pattern indicates sustained buying pressure and a strong reversal or continuation of an uptrend.
- **Example:** In a downtrend, a stock closes at $50 (first bullish candle). The next session opens at $51 and closes at $55 (second bullish candle). The third session opens at $56 and closes at $60, completing the pattern.

Practical Application:

- Confirm the pattern with increased volume or subsequent bullish candlesticks to ensure momentum is intact.
- Use the high of the third candlestick as a potential breakout point for entering a long position.
- Place stop-loss orders below the low of the first candlestick to manage risk.
Note: The Three White Soldiers pattern is most reliable when it forms near a key support level or after oversold conditions.

Three Black Crows

The Three Black Crows pattern is a bearish reversal or continuation formation that appears after an uptrend or a period of consolidation. It consists of three consecutive bearish candlesticks, each with progressively lower closes.

- **Key Characteristics:**
    - o Each candlestick opens within or near the previous candlestick's body and closes below its low.
        - o The candlesticks have long bodies, reflecting strong selling momentum.
        - o Shadows are typically short, indicating limited buying pressure during the session.
    - **Significance:** This pattern highlights sustained selling pressure and signals a strong reversal or continuation of a downtrend.
    - **Example:** In an uptrend, a stock closes at $100 (first bearish candle). The next session opens at $99 and closes at $95 (second bearish candle). The third session opens at $94 and closes at $90, completing the pattern.

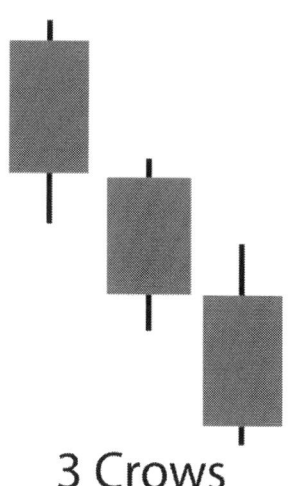

3 Crows

Chapter 7:
Triple Candlestick Patterns

Practical Application:

- Confirm the pattern with a subsequent bearish candlestick or increased volume to validate the trend.
- Use the low of the third candlestick as a signal for entering a short position.
- Place stop-loss orders above the high of the first candlestick to limit potential losses.
  Note: The Three Black Crows pattern is particularly effective when it forms near a key resistance level or after overbought conditions.

Context and Use of Soldier Patterns

- **In Consolidation:** Soldier patterns often signal the end of a consolidation phase and the start of a new trend.
- **In Trends:** When they occur within an established trend, they confirm the continuation of the existing momentum.
- **Volume Confirmation:** These patterns are more reliable when accompanied by high volume, reflecting strong participation in the move.

7.3 THREE METHODS PATTERNS

Three Methods patterns are continuation formations that signal a pause in the trend followed by a resumption of the prevailing direction. These patterns consist of five candlesticks and are divided into two main types: **Rising Three Methods** (bullish continuation) and **Falling Three Methods** (bearish continuation). Recognizing these patterns can help traders capitalize on trend continuation opportunities with greater confidence.

Rising Three Methods

The Rising Three Methods pattern appears in an uptrend and signals that the bullish momentum is intact despite a temporary consolidation.

- **Key Characteristics:**

1. The first candlestick is a large bullish candlestick, reflecting strong upward momentum.

2. The next three candlesticks are small-bodied and bearish, moving downward but staying within the range of the first candlestick.

3. The fifth candlestick is another large bullish candlestick, closing above the high of the first candlestick, confirming the continuation of the uptrend.

- **Significance:** This pattern demonstrates that sellers attempted to push the price lower but failed to overcome the strength of the buyers, leading to a continuation of the uptrend.
- **Example:** A stock in an uptrend closes at $100 (first bullish candle). The next three sessions see small bearish candles that close between $98 and $99. The fifth session closes at $105, completing the pattern.

Practical Application:

- Enter a long position after the fifth candlestick closes above the high of the first candlestick.
- Use the low of the consolidation phase as a stop-loss level.
- Confirm the pattern with increased volume during the fifth candlestick to validate the resumption of the trend.

Falling Three Methods

The Falling Three Methods pattern appears in a downtrend and signals that the bearish momentum is intact despite a brief consolidation.

- **Key Characteristics:**

1. The first candlestick is a large bearish candlestick, reflecting strong downward momentum.

2. The next three candlesticks are small-bodied and bullish, moving upward but staying within the range of the first candlestick.

3. The fifth candlestick is another large bearish candlestick, closing below the low of the first candlestick, confirming the continuation of the downtrend.

- **Significance:** This pattern indicates that buyers attempted to push the price higher but were overpowered by sellers, leading to a continuation of the downtrend.

- **Example:** A stock in a downtrend closes at $50 (first bearish candle). The next three sessions see small bullish candles that close between $51 and $52. The fifth session closes at $45, completing the pattern.

Practical Application:

- Enter a short position after the fifth candlestick closes below the low of the first candlestick.

- Use the high of the consolidation phase as a stop-loss level.
- Confirm the pattern with increased volume during the fifth candlestick to strengthen the signal.

Context and Use of Three Methods Patterns

- **In Trends:** These patterns provide traders with confidence that the trend will continue, even after a brief pause.
- **Volume Confirmation:** Volume is a critical factor. Lower volume during the consolidation phase and higher volume during the fifth candlestick increase the pattern's reliability.
- **Support and Resistance:** These patterns are more reliable when they form within trending markets and align with key support or resistance levels.

7.4 Abandoned Baby Patterns

The Abandoned Baby is a rare but highly reliable triple-candlestick pattern that signals a strong reversal in the market. It can occur as a **bullish reversal** at the end of a downtrend or as a **bearish reversal** at the end of an uptrend. The unique feature of this pattern is the middle candlestick, which is a Doji that "gaps" away from the previous and subsequent candlesticks, creating a clear separation. This gap visually isolates the Doji, resembling an "abandoned baby."

Bullish Abandoned Baby

The Bullish Abandoned Baby forms at the end of a downtrend and signals a reversal to the upside.

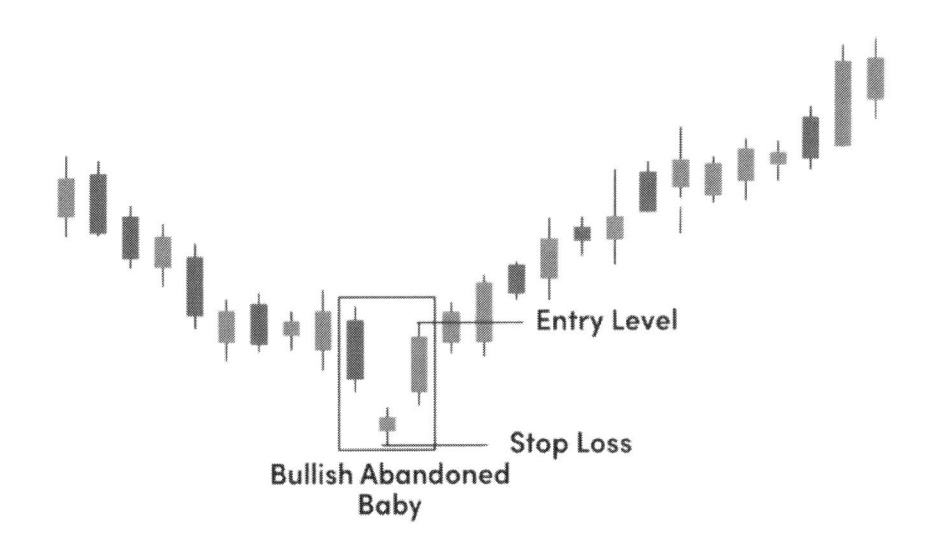

- **Key Characteristics:**
    1. **First Candle:** A large bearish candlestick that reflects strong selling pressure, continuing the downtrend.
    2. **Second Candle:** A Doji candlestick that gaps below the first candle, indicating indecision and a potential shift in momentum.
    3. **Third Candle:** A large bullish candlestick that gaps above the Doji and closes within or above the body of the first candlestick.
- **Significance:** This pattern highlights that sellers are losing control, while buyers are stepping in forcefully to reverse the trend.
- **Example:** A stock in a downtrend closes at $50 (first bearish candle). The next session gaps down to open at $48 and forms a Doji with a high of $49. The following session gaps up to open at $51 and closes at $55, completing the Bullish Abandoned Baby pattern.

Practical Application:

- Enter a long position when the third candlestick closes above the high of the Doji.
- Place a stop-loss order below the low of the Doji to limit potential losses.
- Confirm the pattern with volume analysis; higher volume during the third candlestick strengthens the signal.

Bearish Abandoned Baby

The Bearish Abandoned Baby forms at the end of an uptrend and signals a reversal to the downside.

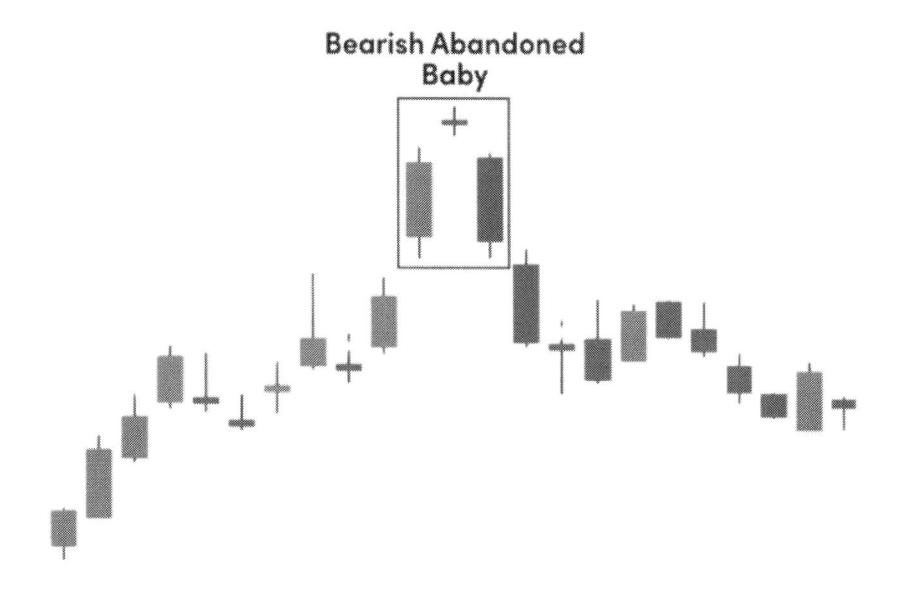

Chapter 7:
Triple Candlestick Patterns

- **Key Characteristics:**
    1. **First Candle:** A large bullish candlestick that reflects strong buying pressure, continuing the uptrend.
    2. **Second Candle:** A Doji candlestick that gaps above the first candle, indicating indecision and potential exhaustion of buying momentum.
    3. **Third Candle:** A large bearish candlestick that gaps below the Doji and closes within or below the body of the first candlestick.
- **Significance:** This pattern shows that buyers are losing control, and sellers are taking over, signaling the start of a downtrend.
- **Example:** A stock in an uptrend closes at $100 (first bullish candle). The next session gaps up to open at $102 and forms a Doji with a low of $101. The following session gaps down to open at $98 and closes at $95, completing the Bearish Abandoned Baby pattern.

Practical Application:

- Enter a short position when the third candlestick closes below the low of the Doji.
- Place a stop-loss order above the high of the Doji to manage risk.
- Look for confirmation through increased volume during the third candlestick to validate the pattern.

Context and Use of Abandoned Baby Patterns

- **High Reliability:** The gaps on either side of the Doji make this pattern particularly reliable for signaling strong reversals.
- **Market Context:** The effectiveness of the pattern increases when it aligns with key support or resistance levels or is confirmed by other technical tools, such as RSI indicating overbought or oversold conditions.
- **Volume Considerations:** High volume on the third candlestick enhances the pattern's reliability, reflecting strong participation in the reversal.

The Abandoned Baby is a potent reversal signal that reflects a decisive change in market sentiment. While it is rare, its appearance offers traders a high-confidence opportunity to act on emerging trends.

The Candlestick Trading Profit Formula

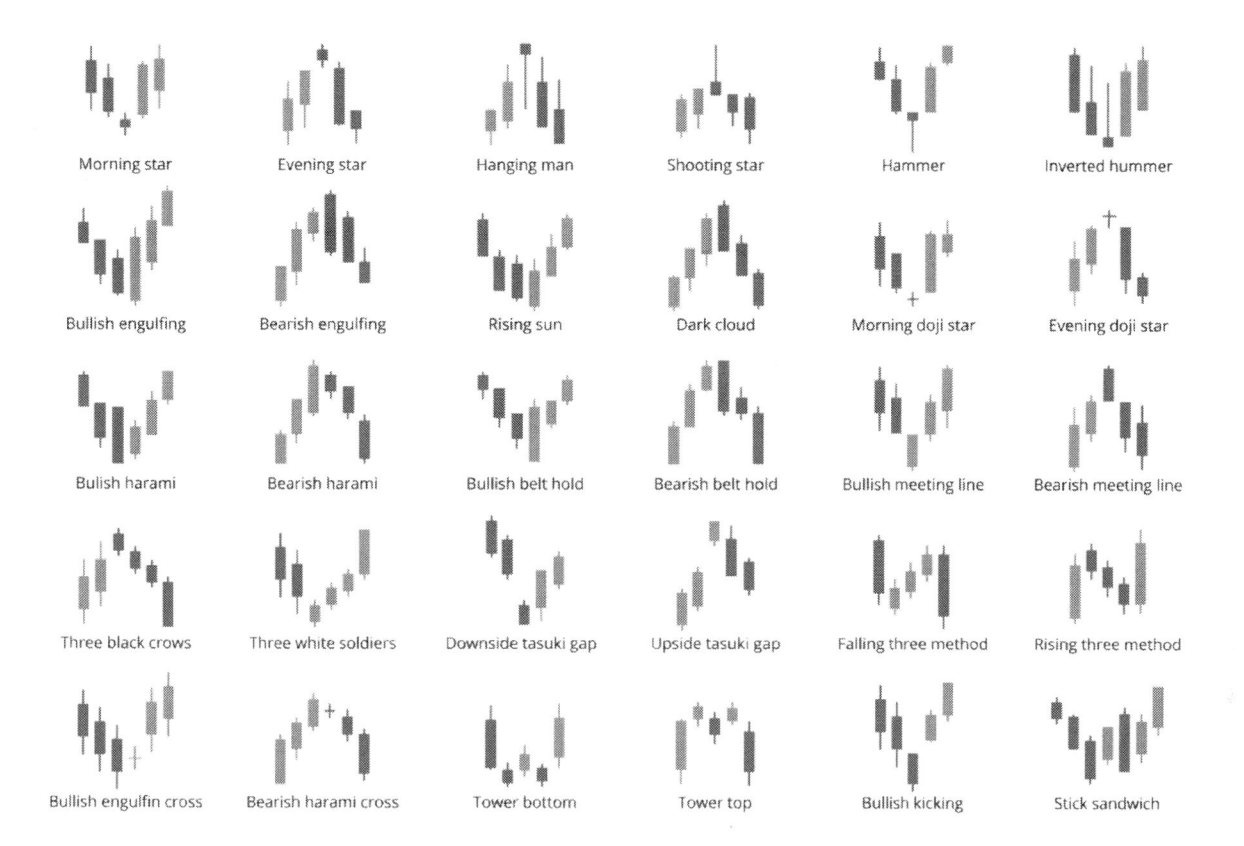

Morning star	Evening star	Hanging man	Shooting star	Hammer	Inverted hammer
Bullish engulfing	Bearish engulfing	Rising sun	Dark cloud	Morning doji star	Evening doji star
Bulish harami	Bearish harami	Bullish belt hold	Bearish belt hold	Bullish meeting line	Bearish meeting line
Three black crows	Three white soldiers	Downside tasuki gap	Upside tasuki gap	Falling three method	Rising three method
Bullish engulfin cross	Bearish harami cross	Tower bottom	Tower top	Bullish kicking	Stick sandwich

Chapter 8:
Complex Pattern Recognition

Chapter 8:
Complex Pattern Recognition

8.1 MULTIPLE TIMEFRAME PATTERN ANALYSIS

Trading is often compared to solving a puzzle, and one of the most effective ways to see the bigger picture is through **multiple timeframe analysis**. By examining patterns across different timeframes, traders can gain a deeper understanding of market dynamics and improve their ability to make well-informed decisions. This approach involves analyzing charts from the smallest (e.g., 1-minute or 5-minute) to the largest (e.g., daily, weekly, or even monthly) timeframes, each offering unique insights into the market's behavior.

Why Multiple Timeframes Matter

Relying on a single timeframe is like examining one piece of a puzzle—it provides some information, but not the full picture. Multiple timeframe analysis helps you:

- **Understand Market Context:** Smaller timeframes reveal granular details, while larger timeframes provide the overarching trend. Together, they offer a comprehensive view.
- **Confirm Patterns:** A pattern forming on a smaller timeframe may lack significance if it contradicts the dominant trend on a larger timeframe. Conversely, a pattern confirmed across multiple timeframes carries more weight.

- **Enhance Precision:** Use larger timeframes to identify major support and resistance levels, and smaller timeframes to pinpoint precise entry and exit points.

How to Conduct Multiple Timeframe Analysis

1. **Start with the Larger Timeframe:**

   Begin by analyzing a higher timeframe (e.g., weekly or daily) to determine the primary trend. Ask yourself:
   - Is the market trending upward, downward, or sideways?
   - Are there any major candlestick patterns (e.g., Morning Star, Three Black Crows) signaling potential reversals?

2. **Drill Down to the Intermediate Timeframe:**

   Move to an intermediate timeframe (e.g., daily or 4-hour) to refine your understanding of the trend. This is where you can identify:
   - Continuation patterns like Rising Three Methods or flags.
   - Intermediate support and resistance levels that may impact short-term movements.

3. **Zoom into the Smaller Timeframe:**

   Finally, examine a smaller timeframe (e.g., 1-hour or 15-minute) to:
   - Spot precise entry and exit opportunities within the context of the larger trend.
   - Observe short-term candlestick formations, such as hammers or engulfing patterns, for actionable signals.

Practical Example: Identifying a Bullish Opportunity

- **Weekly Chart:** Shows a strong bullish trend with the price recently bouncing off a long-term support level.
- **Daily Chart:** Confirms the bullish trend with a Morning Star pattern forming near the support level.
- **1-Hour Chart:** Reveals a bullish engulfing candlestick breaking above a resistance zone, providing a precise entry point.

By aligning all three timeframes, you increase the probability of a successful trade, as each layer supports the bullish case.

Common Pitfalls to Avoid

- **Overcomplicating Analysis:** Too many timeframes can lead to confusion. Stick to three timeframes: large, intermediate, and small.

Chapter 8:
Complex Pattern Recognition

- **Ignoring Contradictions:** If smaller timeframes show a reversal while the larger timeframe trend remains intact, exercise caution. Focus on trades aligned with the dominant trend.
- **Chasing Short-Term Noise:** Avoid acting on patterns in the smallest timeframe without confirming their relevance in the broader context.

Tips for Success

- **Customize Timeframes:** Adjust timeframes based on your trading style. Swing traders may use weekly, daily, and 4-hour charts, while day traders might focus on hourly, 15-minute, and 5-minute charts.
- **Use Key Levels:** Mark support and resistance zones from higher timeframes to guide decisions in smaller timeframes.
- **Leverage Indicators:** Combine multiple timeframe analysis with indicators like moving averages or RSI to validate patterns.

Benefits of Mastering Multiple Timeframe Analysis

- Provides clarity by connecting short-term movements with long-term trends.
- Reduces false signals by confirming patterns across timeframes.
- Enhances confidence in decision-making by offering a holistic market perspective.

The image below illustrates a marked strong resistance level on the Daily timeframe. The trader first identifies this level on a higher timeframe and, once it is broken, shifts to a lower timeframe to search for bullish trading opportunities.

Support and resistance levels identified on higher timeframes tend to be more significant, which is why it's essential to establish these levels on your higher timeframe before proceeding.

The image below displays the 1H timeframe following the breakout of the resistance level. After the breakout, the price moved upward, making it advantageous for the trader to adopt a bullish perspective and seek opportunities to capitalize on bullish trend continuations.

The image below highlights a bullish engulfing candlestick on the higher Daily timeframe, aligning with the overall bullish uptrend. Notably, this candlestick forms directly at the 30 EMA (exponential moving average), a tool commonly used by traders for trend-following and pullback strategies. This candlestick pattern aligns seamlessly with the prevailing trend. After spotting the engulfing candlestick, a trader can transition to a lower timeframe to search for bullish trading signals that align with the higher timeframe bias.

The image below depicts the lower 5-minute timeframe, with the blue zone on the left representing the high of the Daily engulfing candlestick. Following the breakout, the price moved upward,

Chapter 8:
Complex Pattern Recognition

offering a trend-following trader the opportunity to execute a successful breakout long trade and capitalize on the bullish momentum. While some traders may act solely on the Daily signal, using a multi-timeframe approach enables traders to pinpoint an optimal entry price and leverage the short-term momentum triggered by the engulfing candlestick.

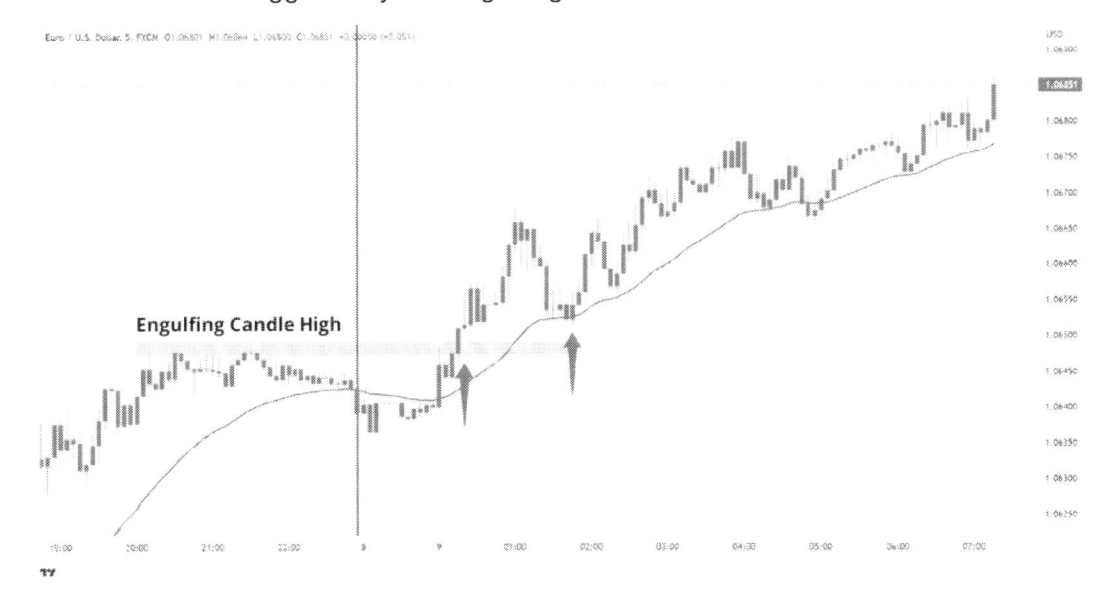

By adopting multiple timeframe analysis, you gain the ability to navigate markets with precision and clarity, aligning your trades with both the immediate opportunities and the broader market narrative. This method not only improves your chances of success but also instills a sense of control and confidence in your trading strategy.

8.2 PATTERN CONFLUENCE

Pattern confluence occurs when multiple technical patterns align or reinforce one another, providing a stronger signal for potential market movements. This concept is a cornerstone of advanced technical analysis, as it enables traders to combine insights from various tools and patterns to make more confident and reliable trading decisions. Confluence leverages the principle that when multiple factors point in the same direction, the probability of a successful trade increases significantly.

The Power of Confluence in Trading

In isolation, a single candlestick or chart pattern may signal a potential reversal or continuation, but it often lacks context. By combining patterns, traders can validate signals and reduce the likelihood of false positives. For example, a Bullish Engulfing pattern forming at a key support level gains credibility when it coincides with a Rising Three Methods continuation pattern or an oversold RSI reading. These layers of agreement add weight to the trade setup, transforming a basic opportunity into a high-probability scenario.

Recognizing Confluence

Confluence can occur at various levels and involves multiple analytical dimensions. For instance, candlestick patterns can align with chart patterns, trendlines, support and resistance levels, or technical indicators. This alignment provides a multi-faceted view of the market and increases the confidence in taking action. A Morning Star pattern, for example, becomes more compelling when it forms near a Fibonacci retracement level and is confirmed by an ascending trendline. Each element complements the other, reinforcing the likelihood of a reversal.

Using Confluence in Trend Trading

Confluence is particularly powerful in trend trading. When a pattern like Three White Soldiers aligns with a breakout above a key resistance level and is supported by strong volume, it signals a robust continuation of the uptrend. Conversely, in a downtrend, a Falling Three Methods pattern that aligns with a breakdown below a critical support level can indicate sustained bearish momentum. These scenarios illustrate how confluence can provide clarity in trend-following strategies.

Confluence in Reversal Scenarios

Reversal setups also benefit from confluence. A Dragonfly Doji at a long-term support level might suggest a potential bullish reversal, but its reliability increases when combined with a Bullish Engulfing pattern and divergence on the MACD. The synergy of these signals confirms the shift in market sentiment and strengthens the case for entering the trade.

Building Confluence into Your Strategy

To effectively use confluence, traders should focus on a balanced combination of elements without overcomplicating their analysis. It is essential to prioritize quality over quantity, identifying two or three key factors that align rather than attempting to validate every possible signal. Overloading the analysis can lead to indecision and missed opportunities.

For instance, a trader might start by identifying a clear chart pattern such as a symmetrical triangle. Next, they could confirm its significance by ensuring the pattern aligns with a candlestick formation, such as a Bullish Engulfing candle at the breakout point. Finally, adding volume confirmation, such as a surge in buying activity, provides the final layer of confluence to justify the trade.

The Benefits of Confluence

Trading with confluence not only increases the probability of success but also builds confidence and discipline. When traders understand the reasons behind their setups and see multiple layers of validation, they are less likely to make impulsive or emotional decisions. This structured approach allows them to approach markets with clarity and focus.

Chapter 8:
Complex Pattern Recognition

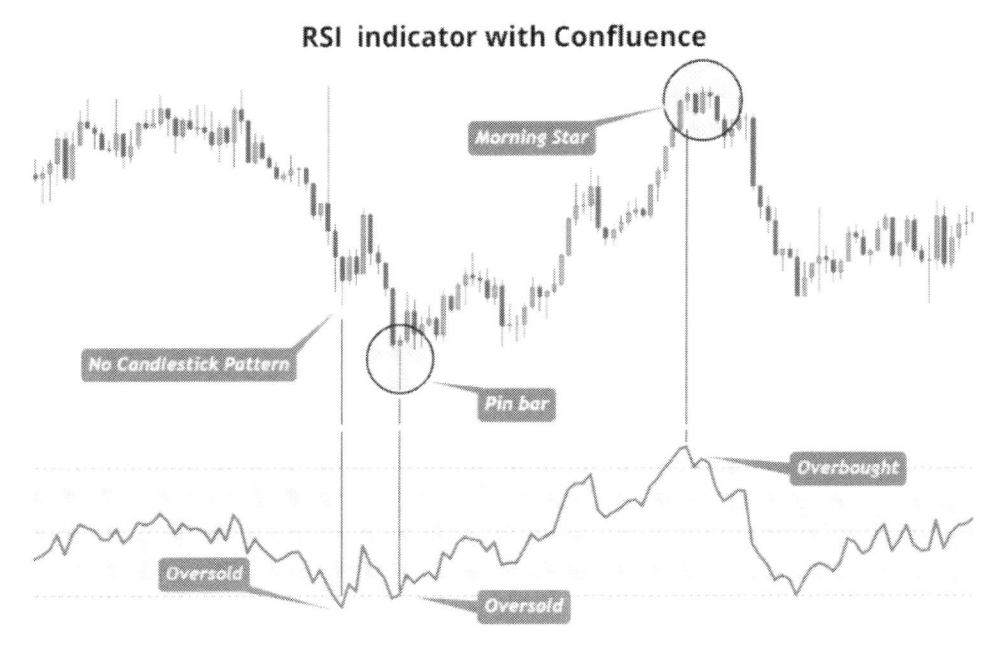

RSI indicator with Confluence chart showing Morning Star, No Candlestick Pattern, Pin bar, Overbought, and Oversold annotations

By mastering pattern confluence, traders can transition from relying on isolated signals to adopting a holistic view of the market, significantly enhancing their ability to identify and execute high-probability trades.

8.3 PATTERN FAILURE ANALYSIS

While recognizing patterns is an essential skill, understanding **pattern failure** is equally critical. Patterns do not guarantee outcomes—they indicate probabilities. Analyzing what happens when patterns fail can provide valuable insights into market behavior and help traders adjust their strategies. Pattern failure often precedes significant moves in the opposite direction, making it a vital concept for advanced traders aiming to refine their skills and minimize risk.

The Relationship Between Confluence and Pattern Failure

Building on the idea of confluence, it's important to recognize that a lack of alignment among key signals increases the likelihood of pattern failure. For instance, a Rising Three Methods pattern that forms without strong volume or breaks below a support level instead of continuing upward could signal a bearish reversal rather than a bullish continuation. This underscores the importance of using confluence to validate patterns and mitigate the risks of acting on incomplete signals.

Why Patterns Fail

Patterns fail for several reasons, many of which are rooted in the dynamic nature of market forces. Key factors include:

- **Market Context:** A pattern forming against the dominant trend or in isolation from broader market dynamics is more likely to fail.

- **Lack of Volume:** Without sufficient volume to confirm the breakout or continuation, the pattern may lack the momentum needed to complete.
- **External Influences:** News events, economic data releases, or geopolitical developments can override technical patterns and cause unexpected moves.
- **Overcrowded Trades:** When too many market participants act on the same pattern, sudden reversals can occur as traders rush to exit their positions.

Recognizing and Interpreting Pattern Failure

Identifying a failed pattern early allows traders to adapt quickly and even capitalize on the situation. Signs of failure include:

- **Breakouts in the Opposite Direction:** A breakout that moves against the expected direction is a clear indicator of pattern failure. For example, a Bullish Engulfing pattern that is followed by a strong bearish candlestick breaking below the pattern's low suggests seller dominance.
- **Inability to Sustain Key Levels:** Patterns that fail to hold support or resistance levels lose their validity. For instance, a Head and Shoulders pattern that doesn't break below the neckline may signal a continuation of the uptrend.
- **Diverging Indicators:** When technical indicators like RSI or MACD contradict the pattern's direction, it often signals impending failure.

Practical Example: Failed Head and Shoulders

Consider a Head and Shoulders pattern forming near a resistance level. The price approaches the neckline but does not break below it. Instead, a bullish engulfing candle forms, pushing the price higher and invalidating the pattern. Recognizing this failure in real-time allows the trader to shift focus from a short-selling opportunity to a potential breakout trade.

Strategies for Managing Pattern Failures

1. **Set Clear Invalidations:** Always define invalidation points before entering a trade based on a pattern. For instance, use the high or low of the pattern as a stop-loss level.
2. **Monitor Volume:** Patterns that fail with low volume are less significant, while those accompanied by high volume often indicate strong counter-moves.
3. **Prepare for Reversals:** Treat pattern failure as an opportunity. A failed breakout, for example, often leads to a strong move in the opposite direction, creating new trading opportunities.
4. **Adapt Dynamically:** Use failure as a signal to reassess market conditions. A failed bearish pattern could mean bullish sentiment is stronger than anticipated, warranting a strategy adjustment.

Chapter 8:
Complex Pattern Recognition

Connecting to Volume and Contextual Strength

Pattern failure ties directly to **volume confirmation** and **contextual pattern strength** (topics covered in subsequent sections). Understanding why a pattern fails can help traders refine their use of volume as a validation tool and assess the strength of patterns in specific contexts. For example, a failed Morning Star at a resistance level, accompanied by low volume, might suggest a temporary pause rather than a full reversal.

By mastering pattern failure analysis, traders can gain a more nuanced understanding of market behavior, improving their ability to adapt and even capitalize on unexpected outcomes. This level of insight not only reduces risks but also opens up new opportunities for profit.

8.4 CONTEXTUAL PATTERN STRENGTH

The strength of a pattern is not determined by its shape alone but by the **context in which it forms**. Contextual pattern strength refers to how market conditions, trend direction, and surrounding technical factors enhance or weaken a pattern's reliability. Understanding the context allows traders to differentiate between high-probability setups and those more likely to fail, improving decision-making and reducing unnecessary risks.

The Role of Market Context

Patterns do not exist in isolation. Their significance is amplified or diminished by the broader market environment. A Bullish Engulfing pattern, for instance, is far more compelling when it forms near a strong support level within an established uptrend than when it appears in a consolidating market. Similarly, a Head and Shoulders pattern carries more weight when accompanied by high trading volume and confirmation from other indicators.

Contextual analysis involves asking key questions:

- **Where is the pattern forming?** Is it near critical support or resistance levels?
- **What is the prevailing trend?** Does the pattern align with the primary trend, or is it counter-trend?
- **Are external factors influencing the market?** News events, earnings reports, or geopolitical developments can affect pattern reliability.

Patterns in Trending Markets

Patterns gain strength when they align with the prevailing trend:

- **Bullish Patterns in Uptrends:** Continuation patterns like Rising Three Methods or bullish candlestick formations near trendline support are more likely to succeed when the market is already moving upward.
- **Bearish Patterns in Downtrends:** Patterns like Three Black Crows or Falling Three Methods forming near trendline resistance are more reliable in a bearish market.

In contrast, reversal patterns (e.g., Morning Star, Evening Star) are most effective when they appear at the end of a prolonged trend, signaling exhaustion.

Patterns in Consolidating Markets

In range-bound markets, patterns near the extremes of the range—such as a Hammer forming at support or a Shooting Star near resistance—carry more significance. Within consolidation zones, patterns like Spinning Tops or Doji candles reflect indecision and can help traders anticipate breakouts or continued consolidation.

The Impact of Time Frames

Time frame plays a critical role in contextual pattern strength. Patterns on higher time frames (e.g., daily, weekly) tend to be more reliable than those on smaller time frames (e.g., 5-minute, 15-minute). For instance:

Chapter 8:
Complex Pattern Recognition

- A Bullish Engulfing pattern on a weekly chart carries more weight than the same pattern on a 1-hour chart, as it reflects broader market sentiment.
- Traders should align smaller time frame patterns with the context provided by larger time frames to enhance reliability.

Combining Context with Volume

Volume acts as a confirming factor for contextual pattern strength. A pattern supported by high volume indicates stronger conviction among market participants. For example:

- A Bullish Morning Star at a support level, accompanied by a volume surge, signals a high-probability reversal.
- Conversely, a similar pattern forming with low volume may lack the momentum needed for a sustained move.

Practical Example: Contextual Analysis

Imagine a trader identifies a Bearish Engulfing pattern on a daily chart. The pattern forms near a resistance level in an overall downtrend and is accompanied by increased selling volume. These contextual factors—trend alignment, key level proximity, and volume confirmation—significantly enhance the pattern's strength and likelihood of success.

Adapting to Weak Context

When patterns form in weak contexts, they should be treated with caution. For example, a Hammer forming in the middle of a consolidating market lacks the significance it would have if it appeared at a long-term support level. In such cases, traders should wait for additional confirmation or consider avoiding the trade.

By understanding contextual pattern strength, traders can refine their ability to filter high-quality setups and avoid weak or unreliable patterns. This approach not only increases the probability of successful trades but also instills a disciplined, context-aware mindset essential for long-term success.

8.5 Volume Confirmation in Patterns

Volume is a critical component of technical analysis, serving as a powerful confirmation tool for candlestick and chart patterns. It reflects the intensity of market activity and provides insight into the conviction of buyers and sellers. Understanding how to use volume in conjunction with patterns can help traders validate signals, identify false moves, and improve the accuracy of their trading decisions.

The Importance of Volume in Pattern Analysis

Patterns alone offer probabilities, but volume adds a layer of confirmation by revealing the level of participation behind price movements. High volume indicates strong conviction, while low volume suggests hesitation or a lack of interest. A Bullish Engulfing pattern, for instance, is more reliable when accompanied by a surge in volume, as it shows that buyers are actively driving the reversal.

Volume confirmation also helps traders distinguish between genuine breakouts and false breakouts. A breakout from a triangle pattern with high volume is likely to sustain its movement, while a low-volume breakout is more prone to reversal.

Using Volume with Key Patterns

1. **Reversal Patterns:**

   Volume is essential for confirming reversal patterns like Morning Star, Evening Star, or Head and Shoulders.

   - A Morning Star near support with increasing volume on the third bullish candlestick signals a strong likelihood of reversal.
   - Conversely, an Evening Star near resistance with declining volume may indicate weak conviction, requiring additional confirmation.

2. **Continuation Patterns:**

   Patterns like Rising Three Methods or Falling Three Methods require consistent or increasing volume to confirm the trend's continuation.

   - In a Rising Three Methods pattern, lower volume during the consolidation phase and higher volume on the breakout candlestick validate the continuation.
   - In a Falling Three Methods pattern, high volume on the breakdown reinforces the bearish signal.

3. **Breakouts:**

   Volume is especially critical for breakout patterns such as triangles or rectangles.

   - High volume during a breakout indicates strong momentum and increases the probability of sustained movement.
   - Low volume suggests potential failure, often leading to false breakouts or re-entries into the pattern's range.

Chapter 8:
Complex Pattern Recognition

Recognizing Divergences

Volume divergences—where price moves in one direction while volume moves in the opposite—can provide early warnings of pattern failure or reversal. For example:

- A Bullish Engulfing pattern forming with decreasing volume may indicate a lack of follow-through, warranting caution.
- Similarly, a breakout above resistance without a corresponding surge in volume is less likely to sustain its upward trajectory.

Volume in Context

The significance of volume depends on the context in which it occurs. A volume spike during a Bullish Engulfing pattern in an uptrend near a support level carries greater weight than a similar pattern forming mid-range in a consolidating market. Aligning volume analysis with broader market context enhances its reliability.

Practical Example: Volume Confirmation

Imagine a stock forming a Head and Shoulders pattern at the top of an uptrend. The right shoulder forms with declining volume, and the neckline breaks with a sudden spike in volume on a bearish candlestick. This volume behavior confirms the bearish breakout and the pattern's validity, signaling a strong opportunity for short positions.

Combining Volume with Indicators

For added precision, volume-based indicators like On-Balance Volume (OBV) or Volume Price Analysis (VPA) can complement raw volume data. These tools help visualize trends in buying and selling pressure, aligning with patterns to provide clearer signals.

The image below illustrates, in the first hour of trading, the stock made an attempt to break out.

Initially, the breakout showed promising volume, but it gradually diminished. This pattern often leads to the stock drifting sideways without any clear direction. While this trade might have ended close to breakeven, your capital would have remained idle. On the bright side, at least it wouldn't have resulted in a loss.

Volume is the heartbeat of market activity, and its integration with pattern analysis provides a powerful edge in trading. By mastering volume confirmation, traders can filter out unreliable setups, validate high-probability trades, and enhance their overall strategy with a deeper understanding of market dynamics.

PART 3:
Chart Pattern Analysis

Automated
Technical Analysis Tool

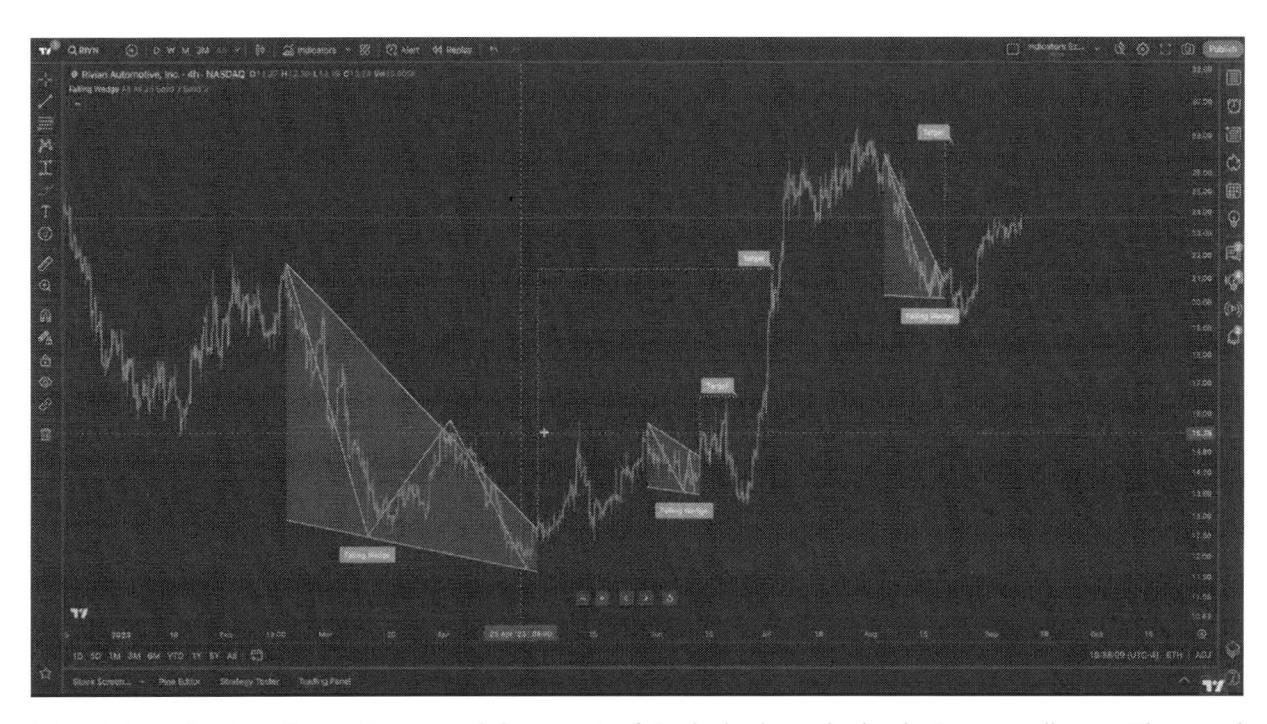

Identifying chart patterns is a crucial aspect of technical analysis, but manually spotting and analyzing them can be time-consuming. To enhance your trading efficiency, I'm excited to introduce the **Automated Technical Analysis** feature on **TradingView**, a tool that brings automation to your chart analysis and empowers you to detect patterns instantly.

What Is the Automated Technical Analysis Tool?

The **Automated Technical Analysis** tool simplifies chart pattern recognition by automatically identifying, drawing, and coloring chart patterns on your TradingView charts. With just a few clicks, you can visualize complex patterns and gain actionable insights, saving valuable time while improving accuracy.

Key Features:
- **Instant Pattern Detection**: Automatically identifies patterns such as triangles, head and shoulders, and more.
- **Time-Saving Efficiency**: Quickly highlights patterns without the need for manual effort.

- **Double-Check Your Work**: Use the tool to validate your own analysis and ensure accuracy.
- **Customizable Options**: Tailor the settings to focus on specific patterns that align with your strategy.
- **Educational Insights**: Study historical patterns to prepare for future market scenarios.

How to Use the Tool

Follow these simple steps to start using the **Automated Technical Analysis** feature:

1. **Scan the QR Code**: Use your smartphone or device to access the tutorial.
2. **Watch the Video Guide**: Learn how to activate and use the tool effectively with a step-by-step explanation.

Scan to Access the Video Guide

Use the QR code below to watch the full tutorial on how to set up and use the **Automated Technical Analysis** tool:

Optimize your trading workflow with the **Automated Technical Analysis** tool. By combining this feature with the strategies in this book, you'll be equipped to spot, analyze, and act on market opportunities more effectively than ever before. This innovative tool bridges the gap between traditional analysis and modern automation, giving you an undeniable edge in the markets.

Chapter 9: Fundamentals of Chart Patterns

9.1 INTRODUCTION TO CHART PATTERNS

Chart patterns are the visual representation of market psychology, reflecting the collective actions and emotions of buyers and sellers. These patterns, formed by price movements over time, are critical tools in technical analysis, providing traders with a roadmap to predict potential market behavior. Whether identifying trend continuations, reversals, or consolidation phases, chart patterns help traders make data-driven decisions with greater confidence.

What Are Chart Patterns?

At their core, chart patterns are recurring shapes and formations that emerge on price charts due to repetitive market behavior. They represent the tug-of-war between bulls and bears, offering clues about the prevailing trend and possible future direction. By recognizing these patterns, traders can anticipate potential price movements and adjust their strategies accordingly.

Chart patterns are broadly categorized into three types:

- **Reversal Patterns:** Indicate a potential change in the existing trend direction (e.g., Head and Shoulders, Double Top).
- **Continuation Patterns:** Suggest the current trend is likely to persist after a temporary pause (e.g., Flags, Pennants).
- **Bilateral Patterns:** Indicate that the price could break out in either direction, requiring additional confirmation (e.g., Symmetrical Triangles).

Understanding these categories allows traders to quickly assess market conditions and select the appropriate response.

Why Are Chart Patterns Important?

Chart patterns serve as a bridge between raw price action and actionable insights. They provide:

- **Clarity Amidst Chaos:** Patterns distill complex market movements into recognizable shapes, making it easier to interpret trends and potential reversals.
- **Strategic Entry and Exit Points:** Patterns often form near critical support and resistance levels, helping traders define precise entry and exit points.

- **A Proven Framework:** These patterns have been studied and validated over decades, offering traders a reliable framework for analyzing markets.

For example, a Bullish Flag forming in an uptrend provides a clear signal to anticipate a continuation of the trend. Similarly, a Double Bottom at a long-term support level suggests a potential reversal to the upside.

Chart Patterns vs. Indicators

While indicators like RSI or MACD provide valuable insights into momentum and overbought/oversold conditions, chart patterns focus on the bigger picture. They reflect the market's structure and provide a narrative for price movements, making them a vital complement to technical indicators. For instance, identifying a Head and Shoulders pattern in conjunction with a bearish divergence on the RSI strengthens the likelihood of a reversal.

The Art and Science of Chart Patterns

Recognizing chart patterns is both an art and a science. The science lies in understanding the rules and characteristics of each pattern—its structure, breakout points, and implications. The art lies in interpreting these patterns within the context of the broader market. A Head and Shoulders pattern is a strong reversal signal, but its reliability increases when it aligns with other factors such as high volume on the breakdown or a confirmed downtrend on a larger timeframe.

Practical Insights

- Always analyze chart patterns within the context of the prevailing trend. For example, a Rising Wedge forming in a downtrend is more reliable as a bearish continuation pattern than if it appears mid-range.

- Combine patterns with other technical tools like support/resistance levels, trendlines, or volume to validate their signals.

- Avoid over-trading based on incomplete patterns. Wait for confirmation, such as a breakout or a close beyond key levels, before taking action.

Chart patterns offer traders a systematic approach to understanding market behavior and identifying profitable opportunities. By mastering these formations and interpreting their context, you can elevate your trading skills and navigate markets with greater confidence and precision. This chapter lays the foundation for deeper exploration of specific patterns, helping you unlock the full potential of chart pattern analysis.

Chapter 9:
Fundamentals of Chart Patterns

9.2 CHART PATTERNS VS. CANDLESTICK PATTERNS

Chart patterns and candlestick patterns are both fundamental tools in technical analysis, yet they serve distinct purposes and offer unique insights into market behavior. Understanding the differences—and how to use them together—can significantly enhance a trader's ability to make informed decisions. While candlestick patterns focus on short-term price action within individual candles or small groups of candles, chart patterns provide a broader view of market trends over extended periods.

Key Differences Between Chart and Candlestick Patterns

1. **Scope of Analysis**
    - **Candlestick Patterns:** These are micro-level tools that highlight specific moments of market sentiment, often signaling immediate price changes. Examples include Doji, Hammer, or Engulfing patterns, which can develop within a single trading session or over a few sessions.
    - **Chart Patterns:** These operate at a macro level, reflecting the cumulative behavior of the market over time. Patterns like Head and Shoulders, Flags, or Triangles unfold over weeks or months and reveal larger trends or trend transitions.

2. **Purpose and Focus**
    - **Candlestick Patterns:** Designed to capture and interpret short-term sentiment shifts, candlestick patterns are ideal for identifying quick reversals or confirming entries and exits.
    - **Chart Patterns:** These focus on the bigger picture, helping traders understand the overall market structure and anticipate longer-term moves.

3. **Formation and Duration**
    - **Candlestick Patterns:** Form within one to three candles, providing immediate insights. For example, a Shooting Star within an uptrend may signal an imminent pullback.
    - **Chart Patterns:** Require more time and data to develop. A Double Bottom, for instance, often takes several weeks to complete, signaling a significant trend reversal when confirmed.

4. **Complexity and Interpretation**
    - **Candlestick Patterns:** Tend to be simpler and easier to spot, making them suitable for traders seeking quick, actionable signals.
    - **Chart Patterns:** Often require a more advanced understanding of market dynamics, as their interpretation depends on context, volume, and trend alignment.

How Chart and Candlestick Patterns Complement Each Other

When used together, chart and candlestick patterns provide a multi-dimensional view of the market. Candlestick patterns can offer early signals within larger chart formations, enhancing a trader's precision and timing.

- **Example 1:** Within a Bullish Flag (a chart pattern indicating trend continuation), a Bullish Engulfing candlestick pattern forming near the lower boundary provides an early entry signal before the breakout.

- **Example 2:** A Double Top (a chart reversal pattern) becomes more compelling if a Shooting Star candlestick forms at the second peak, reinforcing bearish sentiment.

By integrating these tools, traders can align short-term price action with broader market structures, increasing the reliability of their strategies.

Practical Insights for Combining the Two

- Use **candlestick patterns** to fine-tune entries and exits within the framework of a **chart pattern**. For example, wait for a Morning Star candlestick near the support level of a Rectangle pattern to confirm a potential breakout.

- Validate chart patterns with candlestick patterns to avoid false signals. A Head and Shoulders pattern is more convincing when the breakdown is accompanied by a Bearish Marubozu candle.

- Monitor multiple timeframes for alignment. A candlestick pattern forming on a smaller timeframe can provide additional confirmation of a chart pattern on a higher timeframe.

Why Both Matter

Chart patterns help you understand the market's long-term structure, while candlestick patterns provide clarity on immediate sentiment shifts. Together, they form a cohesive toolkit that allows you to navigate the markets with confidence, whether you're identifying reversals, continuations, or key entry points.

Chart patterns and candlestick patterns are not competing tools—they are complementary. By understanding their differences and leveraging their strengths, you can unlock a deeper, more nuanced understanding of market behavior, enabling more precise and profitable trades.

Chapter 9:
Fundamentals of Chart Patterns

9.3 THE PSYCHOLOGY BEHIND CHART PATTERNS

Chart patterns are more than just shapes on a price chart—they are a visual representation of the underlying psychology driving market participants. Every candlestick, trendline, and breakout reflects the actions and emotions of traders and investors. Understanding the psychology behind chart patterns allows traders to anticipate behavior, recognize opportunities, and make more informed decisions.

The Tug-of-War: Buyers vs. Sellers

At their core, chart patterns depict the ongoing battle between buyers and sellers. This constant struggle creates distinct formations that traders can analyze. For instance:

- **Reversal Patterns** (e.g., Double Tops, Head and Shoulders): These occur when one side begins to lose momentum, signaling a potential shift in control. A Double Top reflects a market where buyers attempt to push the price higher but fail to overcome resistance, paving the way for sellers to take charge.

- **Continuation Patterns** (e.g., Flags, Pennants): These patterns show temporary pauses in a prevailing trend. They highlight moments of indecision where both sides regroup before the dominant trend resumes.

Recognizing these dynamics allows traders to better understand the story behind the price action.

Fear, Greed, and Indecision

Market psychology is driven by emotions such as fear, greed, and uncertainty. Chart patterns often form as these emotions play out on a collective scale:

- **Greed in Uptrends:** As prices rise, more participants enter the market, creating bullish patterns like Flags or Ascending Triangles. These patterns reflect optimism and momentum.

- **Fear in Downtrends:** In falling markets, panic selling leads to bearish patterns like Falling Wedges or Descending Triangles, as participants rush to exit positions.

- **Indecision in Consolidation:** During sideways markets, patterns like Symmetrical Triangles or Rectangles reflect hesitation as buyers and sellers wait for new catalysts.

By understanding these emotional drivers, traders can better interpret patterns and predict outcomes.

The Role of Confirmation and Breakouts

Chart patterns reflect a build-up of pressure. Breakouts occur when one side (buyers or sellers) finally gains the upper hand, breaking through support or resistance. For example:

- A **Bullish Flag** shows a brief consolidation before buyers regain control, leading to a continuation of the uptrend.

- A **Descending Triangle** signals increasing selling pressure, with the price eventually breaking lower.

The psychology behind breakouts lies in collective action. When a breakout occurs, traders who were waiting on the sidelines often rush to enter the market, amplifying the move.

Volume as a Window Into Psychology

Volume plays a critical role in revealing the intensity of market sentiment during pattern formation and breakouts:

- **High Volume at Key Levels:** Indicates strong conviction among participants. For instance, a breakout from a Symmetrical Triangle accompanied by a volume surge confirms the pattern's reliability.
- **Low Volume During Consolidation:** Reflects hesitation and lack of commitment, often seen in the middle stages of Flags or Pennants.

By correlating volume with price movements, traders gain deeper insights into the strength and sustainability of a pattern.

Practical Example: Head and Shoulders

Consider a Head and Shoulders pattern forming at the end of an uptrend:

- **Left Shoulder:** Initial optimism drives prices higher, but resistance emerges, and prices pull back slightly.
- **Head:** Buyers attempt to push prices to a new high, fueled by greed and bullish sentiment. However, resistance at the top of the head reflects growing selling pressure.
- **Right Shoulder:** Sellers dominate, and buyers lose confidence, leading to a lower high.
- **Breakdown:** The neckline is broken, confirming the pattern and signaling that sellers have taken control.

Understanding this psychological progression allows traders to anticipate the pattern's development and time their entries or exits effectively.

How to Use Psychology to Your Advantage

- Align your trading with the prevailing sentiment reflected in the pattern. For instance, a Bullish Pennant signals strong optimism, making it an ideal time to look for long entries.
- Be cautious during patterns that suggest indecision, such as Rectangles or Symmetrical Triangles. Wait for clear breakouts before acting.
- Recognize when emotions are at extremes (e.g., panic selling or euphoric buying) and look for patterns that suggest a reversal, such as Double Bottoms or Shooting Stars.

By understanding the psychology behind chart patterns, traders can move beyond mechanical pattern recognition to truly grasp the market's underlying dynamics. This insight not only enhances trading accuracy but also builds confidence in making decisions, even in volatile conditions.

Chapter 10:
Reversal Chart Patterns

10.1 Understanding Pattern Reversals

Reversal patterns are powerful tools in technical analysis, signaling a potential change in the direction of a trend. These patterns mark a transition in market sentiment, where the prevailing trend loses momentum and the opposing force—whether bullish or bearish—begins to take control. Understanding reversal patterns is essential for traders aiming to capitalize on key turning points in the market.

What Are Reversal Patterns?

Reversal patterns appear after an established trend—either uptrend or downtrend—and indicate that the current direction is likely to reverse. They are characterized by specific formations that reflect shifts in market dynamics:

- **In Uptrends:** Reversal patterns such as Head and Shoulders or Double Top signal a transition from bullish to bearish sentiment, often leading to price declines.

- **In Downtrends:** Reversal patterns like Double Bottom or Inverse Head and Shoulders signify a shift from bearish to bullish momentum, often preceding upward movements.

Reversal patterns are most reliable when they form at significant support or resistance levels, where market participants are more likely to reassess their positions.

The Psychology Behind Reversals

At the heart of every reversal pattern is a shift in the balance of power between buyers and sellers:

- In an **uptrend**, buyers initially dominate, driving prices higher. However, as the trend matures, buying pressure wanes, and sellers begin to assert control.

- In a **downtrend**, the opposite occurs: sellers dominate until buying interest resurfaces, often at a key support level.

These shifts are reflected in the structure of reversal patterns, providing traders with visual cues to anticipate the change.

Key Characteristics of Reversal Patterns

To identify and validate reversal patterns, look for these common elements:

- **Trend Preceding the Pattern:** Reversals require an existing trend to reverse. Without a prior trend, the pattern is less meaningful.

- **Clear Formation:** The pattern must exhibit a distinct structure, such as peaks and troughs for Double Tops or a defined neckline for Head and Shoulders.
- **Volume Dynamics:** Volume often plays a critical role. Declining volume during the formation of the pattern followed by a surge at the breakout confirms the reversal.
- **Breakout Direction:** The price must break a key level (e.g., support, resistance, neckline) to confirm the reversal. Without this confirmation, the pattern remains incomplete.

Practical Application of Reversal Patterns

Consider a **Head and Shoulders** pattern forming after a prolonged uptrend. As the pattern develops:

- **Left Shoulder:** Buyers attempt to push prices higher but face resistance, creating the first peak.
- **Head:** Another rally occurs, surpassing the previous high, but resistance remains strong, leading to a second peak.
- **Right Shoulder:** A weaker rally forms a lower high, reflecting diminishing buying pressure.
- **Neckline Break:** The price breaks below the neckline, confirmed by increased volume, signaling a bearish reversal.

Understanding this progression enables traders to anticipate the pattern's completion and prepare for entry or exit opportunities.

Common Reversal Patterns

Some of the most widely recognized reversal patterns include:

- **Double Top/Bottom:** Indicating a failed attempt to break key resistance or support, respectively.
- **Head and Shoulders/Inverse Head and Shoulders:** Signaling a definitive shift in trend direction.
- **Wedges (Rising/Falling):** Highlighting slowing momentum that leads to a reversal.

Each pattern has unique characteristics and implications, which we will explore in detail in subsequent sections.

Enhancing Accuracy with Context

Reversal patterns are most reliable when supported by additional context:

- **Key Levels:** Patterns forming near significant support or resistance zones carry greater weight.
- **Market Environment:** Reversals are more likely to succeed when aligned with broader market conditions, such as a change in fundamental drivers or macroeconomic trends.
- **Technical Confirmation:** Use tools like RSI to identify overbought or oversold conditions, or MACD to spot momentum shifts that reinforce the pattern.

Chapter 10:
Reversal Chart Patterns

Reversal patterns offer traders a unique opportunity to act at pivotal moments in the market. By understanding their structure, psychology, and validation criteria, you can effectively identify and capitalize on trend reversals, transforming uncertainty into strategic advantage. In the following sections, we will dive into specific patterns and their applications, helping you master these critical tools for your trading arsenal.ù

10.2 DOUBLE TOP AND DOUBLE BOTTOM PATTERNS

Double Top and Double Bottom patterns are among the most reliable and widely recognized reversal formations in technical analysis. These patterns reflect critical shifts in market sentiment, signaling that the prevailing trend is losing momentum and a reversal is imminent. Mastering these patterns can help traders identify high-probability entry and exit points, allowing them to capitalize on key turning points in the market.

Double Top Pattern

The Double Top pattern forms after an extended uptrend and signals a bearish reversal. It is characterized by two distinct peaks at a similar price level, separated by a moderate pullback. This pattern highlights that buying pressure has weakened and sellers are gaining control.

- **Key Characteristics:**
    - **Two Peaks:** The peaks should be at approximately the same price level, reflecting strong resistance.
    - **Pullback Between Peaks:** The pullback between the two peaks creates a valley, which serves as a potential neckline.
    - **Neckline Break:** The pattern is confirmed when the price breaks below the neckline (the support level formed by the valley).
    - **Volume Dynamics:** Volume typically decreases during the second peak, signaling waning buying pressure, and increases on the breakdown below the neckline.

- **Example:**
  Suppose a stock trends upward and reaches $100 (first peak), then pulls back to $95 (neckline). It rallies again to $100 (second peak) but fails to break higher. When the price drops below $95 with strong volume, it confirms the Double Top and signals a bearish reversal.

- **Practical Application:**
    - Enter a short position after the neckline breakout.
    - Use the height of the pattern (distance from the neckline to the peaks) to estimate the potential price target.
    - Place stop-loss orders above the second peak to limit risk.

Double Top Chart Pattern

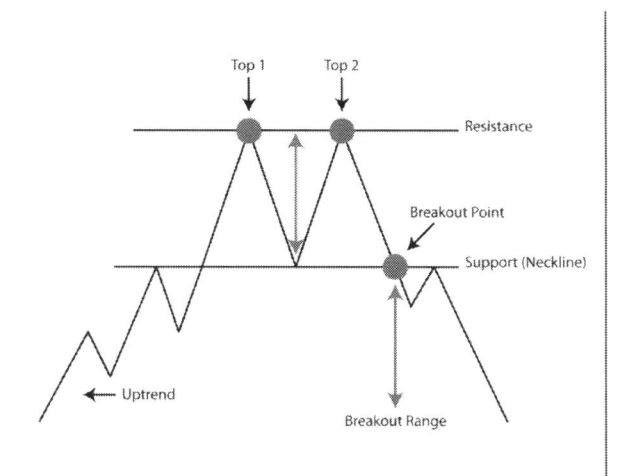

Double Bottom Chart Pattern

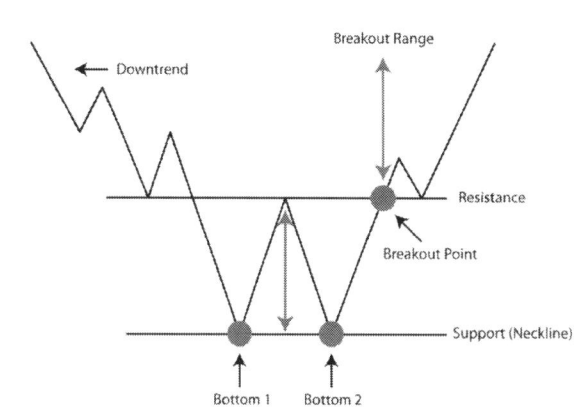

Double Bottom Pattern

The Double Bottom pattern is the bullish counterpart to the Double Top. It forms after a sustained downtrend and signals a reversal to the upside. This pattern is characterized by two troughs at a similar price level, separated by a moderate rally.

- **Key Characteristics:**
    - **Two Troughs:** The troughs should occur at approximately the same price level, reflecting strong support.
    - **Rally Between Troughs:** The rally between the two troughs creates a peak, which serves as a potential neckline.
    - **Neckline Break:** The pattern is confirmed when the price breaks above the neckline (the resistance level formed by the rally).
    - **Volume Dynamics:** Volume often increases during the rally following the second trough, indicating renewed buying interest.
- **Example:**
  A stock in a downtrend falls to $50 (first trough), rallies to $55 (neckline), and then drops back to $50 (second trough). When the price breaks above $55 with strong volume, it confirms the Double Bottom and signals a bullish reversal.
- **Practical Application:**
    - Enter a long position after the neckline breakout.
    - Use the height of the pattern (distance from the neckline to the troughs) to estimate the potential price target.
    - Place stop-loss orders below the second trough to manage risk.

Chapter 10:
Reversal Chart Patterns

Interpreting Double Tops and Bottoms in Context

- **Support and Resistance Levels:** These patterns are most reliable when the peaks or troughs align with significant resistance or support levels.

- **Trend Preceding the Pattern:** Double Tops are valid only after a clear uptrend, and Double Bottoms require a preceding downtrend. Without these conditions, the patterns lose their significance.

- **Volume Confirmation:** A spike in volume during the neckline breakout strengthens the reliability of the pattern.

Common Pitfalls to Avoid

- **Premature Entries:** Wait for a clear breakout above or below the neckline to confirm the pattern. Acting too early can result in false signals.

- **Ignoring Market Context:** Double Tops or Bottoms forming in the middle of a range are less reliable than those near key support or resistance levels.

Double Top and Double Bottom patterns are invaluable tools for traders, providing clear and actionable signals of trend reversals. By understanding their structure, context, and confirmation criteria, you can effectively integrate these patterns into your trading strategy and seize opportunities at critical market junctures.

10.3 HEAD AND SHOULDERS PATTERNS

The **Head and Shoulders pattern** is one of the most reliable and well-known reversal patterns in technical analysis. It signals a significant shift in market sentiment, marking the transition from an uptrend to a downtrend. Its counterpart, the **Inverse Head and Shoulders**, represents the opposite scenario, signaling a reversal from a downtrend to an uptrend. Both patterns offer traders high-probability setups for identifying reversals at critical market turning points.

Classic Head and Shoulders

The Classic Head and Shoulders pattern is a bearish reversal formation that typically develops after a prolonged uptrend. Its structure consists of three peaks: a central, higher peak (the "head") flanked by two lower peaks (the "shoulders"). The line connecting the troughs between these peaks is called the **neckline**, and its breakout confirms the pattern.

- **Key Characteristics:**
    1. **Left Shoulder:** The price rises, peaks, and then pulls back, creating the first high point.

2. **Head:** The price rises again, surpassing the left shoulder, and forms a higher peak before pulling back.

3. **Right Shoulder:** The price rises for a third time, forming a peak lower than the head and roughly equivalent to the left shoulder, followed by another pullback.

4. **Neckline:** The support level connecting the troughs between the shoulders and the head. A break below this line confirms the pattern.

5. **Volume Dynamics:** Volume typically decreases as the pattern forms, reflecting weakening buying interest, but increases significantly during the neckline breakout, confirming the reversal.

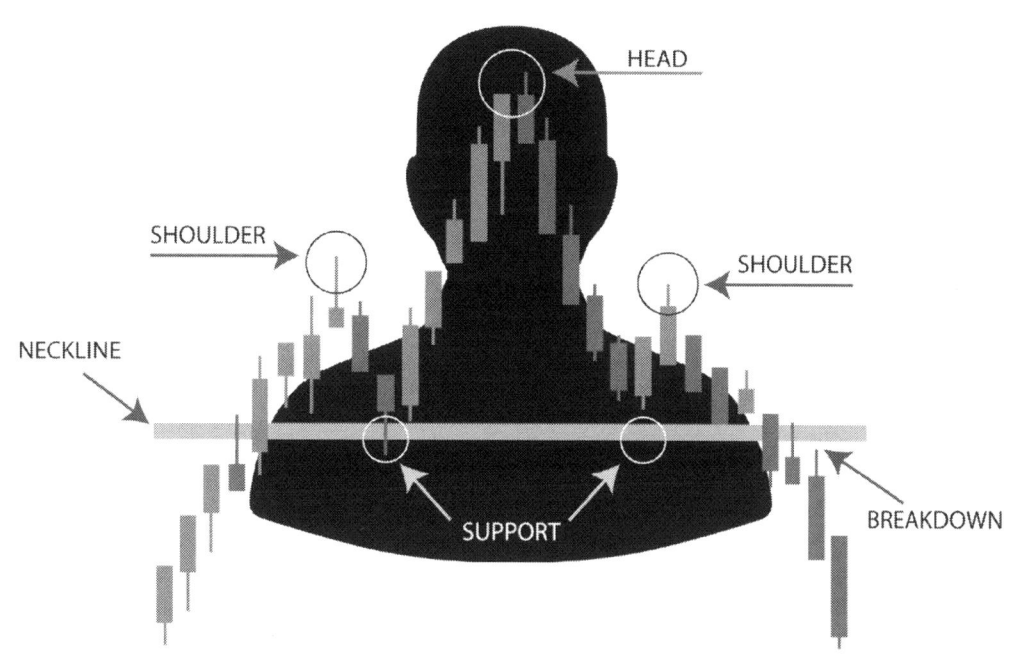

Example: Imagine a stock trending upward, forming a peak at $100 (left shoulder), pulling back to $95, then rallying to $110 (head). It pulls back again to $95, rallies to $102 (right shoulder), and finally breaks below $95 with high volume. This confirms the bearish reversal.

Practical Application:

- **Entry Point:** Enter a short position when the price breaks below the neckline with strong volume.

- **Price Target:** Measure the distance from the head to the neckline and project it downward from the breakout point to estimate the target.

- **Stop-Loss Placement:** Place stop-loss orders above the right shoulder to limit risk.

Chapter 10:
Reversal Chart Patterns

Inverse Head and Shoulders

The Inverse Head and Shoulders is the bullish counterpart to the Classic Head and Shoulders. It typically forms after a downtrend and signals a reversal to the upside. Its structure mirrors the classic pattern, with three troughs: a central, deeper trough (the "head") flanked by two shallower troughs (the "shoulders"). The **neckline** in this case acts as resistance, and its breakout confirms the bullish reversal.

- **Key Characteristics:**
    1. **Left Shoulder:** The price drops, forms a trough, and then rises.
    2. **Head:** The price drops further, forming a deeper trough, followed by a rise.
    3. **Right Shoulder:** The price drops again, forming a shallower trough similar to the left shoulder, and then rises.
    4. **Neckline:** The resistance level connecting the peaks between the troughs. A break above this line confirms the pattern.
    5. **Volume Dynamics:** Volume decreases as the pattern forms but increases significantly during the breakout above the neckline, confirming the reversal.

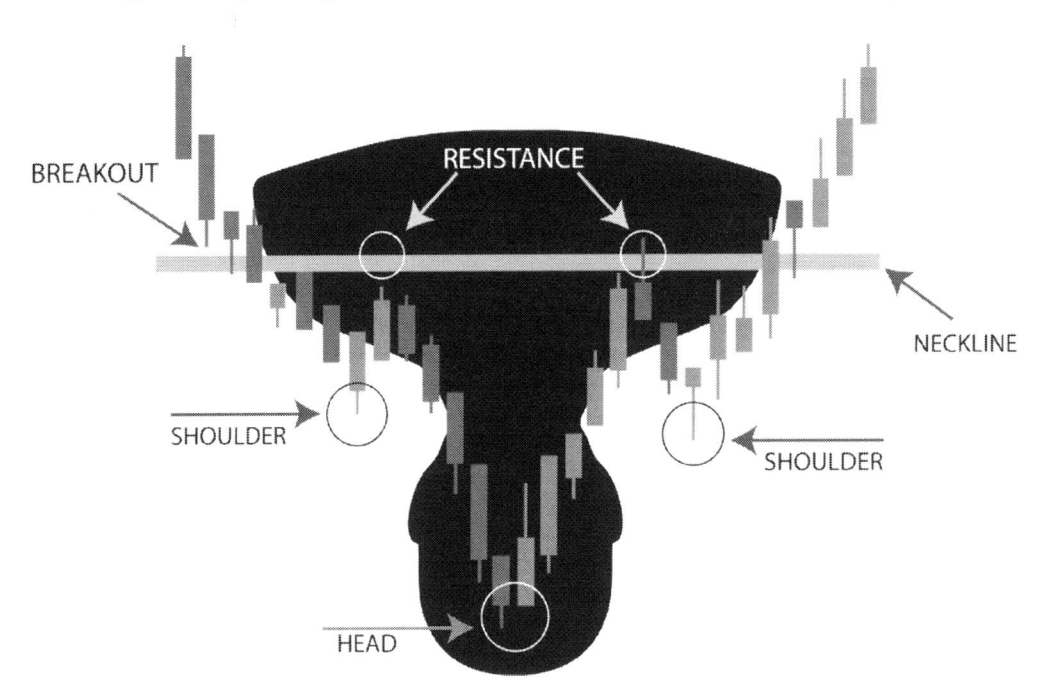

Example: Imagine a stock in a downtrend forms a trough at $50 (left shoulder), rises to $55, then drops to $45 (head). It rises again to $55, drops to $48 (right shoulder), and finally breaks above $55 with high volume, confirming the bullish reversal.

- **Practical Application:**
    - **Entry Point:** Enter a long position when the price breaks above the neckline with strong volume.

- **Price Target:** Measure the distance from the head to the neckline and project it upward from the breakout point to estimate the target.
- **Stop-Loss Placement:** Place stop-loss orders below the right shoulder to manage risk.

Context and Confirmation

Both patterns are most effective when they form near significant support or resistance levels or align with broader market trends. Volume confirmation is critical, as breakouts without sufficient volume may indicate false signals.

Mastering the Head and Shoulders patterns equips traders with a powerful tool for spotting trend reversals and seizing high-probability trading opportunities. By combining these patterns with contextual analysis and volume confirmation, traders can build confidence in their decisions and improve their overall trading performance.

10.4 WEDGE PATTERNS

Wedge patterns are versatile chart formations that signal a potential reversal or continuation of the prevailing trend, depending on their context. These patterns are characterized by converging trendlines that slope either upward or downward, creating a wedge-like shape. Understanding **Rising Wedges** and **Falling Wedges** can help traders anticipate significant market movements and position themselves accordingly.

Rising Wedge

The **Rising Wedge** is typically a bearish pattern, signaling a reversal in an uptrend or a continuation in a downtrend. It is formed when the price makes higher highs and higher lows within a narrowing upward-sloping channel. This pattern reflects waning bullish momentum, with sellers gradually gaining strength.

- **Key Characteristics:**
    1. **Converging Trendlines:** The upper and lower trendlines slope upward and converge as the pattern develops.
    2. **Declining Volume:** Volume often decreases during the pattern's formation, reflecting reduced enthusiasm among buyers.
    3. **Breakout Direction:** The pattern is confirmed when the price breaks below the lower trendline, signaling a bearish move.

Chapter 10:
Reversal Chart Patterns

- **Reversal Context:**

    In an uptrend, the Rising Wedge indicates that buyers are losing control, often leading to a bearish reversal.

- **Continuation Context:**

    In a downtrend, the Rising Wedge suggests that the bearish momentum will resume after a brief consolidation.

Example: A stock in an uptrend forms a Rising Wedge between $100 and $120, with higher highs and higher lows. The price breaks below the lower trendline at $105, accompanied by increased selling volume, confirming a bearish reversal.

Practical Application:

- **Entry Point:** Enter a short position when the price breaks below the lower trendline with strong volume.
- **Price Target:** Measure the height of the wedge at its widest point and project it downward from the breakout point.
- **Stop-Loss Placement:** Place a stop-loss order above the most recent high within the wedge.

Falling Wedge

The **Falling Wedge** is generally a bullish pattern, signaling a reversal in a downtrend or a continuation in an uptrend. It is formed when the price makes lower highs and lower lows within a narrowing downward-sloping channel. This pattern reflects waning bearish momentum, with buyers gradually regaining control.

- **Key Characteristics:**

1. **Converging Trendlines:** The upper and lower trendlines slope downward and converge as the pattern develops.
2. **Declining Volume:** Volume typically decreases during the pattern's formation, reflecting reduced selling pressure.
3. **Breakout Direction:** The pattern is confirmed when the price breaks above the upper trendline, signaling a bullish move.

- **Reversal Context:**

In a downtrend, the Falling Wedge indicates that sellers are losing control, often leading to a bullish reversal.

- **Continuation Context:**

In an uptrend, the Falling Wedge suggests that the bullish momentum will resume after a brief consolidation.

Example:
A stock in a downtrend forms a Falling Wedge between $50 and $40, with lower highs and lower lows. The price breaks above the upper trendline at $45, accompanied by increased buying volume, confirming a bullish reversal.

Practical Application:
- **Entry Point:** Enter a long position when the price breaks above the upper trendline with strong volume.
- **Price Target:** Measure the height of the wedge at its widest point and project it upward from the breakout point.
- **Stop-Loss Placement:** Place a stop-loss order below the most recent low within the wedge.

Context and Interpretation

The effectiveness of wedge patterns depends heavily on their context:

- **In Trending Markets:** A Rising Wedge in an uptrend or a Falling Wedge in a downtrend provides strong reversal signals.
- **In Consolidation Phases:** Wedge patterns often act as continuation signals, helping traders anticipate the resumption of the prevailing trend.

Volume confirmation is crucial for validating breakouts in both patterns. A breakout without sufficient volume increases the likelihood of a false signal.

Wedge patterns are valuable tools for identifying market turning points and trend continuations. By understanding their structure, context, and volume characteristics, traders can confidently integrate these patterns into their trading strategies and enhance their ability to navigate the markets effectively.

10.5 COMPLEX REVERSAL PATTERNS

Complex reversal patterns are advanced formations that indicate significant trend changes, often marked by intricate structures and multiple phases. These patterns go beyond the simplicity of Double Tops or Head and Shoulders, incorporating additional elements that provide deeper insights into market behavior. Understanding complex reversal patterns allows traders to navigate nuanced market dynamics and capitalize on pivotal moments.

Characteristics of Complex Reversal Patterns

Unlike basic reversal patterns, complex reversal patterns often involve:

- **Prolonged Formation Periods:** These patterns take longer to develop, reflecting a drawn-out battle between buyers and sellers.

- **Multiple Peaks or Troughs:** Instead of two or three distinct points, these patterns may include several smaller peaks or troughs within their structure.

- **Interplay of Levels:** Complex patterns often interact with multiple support and resistance levels, requiring traders to pay close attention to key zones.

These characteristics make complex reversal patterns particularly reliable when they align with other technical tools like volume analysis or momentum indicators.

Key Complex Reversal Patterns

1. **Triple Top and Triple Bottom**

    These patterns extend the concept of Double Tops and Double Bottoms by including a third peak or trough, offering a more drawn-out confirmation of a trend reversal.

    o **Triple Top:** Reflects three failed attempts by buyers to break a resistance level, signaling a bearish reversal.

    o **Triple Bottom:** Indicates three failed attempts by sellers to break a support level, signaling a bullish reversal.

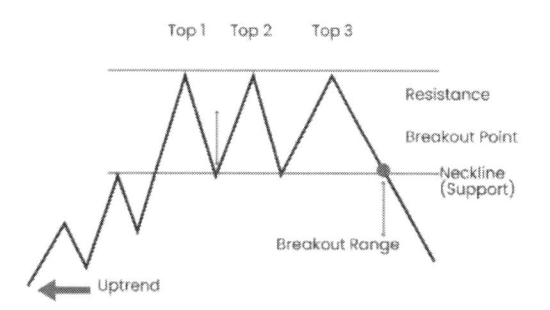

Chapter 10:
Reversal Chart Patterns

Example:
A stock in an uptrend forms three peaks at $100, with pullbacks to $95 after each attempt. When the price breaks below $95 with high volume, the Triple Top confirms a bearish reversal.

2. **Diamond Top and Diamond Bottom**

    These rare patterns resemble a diamond shape on the chart and are considered strong reversal signals.

    - **Diamond Top:** Forms after an uptrend and indicates a bearish reversal. It starts with widening price swings, followed by a narrowing consolidation.

    - **Diamond Bottom:** Forms after a downtrend and signals a bullish reversal, following the same widening and narrowing structure.

Example:
After a sharp rally, a stock's price forms a Diamond Top, with the widest swings in the middle of the pattern. A breakout below the lower trendline confirms the reversal.

3. **Broadening Formation**

    Also known as a megaphone pattern, this structure features progressively higher highs and lower lows, signaling increasing volatility before a reversal.

    - **Bearish Broadening Formation:** Occurs after an uptrend, with a breakdown below the lower boundary confirming the reversal.

    - **Bullish Broadening Formation:** Occurs after a downtrend, with a breakout above the upper boundary confirming the reversal.

Example:
A stock in an uptrend forms a Broadening Formation, with highs at $100, $110, and $115 and lows at $90, $85, and $80. A sharp breakdown below $80 signals a bearish reversal.

Volume and Context in Complex Reversal Patterns

Volume analysis plays a crucial role in confirming complex reversal patterns:

- **Triple Tops and Bottoms:** Volume typically decreases during the formation and surges at the breakout.

- **Diamond Patterns:** Volume is high during the initial widening phase and decreases as the pattern narrows. A breakout is validated by a volume spike.

- **Broadening Formations:** Increasing volume during the formation signals heightened market activity. The breakout or breakdown should be accompanied by a volume surge.

Context is equally important. Complex reversal patterns are most reliable when they form near significant support or resistance levels or align with broader market trends. For instance, a Diamond Bottom near a long-term support zone carries more weight than one forming mid-range.

Common Pitfalls to Avoid

- **Overlooking Time Frames:** These patterns require patience to develop. Traders who act prematurely may fall victim to false signals.

- **Ignoring Volume Dynamics:** A breakout or breakdown without sufficient volume often leads to pattern failure.

- **Forcing Patterns:** Not all price movements form complex structures. Avoid interpreting random fluctuations as patterns.

Practical Tips for Trading Complex Patterns

- **Confirm with Indicators:** Use tools like RSI or MACD to validate momentum shifts within the pattern.

- **Define Clear Levels:** Identify key breakout or breakdown points and wait for price confirmation before entering a trade.

- **Set Realistic Targets:** Measure the pattern's height and project it from the breakout point to estimate potential price moves.

Complex reversal patterns provide traders with nuanced insights into market transitions. By mastering these advanced formations and integrating them with broader analysis, traders can identify high-probability opportunities and execute trades with greater confidence, even in challenging market conditions.

Chapter 10:
Reversal Chart Patterns

Bullish Chart Patterns

Falling Wedge	Symmetrical Triangle
Inverse Head & Shoulder	Cup and Handle
Ascending Triangle	Bullish Rectangle

Bearish Chart Pattern

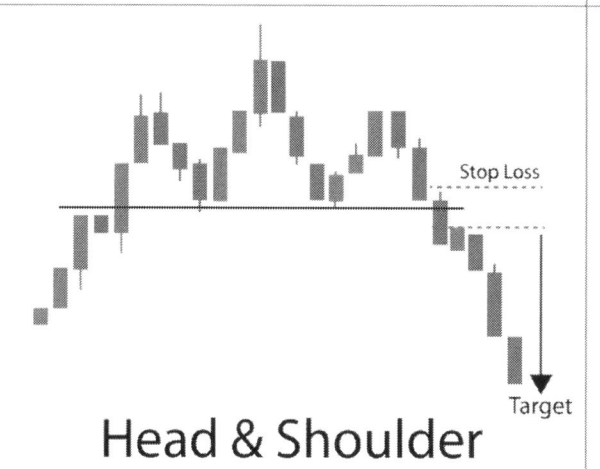

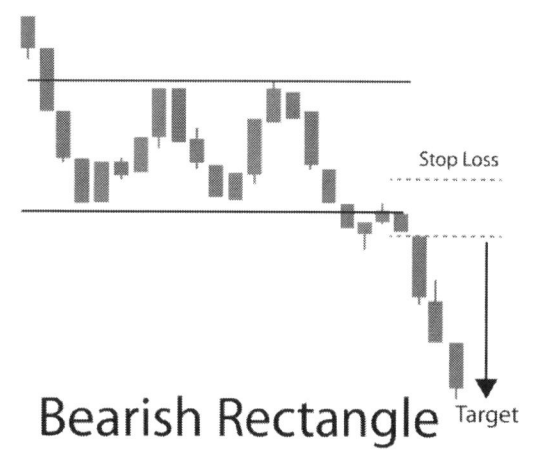

Rising Wedge — Stop Loss, Target

Inverted Flag — Stop Loss, Target

Head & Shoulder — Stop Loss, Target

Bearish Rectangle — Stop Loss, Target

Descending Triangle — Stop Loss, Target

Symmetrical Triangle — Stop Loss, Target

Chapter 11:
Continuation Chart Patterns

11.1 THE NATURE OF CONTINUATION PATTERNS

Continuation patterns are essential tools in technical analysis, offering traders insights into the potential resumption of an existing trend after a brief pause or consolidation phase. Unlike reversal patterns, which signal a change in trend direction, continuation patterns indicate that the current trend is likely to persist, providing traders with opportunities to enter positions aligned with the dominant market movement.

What Are Continuation Patterns?

Continuation patterns occur when the price temporarily consolidates within a defined range, reflecting a balance between buyers and sellers. During this phase, the market is "catching its breath" before resuming the primary trend. These patterns are characterized by their ability to:

- **Pause Without Reversing:** The trend slows or consolidates but does not exhibit clear signs of a reversal.
- **Retain Trend Momentum:** Despite the pause, the underlying trend's momentum remains intact.
- **Provide Entry Opportunities:** These patterns often signal an optimal point to enter trades in the direction of the trend.

Why Do Continuation Patterns Form?

Continuation patterns form due to the natural ebb and flow of market dynamics:

- **Profit-Taking:** Traders who entered the trend earlier may take profits, causing the price to temporarily stabilize.
- **Accumulation or Distribution:** Institutional players may use these phases to accumulate or distribute large positions without significantly impacting the price.
- **Market Sentiment:** The pause reflects a period of indecision or equilibrium as participants wait for additional confirmation or catalysts.

Key Characteristics of Continuation Patterns

1. **Trend Context:** Continuation patterns must occur within the context of a clearly defined trend—either bullish or bearish.

2. **Defined Structure:** These patterns have distinct shapes, such as rectangles, flags, or pennants, that are easily recognizable.

3. **Breakout Direction:** The breakout typically occurs in the direction of the prevailing trend, signaling the pattern's completion.

4. **Volume Dynamics:** Volume often decreases during the consolidation phase and increases sharply at the breakout, confirming the pattern.

Examples of Continuation Patterns

Common continuation patterns include:

- **Rectangles:** The price moves sideways within parallel support and resistance levels before breaking out in the trend's direction.

- **Flags and Pennants:** The price consolidates in a tight range, forming small, angular patterns that precede a resumption of the trend.

Continuation vs. Reversal Patterns

The key difference lies in the breakout direction. While reversal patterns signal a trend change, continuation patterns confirm the existing trend's persistence. For example:

- A Head and Shoulders pattern at the top of an uptrend signals a bearish reversal.

- A Bullish Flag pattern within the same uptrend suggests the trend will continue upward after the breakout.

Practical Insights for Traders

- **Align with the Trend:** Ensure that the continuation pattern is consistent with the prevailing trend.

- **Wait for Confirmation:** Enter trades only after the breakout is confirmed, either above resistance or below support, depending on the trend.

- **Use Volume as a Guide:** Rising volume during the breakout strengthens the pattern's reliability.

Continuation patterns are vital for traders looking to capitalize on trend persistence. By understanding their nature and applying disciplined analysis, traders can identify high-probability entry points and position themselves to profit from the market's continuation in its primary direction.

Chapter 11:
Continuation Chart Patterns

11.2 RECTANGLE PATTERNS

Rectangle patterns are straightforward yet powerful continuation patterns that signal a temporary consolidation phase before the prevailing trend resumes. These patterns are characterized by price moving sideways within parallel support and resistance levels. Rectangle patterns provide traders with clear breakout points, making them valuable tools for identifying high-probability trading opportunities.

What Are Rectangle Patterns?

Rectangle patterns form when the price oscillates between a defined support level (bottom of the rectangle) and a resistance level (top of the rectangle), creating a box-like structure. This pattern reflects a period of market indecision, during which buyers and sellers are evenly matched. Once the breakout occurs, the price typically continues in the direction of the prevailing trend.

- **Trend Context:** Rectangle patterns are most reliable when they appear as part of a larger trend, signaling a continuation after the consolidation.
- **Volume Dynamics:** Volume often decreases during the formation of the rectangle and increases sharply at the breakout, confirming the pattern.

Rectangle patterns can be classified into two types based on the breakout direction: **Bullish Rectangle** and **Bearish Rectangle**.

Bullish Rectangle

A Bullish Rectangle forms during an uptrend and signals a continuation of the bullish momentum. The price consolidates between horizontal support and resistance levels, reflecting a pause before the next leg higher.

- **Structure:**
    - The price oscillates between a well-defined resistance level (ceiling) and support level (floor), forming a horizontal range.
    - The breakout occurs when the price closes above the resistance level.
- **Volume Characteristics:**
    - Volume decreases during the consolidation phase, indicating reduced activity.
    - A surge in volume at the breakout confirms the pattern's validity.
- **Example:** Imagine a stock in an uptrend reaches $100, pulls back to $95, and oscillates between $95 and $100 for several sessions. When the price breaks above $100 with high volume, the Bullish Rectangle is confirmed, signaling a continuation of the uptrend.

The Candlestick Trading Profit Formula

Bullish Rectangle

- **Practical Application:**
    - **Entry Point:** Enter a long position when the price breaks above the resistance level with strong volume.
    - **Price Target:** Measure the height of the rectangle (distance between support and resistance) and project it upward from the breakout point to estimate the target.
    - **Stop-Loss Placement:** Place a stop-loss order below the support level to limit risk.

Bearish Rectangle

A Bearish Rectangle forms during a downtrend and signals a continuation of bearish momentum. The price consolidates between horizontal support and resistance levels, reflecting a temporary pause before resuming the downward movement.

- **Structure:**
    - The price oscillates between a resistance level (ceiling) and support level (floor) within a horizontal range.
    - The breakout occurs when the price closes below the support level.
- **Volume Characteristics:**
    - Volume declines during the consolidation phase, reflecting reduced trading activity.

Chapter 11:
Continuation Chart Patterns

- o A spike in volume during the breakdown confirms the pattern's reliability.
- **Example:** Suppose a stock in a downtrend drops to $50, bounces to $55, and oscillates between $50 and $55 for several sessions. When the price breaks below $50 with high volume, the Bearish Rectangle is confirmed, signaling a continuation of the downtrend.

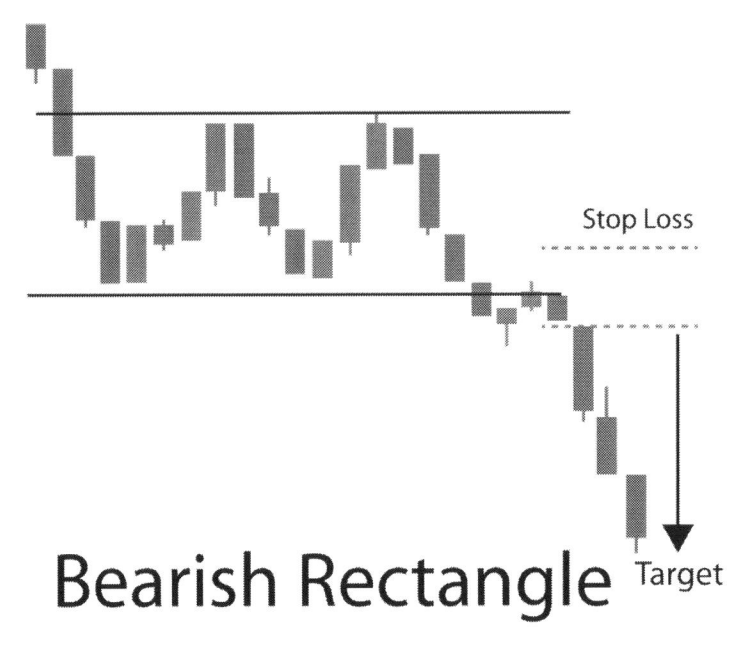

Bearish Rectangle

- **Practical Application:**
  - o **Entry Point:** Enter a short position when the price breaks below the support level with strong volume.
  - o **Price Target:** Measure the height of the rectangle (distance between support and resistance) and project it downward from the breakdown point to estimate the target.
  - o **Stop-Loss Placement:** Place a stop-loss order above the resistance level to manage risk.

Tips for Trading Rectangle Patterns

- **Wait for Confirmation:** Always wait for a decisive breakout with volume confirmation before entering a trade.
- **Combine with Indicators:** Use momentum indicators like RSI or MACD to gauge whether the breakout aligns with market strength.
- **Context Matters:** Rectangle patterns forming near key support or resistance levels carry more significance.

Rectangle patterns offer traders a straightforward yet effective way to capitalize on trend continuation. By mastering their structure and confirmation criteria, you can enhance your ability to identify high-probability setups and position yourself for success in trending markets.

11.3 FLAG AND PENNANT PATTERNS

Flag and Pennant patterns are highly reliable continuation patterns that indicate brief consolidations within strong trends. These formations typically occur after sharp price movements, known as the flagpole, and signal that the prevailing trend is likely to resume. Despite their similarities, Flags and Pennants have distinct shapes that make them valuable tools for traders aiming to enter trends with high probability.

Bullish and Bearish Flags

Bullish Flag:

A Bullish Flag forms during an uptrend, following a strong upward move. The price consolidates in a rectangular pattern that slopes slightly downward or remains horizontal. This consolidation reflects a pause as traders take profits before the trend resumes.

- **Structure:** The flagpole represents the initial sharp price movement, followed by a rectangle formed by parallel trendlines that contain the consolidation phase. A breakout above the upper trendline signals the continuation of the uptrend.
- **Volume Dynamics:** Volume typically decreases during the consolidation phase and surges at the breakout, confirming the pattern.

Example: A stock rallies from $50 to $70, then consolidates between $68 and $72. When the price breaks above $72 with increased volume, the Bullish Flag is confirmed.

Practical Application: Enter a long position when the price breaks above the upper trendline with strong volume. Measure the height of the flagpole and add it to the breakout point to project the target. Place a stop-loss order below the lower boundary of the flag.

Bearish Flag:

A Bearish Flag forms during a downtrend, following a sharp downward move. The price consolidates in a rectangle that slopes slightly upward or remains horizontal. This consolidation reflects a pause before the downtrend resumes.

- **Structure:** The flagpole represents the sharp initial decline, followed by a rectangle formed by parallel trendlines containing the consolidation. A breakdown below the lower trendline signals the continuation of the downtrend.

Chapter 11:
Continuation Chart Patterns

- **Volume Dynamics:** Volume typically decreases during consolidation and surges at the breakdown.

Example:
A stock drops from $100 to $80, then consolidates between $78 and $82. When the price breaks below $78 with strong volume, the Bearish Flag is confirmed.

Practical Application: Enter a short position when the price breaks below the lower trendline with strong volume. Measure the height of the flagpole and subtract it from the breakdown point to project the target. Place a stop-loss order above the upper boundary of the flag.

Bullish and Bearish Pennants

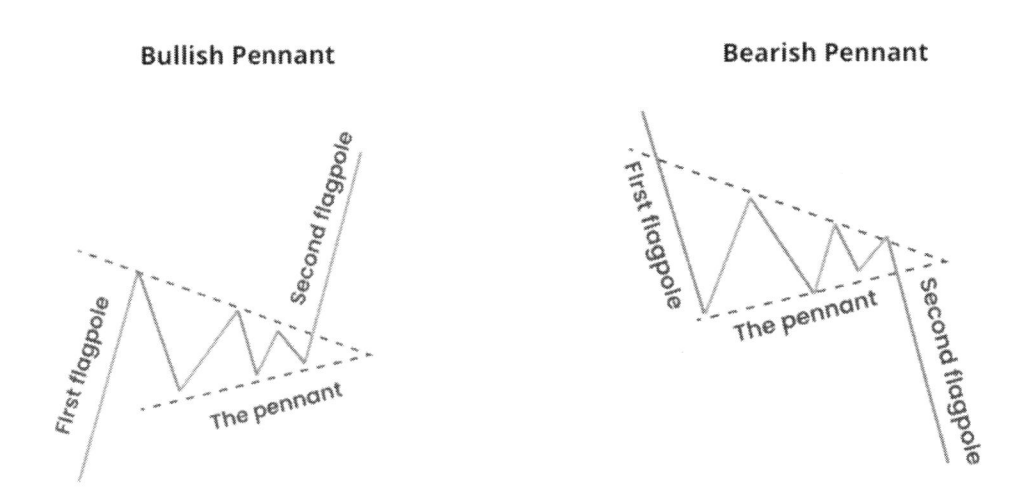

Bullish Pennant:

A Bullish Pennant forms during an uptrend after a sharp rally. Unlike Flags, Pennants are triangular, with trendlines converging as the price consolidates. This pattern reflects a pause in bullish momentum before the uptrend resumes.

- **Structure:** The flagpole represents the initial sharp price movement, followed by a small symmetrical triangle. A breakout above the upper trendline signals a continuation of the uptrend.
- **Volume Dynamics:** Volume decreases during the consolidation phase and spikes at the breakout.

Example: A stock rallies from $50 to $75, then consolidates into a Pennant with converging trendlines between $73 and $76. When the price breaks above $76 with high volume, the Bullish Pennant is confirmed.

124

Practical Application: Enter a long position at the breakout above the upper trendline with strong volume. Use the height of the flagpole to project the price target. Place a stop-loss order below the lower boundary of the Pennant.

Bearish Pennant:

A Bearish Pennant forms during a downtrend, following a sharp price decline. The triangular consolidation reflects a pause in bearish momentum before the trend resumes downward.

- **Structure:** The flagpole represents the sharp initial decline, followed by a small symmetrical triangle. A breakdown below the lower trendline signals the continuation of the downtrend.

- **Volume Dynamics:** Volume decreases during the consolidation phase and spikes at the breakdown.

Example: A stock drops from $90 to $70, then consolidates into a Pennant with converging trendlines between $68 and $72. When the price breaks below $68 with strong volume, the Bearish Pennant is confirmed.

Practical Application: Enter a short position when the price breaks below the lower trendline with strong volume. Use the height of the flagpole to project the price target. Place a stop-loss order above the upper boundary of the Pennant.

Flag and Pennant patterns are highly effective for identifying trend continuation opportunities. By understanding their distinct structures and volume dynamics, traders can confidently anticipate the resumption of a trend and align their strategies for maximum profitability.

11.4 MEASURING MOVES AND PRICE TARGETS

Measuring moves and calculating price targets is a fundamental skill in trading continuation patterns. These calculations allow traders to estimate the potential movement of an asset following a breakout, providing clear objectives for entry, exit, and stop-loss placement. By using a systematic approach, traders can set realistic expectations and optimize their trading strategies.

Why Measuring Moves Is Important

Accurately estimating price targets:

- Provides clarity on whether a trade aligns with your risk-to-reward ratio.

- Helps set precise entry and exit points, reducing emotional decision-making.

- Ensures a disciplined approach to profit-taking.

Steps to Measure Moves and Calculate Price Targets

1. Measure the Pattern's Height (Flagpole or Pattern Range):

Chapter 11:
Continuation Chart Patterns

The first step is to measure the vertical distance of the pattern, which often represents the potential price movement after the breakout.

- For **Flags and Pennants**, measure the height of the flagpole (the initial sharp move leading to the pattern).
- For **Rectangles**, calculate the vertical distance between the support and resistance levels.
- For **Wedges**, measure the height at the widest point of the pattern.

2. Apply the Measured Move to the Breakout Point:

Add (or subtract, for bearish patterns) the measured height to the breakout price to calculate the price target.

- For **Bullish Patterns**, add the height to the breakout point above resistance.
- For **Bearish Patterns**, subtract the height from the breakout point below support.

3. Adjust for Market Context:

Consider broader market factors, such as key support and resistance zones, to refine the price target. If the calculated target aligns with a significant level, it reinforces the target's reliability.

Practical Examples

Example 1: Bullish Flag Target Measurement

A stock rallies from $50 to $70, forming a Bullish Flag. The height of the flagpole is $20 ($70 - $50). The price consolidates between $68 and $72 before breaking out above $72.

- **Price Target:** Add the flagpole's height ($20) to the breakout point ($72). The target price is $92.
- **Stop-Loss Placement:** Position the stop-loss below the lower boundary of the flag ($68) to limit risk.

Example 2: Bearish Rectangle Target Measurement

A stock declines from $100 to $80, forming a Bearish Rectangle with a range between $82 and $86. The height of the rectangle is $4 ($86 - $82). The price breaks below $82.

- **Price Target:** Subtract the rectangle's height ($4) from the breakout point ($82). The target price is $78.
- **Stop-Loss Placement:** Position the stop-loss above the upper boundary of the rectangle ($86) to protect against a false breakout.

Using Volume to Confirm Price Targets

Volume acts as a secondary confirmation for price targets. A breakout with high volume increases the likelihood of reaching the calculated target, while low-volume breakouts may signal reduced momentum, requiring caution.

- **High Volume at Breakout:** Indicates strong conviction among market participants, making the target more achievable.

- **Low Volume at Breakout:** Suggests potential weakness; traders should consider adjusting expectations or waiting for further confirmation.

Common Pitfalls to Avoid

- **Ignoring Context:** Blindly applying the measured move without considering broader market factors (e.g., nearby support/resistance levels) can lead to unrealistic targets.
- **Overestimating Potential Moves:** Not all breakouts will achieve their full measured move. Be prepared to adjust expectations based on market conditions.
- **Premature Exits:** Exiting too early without allowing the trade to reach its target undermines the strategy's effectiveness. Use trailing stops or partial profit-taking to balance risk and reward.

Measuring moves and setting price targets is an essential skill that ensures traders approach the market with discipline and precision. By mastering these techniques and integrating them with contextual analysis, you can confidently align your trading objectives with the market's dynamics and maximize your potential for success.

11.5 FAILED CONTINUATION PATTERNS

While continuation patterns are reliable tools for predicting trend persistence, they are not infallible. Failed continuation patterns occur when the price breaks out in the opposite direction of the expected move or fails to sustain the anticipated breakout. Recognizing and managing failed patterns is a crucial skill that can help traders minimize losses and adapt to evolving market conditions.

What Causes Failed Continuation Patterns?

Failed continuation patterns can result from various factors, including:

- **Weak Market Momentum:** Insufficient volume or lack of participation may lead to incomplete or unsustainable breakouts.
- **External Events:** News, economic reports, or unexpected market catalysts can disrupt established trends and invalidate patterns.
- **Overextended Trends:** Trends that are already stretched may lack the strength to continue, causing a pattern to fail.
- **False Breakouts:** Temporary price movements beyond pattern boundaries that lack follow-through are common in volatile markets.

How to Identify Failed Patterns

1. **Volume Mismatch:** A breakout or breakdown that occurs without a corresponding increase in volume is often unreliable and prone to failure.

2. **Re-Entry Into the Pattern:** If the price re-enters the consolidation range after an initial breakout, it is a strong indication of a failed continuation.

3. **Opposite Breakouts:** When the price breaks out in the opposite direction of the expected move, the pattern is invalidated.

4. **Divergence with Indicators:** Momentum indicators like RSI or MACD showing divergence (e.g., a Bullish Flag with bearish divergence) can signal a higher likelihood of failure.

Practical Examples of Failed Patterns

Example 1: Bullish Flag Failure

A stock rallies from $100 to $120 and consolidates into a Bullish Flag between $118 and $122. It breaks below $118 with weak volume and re-enters the consolidation range. This failure suggests that the uptrend is losing momentum, and traders should reconsider their bullish bias.

Example 2: Bearish Rectangle Failure

A stock in a downtrend consolidates between $50 and $55, forming a Bearish Rectangle. The price breaks above $55 with high volume instead of breaking lower, invalidating the bearish setup and signaling a potential reversal.

Strategies for Managing Failed Patterns

- **Cut Losses Quickly:** When a pattern fails, it's essential to exit the trade promptly to minimize losses. Use stop-loss orders placed just outside the pattern boundaries.

- **Confirm Before Acting:** Avoid preemptive entries by waiting for a decisive breakout confirmed by volume. This reduces the likelihood of acting on false signals.

- **Adapt to Market Changes:** A failed continuation pattern often signals a shift in market dynamics. For instance, a failed Bullish Flag may indicate a reversal or transition into a sideways market. Adjust your strategy accordingly.

- **Monitor Nearby Levels:** Failed patterns often lead to tests of key support or resistance levels. Watch these areas for new trading opportunities.

Turning Failed Patterns Into Opportunities

Failed continuation patterns can themselves become actionable setups. A Bullish Flag that breaks down instead of up may signal the start of a bearish reversal, offering opportunities for short positions. Similarly, a Bearish Pennant that breaks upward could indicate the beginning of a bullish trend.

Example:
If a Bearish Flag breaks upward with strong volume, treat the failed pattern as a reversal signal and consider entering a long position aligned with the new trend.

Key Takeaways

- Failed continuation patterns are a normal part of trading and should not be viewed as setbacks but as signals of changing market conditions.
- Disciplined use of stop-loss orders and careful confirmation of breakouts can minimize the impact of failures.
- Learning to interpret failed patterns as opportunities can turn potential losses into strategic advantages.

By recognizing and managing failed continuation patterns, traders can protect their capital, refine their strategies, and stay adaptable in dynamic markets. This understanding ensures that even when patterns fail, traders remain poised to capitalize on the next opportunity.

Chapter 12:
Bilateral Chart Patterns

12.1 Understanding Bilateral Patterns

Bilateral chart patterns are unique formations that signal potential breakouts in either direction, making them both intriguing and challenging for traders. Unlike continuation or reversal patterns, which typically suggest a specific directional bias, bilateral patterns highlight market indecision and the possibility of significant moves in either direction. Understanding these patterns equips traders with the tools to respond effectively to breakout scenarios, regardless of the direction.

What Are Bilateral Patterns?

Bilateral patterns occur when the price consolidates within a narrowing range, creating uncertainty about the next move. This consolidation reflects a balance between buying and selling pressures, as neither side has established dominance. As the range tightens, the market reaches a tipping point where a breakout becomes inevitable.

- **Directional Neutrality:** Bilateral patterns don't inherently suggest whether the breakout will be bullish or bearish. Traders must be prepared for either outcome.

- **High Potential Energy:** The tighter the range, the greater the potential for a strong breakout once the price escapes the pattern.

- **Volume Clues:** While the pattern itself doesn't predict direction, volume dynamics during the breakout often confirm the move.

Common Bilateral Patterns

The most widely recognized bilateral patterns are **Triangles**, including Ascending Triangles, Descending Triangles, and Symmetrical Triangles. These formations reflect a market at a crossroads, ready to move significantly once the consolidation resolves.

- **Ascending Triangles:** Typically bullish but can break downward in weak market conditions.

- **Descending Triangles:** Typically bearish but can break upward if bullish sentiment prevails.

- **Symmetrical Triangles:** Purely neutral and equally likely to break in either direction.

Psychology Behind Bilateral Patterns

At the heart of bilateral patterns lies market indecision:

- Buyers and sellers are locked in a tug-of-war, leading to smaller and smaller price movements.
- The pattern represents a period of "wait and see" as traders monitor key levels for signs of dominance.
- When the breakout occurs, it reflects a decisive shift in sentiment, with one side finally taking control.

Why Are Bilateral Patterns Important?

Bilateral patterns are significant because they offer high-probability setups when combined with disciplined breakout trading strategies:

- **Preparation for Both Outcomes:** These patterns force traders to prepare for both bullish and bearish scenarios, encouraging a flexible approach.
- **Clear Entry and Exit Points:** The well-defined boundaries of bilateral patterns provide clear levels for entries, exits, and stop-loss placement.
- **Potential for Strong Moves:** The compression of price within the pattern often results in explosive breakouts, offering substantial profit opportunities.

Practical Example: Symmetrical Triangle

A stock trading at $50 forms a Symmetrical Triangle, with the price oscillating between lower highs and higher lows. The range narrows over several sessions, creating converging trendlines. When the price breaks above $52 with increased volume, it signals a bullish breakout. Alternatively, a breakdown below $48 with high volume would signal a bearish move.

Tips for Trading Bilateral Patterns

- **Set Conditional Orders:** Use stop orders above and below the pattern boundaries to automatically enter trades in the breakout direction.
- **Monitor Volume Closely:** A breakout accompanied by high volume is more likely to succeed, while low-volume breakouts may signal false moves.
- **Combine with Indicators:** Use tools like RSI or MACD to gauge momentum and confirm the breakout's strength.

Bilateral patterns challenge traders to remain neutral and disciplined, offering valuable opportunities for profit when approached with a structured strategy. By understanding their structure and psychology, you can position yourself to capitalize on the market's next big move, regardless of its direction.

Chapter 12:
Bilateral Chart Patterns

12.2 TRIANGLE PATTERNS

Triangle patterns are some of the most common and reliable bilateral chart patterns in technical analysis. They form when price action consolidates into a narrowing range, bounded by converging trendlines. The three primary types of triangle patterns—Ascending, Descending, and Symmetrical—offer insights into market indecision and the potential for significant breakouts. While Ascending and Descending Triangles often have a directional bias, Symmetrical Triangles are more neutral and can break in either direction.

Ascending Triangles

Definition:
Ascending Triangles are typically bullish patterns that form during an uptrend, signaling potential continuation. The upper boundary of the triangle is a horizontal resistance level, while the lower boundary slopes upward, indicating increasing buying pressure.

- **Structure:**
    - The price forms higher lows, creating an upward-sloping trendline.
    - Resistance remains constant, forming a horizontal upper boundary.
    - The pattern is complete when the price breaks above the resistance level.

- **Psychology Behind the Pattern:** Buyers are becoming more aggressive, as evidenced by the higher lows. Sellers are defending the resistance level, but the increasing buying pressure often leads to a bullish breakout.

- **Volume Dynamics:**
    - Volume typically decreases during the pattern's formation, reflecting reduced activity as the price consolidates.
    - A breakout above the resistance is confirmed by a surge in volume.

Ascending Triangle

- **Example:**
  A stock trades between $50 (resistance) and $45 (support). Over time, the lows rise to $46, $47, and $48, forming an Ascending Triangle. When the price breaks above $50 with high volume, it signals a bullish continuation.

- **Practical Application:**
  - **Entry Point:** Enter a long position when the price closes above the resistance level.
  - **Price Target:** Measure the height of the triangle at its widest point and add it to the breakout level to estimate the target.
  - **Stop-Loss Placement:** Place a stop-loss order just below the last higher low.

Descending Triangle vs Ascending Triangle

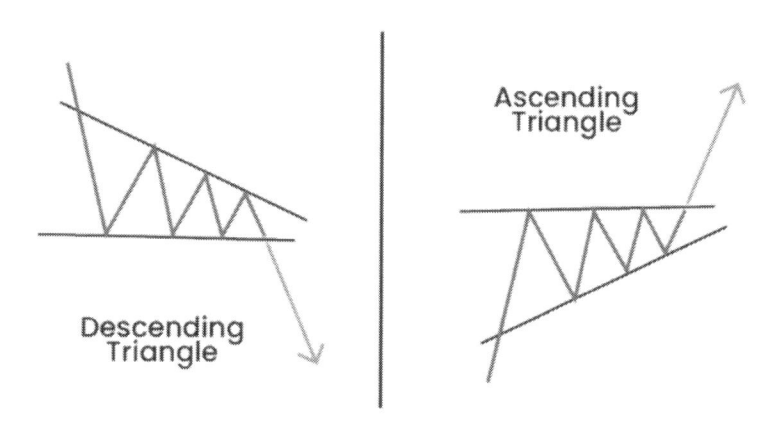

Descending Triangles

Definition:
Descending Triangles are typically bearish patterns that form during a downtrend, signaling potential continuation. The lower boundary of the triangle is a horizontal support level, while the upper boundary slopes downward, indicating increasing selling pressure.

- **Structure:**
  - The price forms lower highs, creating a downward-sloping trendline.
  - Support remains constant, forming a horizontal lower boundary.
  - The pattern is complete when the price breaks below the support level.

Chapter 12:
Bilateral Chart Patterns

- **Psychology Behind the Pattern:** Sellers are becoming more dominant, as evidenced by the lower highs. Buyers are defending the support level, but the increasing selling pressure often leads to a bearish breakout.
- **Volume Dynamics:**
    - Volume typically decreases during the pattern's formation.
    - A breakout below the support is confirmed by a surge in volume.
- **Example:**
A stock trades between $100 (support) and $110 (resistance). Over time, the highs drop to $108, $106, and $104, forming a Descending Triangle. When the price breaks below $100 with high volume, it signals a bearish continuation.
- **Practical Application:**
    - **Entry Point:** Enter a short position when the price closes below the support level.
    - **Price Target:** Measure the height of the triangle at its widest point and subtract it from the breakout level to estimate the target.
    - **Stop-Loss Placement:** Place a stop-loss order just above the last lower high.

Symmetrical Triangles

Definition:
Symmetrical Triangles are neutral patterns that form when price action narrows within converging trendlines. This pattern reflects a period of indecision where neither buyers nor sellers dominate, and the breakout can occur in either direction.

- **Structure:**
    - The price forms lower highs and higher lows, creating converging trendlines.
    - The pattern is complete when the price breaks out above or below the triangle.
- **Psychology Behind the Pattern:** Both buyers and sellers are losing conviction, causing the price to consolidate. The breakout direction depends on which side ultimately gains control.
- **Volume Dynamics:**
    - Volume typically decreases as the pattern forms.
    - A breakout in either direction is confirmed by a surge in volume.
- **Example:**
A stock trades between $50 and $40, with highs and lows converging toward $45. When the price breaks above $50 with strong volume, it signals a bullish breakout. Alternatively, a breakdown below $40 with high volume signals a bearish move.
- **Practical Application:**

- **Entry Point:** Use stop orders above the upper trendline and below the lower trendline to prepare for either breakout direction.
- **Price Target:** Measure the height of the triangle at its widest point and apply it to the breakout level to estimate the target.
- **Stop-Loss Placement:** Place stop-loss orders just outside the opposite trendline.

Tips for Trading Triangle Patterns

- Confirm breakouts with volume to avoid false signals.
- Align trades with the prevailing trend for higher probability setups.
- Use technical indicators like RSI or MACD to gauge momentum and breakout strength.

By mastering the structure and psychology of triangle patterns, traders can identify high-potential setups and respond effectively to market conditions, whether the breakout is bullish or bearish.

12.3 VOLUME ANALYSIS IN TRIANGLE PATTERNS

Volume analysis plays a critical role in confirming the validity and potential of triangle patterns. While the shape and structure of triangles provide visual cues about price consolidation, volume dynamics offer insight into market participation and the likelihood of a successful breakout. By understanding the relationship between volume and triangle patterns, traders can increase their confidence in trading decisions and filter out false signals.

Why Volume Matters in Triangle Patterns

Volume serves as a barometer of market sentiment and momentum:

- **Decreasing Volume During Formation:** As price action narrows within the triangle, volume typically declines, reflecting reduced activity as traders wait for the breakout. This decreasing volume indicates consolidation and equilibrium between buyers and sellers.
- **Volume Surge at Breakout:** A breakout from the triangle, whether bullish or bearish, is usually accompanied by a sharp increase in volume. This surge confirms that market participants are committed to the new direction.
- **False Breakouts and Low Volume:** A breakout without a significant volume increase often indicates a lack of conviction, raising the likelihood of a false breakout.

Volume Behavior in Different Triangle Types

1. Ascending Triangles:

- **Bullish Breakouts:** Volume tends to decrease during the consolidation phase and then spikes as the price breaks above the horizontal resistance line. This surge confirms strong buying interest.

Chapter 12:
Bilateral Chart Patterns

- **Key Observation:** If the breakout occurs without a notable volume increase, traders should remain cautious, as the breakout may lack sustainability.

2. Descending Triangles:

- **Bearish Breakouts:** Similar to Ascending Triangles, volume decreases during the pattern's formation. A surge in volume as the price breaks below the horizontal support line confirms strong selling pressure.

- **Key Observation:** Low volume during the breakdown suggests hesitation among sellers, which could lead to a retracement.

3. Symmetrical Triangles:

- **Neutral Breakouts:** Volume decreases as the price oscillates between converging trendlines. A breakout in either direction should be accompanied by a sharp increase in volume to confirm the move.

- **Key Observation:** If volume remains muted after the breakout, traders should watch for a potential re-entry into the pattern, signaling a failed breakout.

Practical Example: Volume in a Bullish Ascending Triangle

A stock consolidates within an Ascending Triangle with resistance at $100. As the price narrows, volume declines steadily, indicating reduced activity. When the price breaks above $100 with a surge in volume, it confirms the bullish breakout and signals strong buying interest. Traders can confidently enter a long position, setting a stop-loss below the last higher low.

Using Volume Indicators with Triangles

Volume-based indicators can enhance triangle pattern analysis by providing additional confirmation:

- **On-Balance Volume (OBV):** Tracks cumulative buying and selling pressure. Rising OBV during an Ascending Triangle supports a bullish breakout.

- **Volume Price Trend (VPT):** Combines volume and price trends to gauge momentum. An upward VPT trend in a Symmetrical Triangle suggests bullish bias.

- **Accumulation/Distribution Line:** Highlights whether smart money is accumulating or distributing within the pattern.

Red Flags in Volume Dynamics

- **Breakouts Without Volume:** A breakout with low volume indicates weak participation and a higher risk of reversal.

- **Volume Surges Without Breakouts:** An unexpected volume increase during consolidation may signal insider activity or an impending fake-out.

Actionable Insights for Traders

- Always confirm breakouts with a significant increase in volume to reduce the risk of false signals.

- Combine volume analysis with other technical tools like trendlines and momentum indicators for a comprehensive view.
- Use volume dynamics to set realistic expectations for breakout strength and target distances.

Volume analysis is an indispensable aspect of trading triangle patterns, providing the necessary context to validate breakouts and assess their strength. By incorporating volume dynamics into your trading strategy, you can approach triangle patterns with greater confidence and precision, enhancing your overall market performance.

12.4 TRADING TRIANGLE BREAKOUTS

Trading triangle breakouts is a critical skill that can yield high-probability opportunities when executed with precision. Triangle patterns—whether Ascending, Descending, or Symmetrical—represent periods of market consolidation that precede significant price moves. Successfully trading these breakouts requires a methodical approach, combining pattern recognition, volume analysis, and risk management.

Understanding Breakout Dynamics

Breakouts occur when the price breaches the boundaries of a triangle pattern, signaling the resolution of consolidation. The breakout direction—upward or downward—indicates the prevailing force between buyers and sellers.

- **Bullish Breakouts:** Price moves above resistance, signaling buying dominance.
- **Bearish Breakouts:** Price moves below support, indicating selling pressure.
- **Volume Confirmation:** A breakout is more reliable when accompanied by a surge in volume, reflecting strong participation by market participants.

Steps for Trading Triangle Breakouts

1. Identify the Pattern Early

Begin by spotting the formation of a triangle pattern. Look for converging trendlines that highlight narrowing price action. Confirm the pattern's structure using multiple touches of support and resistance lines.

- For Ascending Triangles, focus on horizontal resistance and rising support.
- For Descending Triangles, focus on horizontal support and falling resistance.
- For Symmetrical Triangles, monitor both trendlines for convergence.

2. Determine the Breakout Direction

While Ascending and Descending Triangles have directional biases, Symmetrical Triangles are neutral. Be prepared for breakouts in either direction.

- Use momentum indicators like RSI or MACD to anticipate potential breakout direction.
- Analyze the prevailing trend, as breakouts often align with the broader market movement.

3. Set Conditional Orders

Place conditional orders to automate trade execution in the breakout direction. Use stop orders slightly above the upper trendline for bullish breakouts and slightly below the lower trendline for bearish breakouts.

- Example: In a Symmetrical Triangle with boundaries at $50 and $55, place a buy-stop order at $55.10 and a sell-stop order at $49.90.

4. Confirm with Volume

Wait for a surge in volume to confirm the breakout. Breakouts with low volume are more likely to fail or result in false signals.

- Example: If the price breaks above resistance in an Ascending Triangle, but volume remains muted, exercise caution before entering the trade.

5. Calculate the Price Target

Use the height of the triangle at its widest point to estimate the breakout's price target.

- For bullish breakouts, add the height to the breakout level.
- For bearish breakouts, subtract the height from the breakout level.
- Example: If an Ascending Triangle has a height of $10 and the breakout occurs at $50, the target price is $60 for a bullish breakout.

6. Manage Risk with Stop-Loss Orders

Place stop-loss orders just outside the opposite trendline to limit losses in case of a failed breakout.

- Example: For a bullish breakout above $50 in an Ascending Triangle, set a stop-loss order below the most recent higher low.

Common Pitfalls to Avoid

- **Premature Entries:** Avoid entering trades before the price decisively breaks out of the pattern. Wait for confirmation with a strong close above or below the trendlines.
- **Ignoring Volume:** Breakouts without volume confirmation are less reliable. Ensure that the breakout aligns with increased trading activity.
- **Overestimating Targets:** Not all breakouts achieve their full measured move. Monitor price action and adjust targets as needed.

Practical Example: Symmetrical Triangle Breakout

A stock consolidates into a Symmetrical Triangle between $40 and $50. The price breaks above $50 with strong volume, signaling a bullish breakout.

- Place a long entry at $50.10 with a price target of $60 (calculated using the triangle's $10 height).
- Set a stop-loss at $45, below the lower trendline, to manage risk.
- Monitor the trade, adjusting stops or taking partial profits as the price approaches the target.

Tips for Success

- Use conditional orders to capitalize on breakouts in either direction, especially with neutral patterns like Symmetrical Triangles.
- Combine technical tools, such as trendlines, volume analysis, and indicators, to strengthen your trade setups.
- Remain disciplined, exiting trades promptly if the breakout fails or invalidates the pattern.

Trading triangle breakouts is a disciplined process that, when executed correctly, can lead to significant rewards. By following a systematic approach and integrating volume confirmation and risk management, you can navigate breakouts with confidence and capture substantial market opportunities.

Chapter 12:
Bilateral Chart Patterns

12.5 MANAGING TRIANGLE PATTERN FAILURES

Even the most reliable triangle patterns can fail, leading to unexpected moves that catch unprepared traders off guard. Triangle pattern failures occur when price action breaks out of the pattern but fails to follow through or reverses direction shortly afterward. Understanding how to identify, interpret, and respond to failed triangle patterns is essential for minimizing losses and capitalizing on new opportunities.

Why Triangle Patterns Fail

Triangle pattern failures can happen for several reasons:

- **Low Volume Breakouts:** A breakout without sufficient volume lacks the market participation needed to sustain the move, increasing the risk of failure.

- **Market Reversals:** Changes in underlying market conditions, such as unexpected news or economic events, can invalidate the pattern.

- **Overextended Trends:** When a trend is already overextended, the market may lack the momentum to continue in the expected direction.

- **False Breakouts:** Temporary price movements beyond the trendlines may lack conviction, resulting in a re-entry into the triangle or a reversal.

Recognizing a Failed Triangle Pattern

1. **Re-Entry Into the Pattern:** After a breakout, the price falls back within the triangle's boundaries, indicating a lack of follow-through.

2. **Breakout Without Momentum:** A breakout occurs, but the price stalls or moves sideways without achieving the expected measured move.

3. **Opposite Direction Breakout:** The price initially breaks out in one direction but quickly reverses, breaking out in the opposite direction with stronger momentum.

4. **Volume Mismatch:** Low or declining volume during and after the breakout often signals a weak or unsustainable move.

Strategies for Managing Failures

1. Use Stop-Loss Orders Effectively

Stop-loss orders are your first line of defense against pattern failures. Place them strategically just outside the pattern boundaries to minimize losses.

- For **bullish breakouts**, place stop-loss orders just below the most recent low or the lower trendline.

- For **bearish breakouts**, place stop-loss orders just above the most recent high or the upper trendline.

Example: In an Ascending Triangle with a breakout above $100, set a stop-loss order below the last higher low at $95. If the price re-enters the triangle and hits the stop-loss, exit the trade promptly.

2. Wait for Volume Confirmation

A breakout with low volume should be treated cautiously. If volume does not increase shortly after the breakout, consider exiting the trade or tightening your stop-loss.

- Monitor the breakout's progress closely; if momentum wanes, it may signal an impending failure.

3. Look for Reversal Opportunities

Failed triangle patterns often signal a shift in market sentiment, creating opportunities for trading in the opposite direction.

- **Example:** A failed bullish breakout in an Ascending Triangle that re-enters the pattern and breaks below the lower trendline may present a short-selling opportunity.
- Use confirmation from indicators like RSI or MACD to validate the reversal.

4. Adapt to Market Conditions

If a breakout fails due to broader market reversals or news, consider the new market context before re-entering a trade.

- For instance, a Symmetrical Triangle breakout may fail if macroeconomic data contradicts the prevailing trend. Adjust your strategy to align with the new information.

5. Adjust Targets and Expectations

Failed patterns may still provide opportunities for smaller moves within the triangle. If the breakout does not achieve the full measured move, scale back your target expectations or take partial profits early.

Practical Example: Managing a Failed Bullish Breakout

A stock forms an Ascending Triangle with resistance at $50. The price breaks above $50 but re-enters the triangle and breaks below $48 with low volume. Recognizing the failure:

- Exit the long position at the stop-loss set below $48.
- Consider entering a short position if the price breaks below the lower trendline with strong volume.
- Use the triangle's height to estimate the potential downside target for the short trade.

Tips for Avoiding Costly Failures

- Always wait for volume confirmation before committing to a breakout trade.
- Avoid trading triangles in choppy or low-liquidity markets, where patterns are more prone to failure.
- Use conditional orders to ensure disciplined entries and exits.

Chapter 12:
Bilateral Chart Patterns

Key Takeaways

- Triangle pattern failures are inevitable, but they provide valuable insights into market dynamics and potential reversals.
- By using stop-loss orders, volume analysis, and adaptive strategies, you can minimize losses and turn failures into opportunities.
- Staying flexible and disciplined is essential when navigating pattern failures, ensuring that you remain poised to capitalize on the next high-probability setup.

Managing triangle pattern failures is an essential component of a robust trading strategy. With the right tools and mindset, you can turn setbacks into learning experiences and maintain a strategic edge in the markets.

PART 4:
Technical Indicators and Integration

Chapter 13: Understanding Technical Indicators

13.1 TYPES OF TECHNICAL INDICATORS

Technical indicators are essential tools for traders, providing insights into market behavior that might not be immediately apparent from price action alone. By analyzing historical data such as price, volume, and volatility, indicators help traders identify trends, momentum, and potential turning points. Understanding the different types of technical indicators is the first step in building a robust trading strategy.

What Are Technical Indicators?

Technical indicators are mathematical calculations applied to price and volume data. They serve as visual aids, simplifying complex market dynamics and helping traders make informed decisions. Indicators can be categorized based on their purpose and how they interact with market data.

Categories of Technical Indicators

Technical indicators fall into four primary categories, each serving a distinct purpose:

1. Trend-Following Indicators:

These indicators help identify the direction and strength of a trend, enabling traders to align their strategies with the prevailing market movement. They are most effective in trending markets and less useful during consolidation phases.

- **Examples:** Moving Averages, Moving Average Convergence Divergence (MACD), Average Directional Index (ADX).
- **Practical Use:** A trader might use a 50-day Moving Average to confirm that an uptrend is intact before entering a long position.

2. Momentum Indicators:

Momentum indicators measure the speed of price movements, indicating whether the market is overbought or oversold. These indicators are particularly useful for identifying potential reversals or entry points during pullbacks.

- **Examples:** Relative Strength Index (RSI), Stochastic Oscillator, Williams %R.

- **Practical Use:** RSI values above 70 suggest overbought conditions, while values below 30 indicate oversold conditions.

3. Volume-Based Indicators:

Volume-based indicators analyze trading activity to confirm trends or warn of potential reversals. They show whether buyers or sellers are driving the market and provide context for price movements.

- **Examples:** On-Balance Volume (OBV), Accumulation/Distribution Line, Money Flow Index (MFI).
- **Practical Use:** A rising OBV alongside an uptrend signals strong buying interest, confirming the trend's strength.

4. Volatility Indicators:

Volatility indicators measure the rate of price changes, helping traders identify periods of high or low market activity. These indicators are particularly useful for setting stop-loss levels or determining optimal entry and exit points.

- **Examples:** Bollinger Bands, Average True Range (ATR).
- **Practical Use:** Bollinger Bands expand during high volatility, signaling potential breakout opportunities.

Choosing the Right Indicators

With so many indicators available, it's crucial to choose the ones that align with your trading style and goals. For instance:

- **Trend Traders:** Focus on Moving Averages or MACD to ride established trends.
- **Swing Traders:** Use RSI or Stochastic Oscillator to identify short-term reversals.
- **Day Traders:** Rely on volume-based indicators like OBV to gauge intraday momentum.

Avoiding Indicator Overload

Using too many indicators can lead to confusion and analysis paralysis. Instead, select a few complementary indicators that provide unique insights. For example, pairing a trend-following indicator like Moving Averages with a momentum indicator like RSI offers a balanced view of the market.

Technical indicators are powerful allies in trading, transforming raw data into actionable insights. By understanding the purpose and strengths of each type, you can select the tools that best support your trading strategy, enabling you to navigate the markets with confidence and precision.

13.2 LEADING VS. LAGGING INDICATORS

Chapter 13:
Understanding Technical Indicators

A solid understanding of leading and lagging indicators is essential for traders who aim to make well-timed decisions. These two categories of indicators serve distinct purposes, offering complementary insights into market behavior. By knowing how and when to use each type, traders can better navigate trends, anticipate reversals, and avoid false signals.

What Are Leading Indicators?

Leading indicators are designed to predict future price movements, providing signals before a trend change occurs. They are especially useful for identifying potential entry and exit points early in a market cycle. However, their predictive nature makes them prone to generating false signals, particularly in choppy or range-bound markets.

- **Purpose:** To anticipate future price direction.
- **Strengths:** They allow traders to act early, often capturing the beginning of a trend or reversal.
- **Weaknesses:** Their predictive nature can lead to inaccuracies if the market does not follow the anticipated direction.

Examples of Leading Indicators

- **Relative Strength Index (RSI):** Identifies overbought or oversold conditions, signaling potential reversals.
- **Stochastic Oscillator:** Measures the relationship between a closing price and its price range over a specified period, highlighting momentum shifts.
- **Williams %R:** Similar to the Stochastic Oscillator, it helps pinpoint reversals by identifying extreme conditions.

Practical Use

Imagine a stock with an RSI that reaches 75, indicating overbought conditions. A trader might anticipate a price pullback and prepare to exit or short the position.

What Are Lagging Indicators?

Lagging indicators confirm trends and provide signals after a movement has occurred. They are particularly valuable for validating a trend's strength and reducing the likelihood of false signals. However, their delayed nature means traders may miss the earliest part of a move.

- **Purpose:** To confirm existing trends and provide reliable signals.
- **Strengths:** They excel in trending markets by reducing the impact of noise and false breakouts.
- **Weaknesses:** Their delayed nature can cause traders to enter late or miss reversals.

Examples of Lagging Indicators

- **Moving Averages:** Smooth out price data to confirm the direction of a trend.

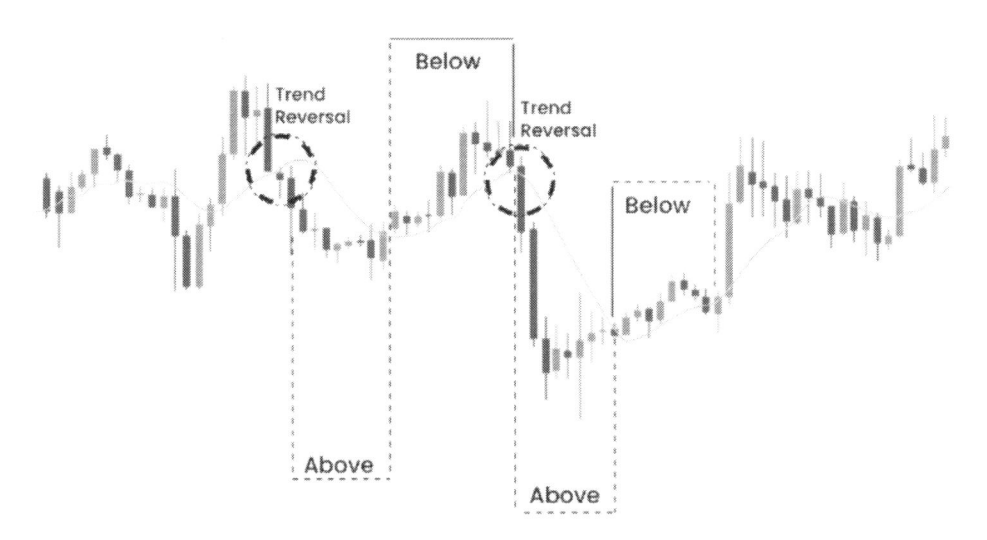

Moving Average

- **MACD (Moving Average Convergence Divergence):** Tracks the relationship between two moving averages to identify trend strength and direction.

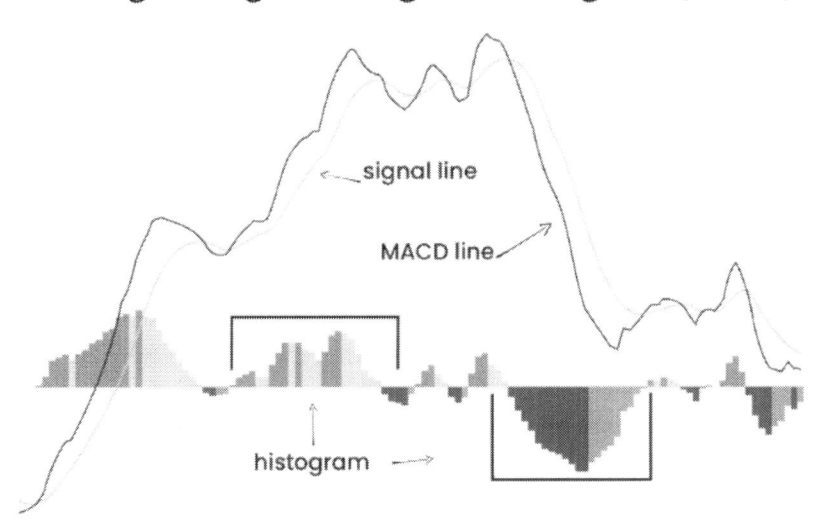

Moving Average Convergence Divergence (MACD)

Chapter 13:
Understanding Technical Indicators

- **Bollinger Bands:** Measure volatility and trend confirmation through the width of the bands.

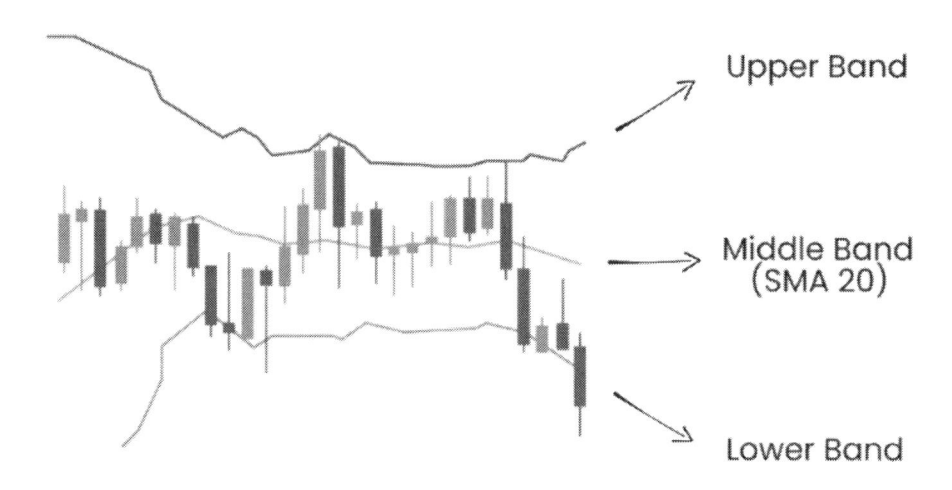

Bollinger Bands

Practical Use

If a stock's price crosses above its 200-day Moving Average, a trader might use this lagging indicator to confirm that an uptrend is firmly in place before entering a long position.

Key Differences Between Leading and Lagging Indicators

1. **Timing of Signals:**
   - Leading indicators generate signals before a trend begins.
   - Lagging indicators generate signals after a trend is established.

2. **Risk vs. Reliability:**
   - Leading indicators are riskier due to false signals but offer the potential for earlier entries.
   - Lagging indicators are more reliable but may result in delayed actions.

3. **Market Suitability:**
   - Leading indicators perform best in range-bound or early-stage trends.
   - Lagging indicators excel in strong, well-established trends.

Combining Leading and Lagging Indicators

For a balanced trading strategy, use a combination of leading and lagging indicators to confirm signals and reduce risks. For example, pair a leading indicator like RSI with a lagging indicator like a Moving Average. RSI can help identify a potential reversal, while the Moving Average confirms whether the broader trend aligns with the anticipated move.

Example Strategy

- Use RSI to identify an oversold condition, signaling a potential bullish reversal.
- Wait for the price to cross above a 50-day Moving Average to confirm the uptrend before entering a trade.

By understanding the strengths and limitations of leading and lagging indicators, traders can create a well-rounded strategy that balances early entries with reliable confirmations. This approach ensures more informed decision-making and enhances the ability to adapt to various market conditions.

13.3 AVOIDING INDICATOR REDUNDANCY

When building a trading strategy, one common mistake is using too many technical indicators that provide overlapping information. This redundancy can lead to analysis paralysis, conflicting signals, and reduced confidence in decision-making. Learning to avoid indicator redundancy ensures a cleaner, more efficient approach to market analysis, allowing traders to focus on the most actionable insights.

What Is Indicator Redundancy?

Indicator redundancy occurs when multiple indicators on your chart measure the same market dynamics, such as trend, momentum, or volatility. While it might seem beneficial to "double-check" signals with similar indicators, this approach often results in cluttered charts and overconfidence in redundant confirmations.

Example of Redundancy

Using both the RSI and the Stochastic Oscillator simultaneously can be redundant, as both measure momentum and overbought/oversold conditions. Similarly, pairing the MACD with a Moving Average often duplicates trend-following information.

Why Avoiding Redundancy Matters

1. **Clarity in Analysis:** A simpler chart is easier to interpret, reducing cognitive load and enabling faster decision-making.
2. **Avoiding Conflicting Signals:** Overlapping indicators may provide conflicting signals due to slight variations in their calculations, leading to confusion.
3. **Efficiency in Execution:** A streamlined approach reduces the time spent analyzing charts and increases the focus on executing trades effectively.
4. **Improved Confidence:** By relying on non-overlapping indicators, traders can have greater trust in their signals.

Steps to Avoid Indicator Redundancy

Chapter 13:
Understanding Technical Indicators

1. Understand the Purpose of Each Indicator

Before adding an indicator to your chart, identify its primary purpose. Indicators generally fall into one of the following categories:

- **Trend Indicators:** Identify the direction and strength of the trend (e.g., Moving Averages, MACD).
- **Momentum Indicators:** Measure the speed and strength of price movements (e.g., RSI, Stochastic Oscillator).
- **Volume Indicators:** Analyze trading activity to confirm price moves (e.g., OBV, Volume Price Analysis).
- **Volatility Indicators:** Assess the rate of price change (e.g., Bollinger Bands, ATR).

Choose one or two indicators from each category to cover all aspects of market analysis without duplication.

2. Combine Complementary Indicators

Instead of using multiple indicators that measure the same element, combine complementary indicators that address different aspects of the market.

- **Example:** Pair a trend indicator (Moving Average) with a momentum indicator (RSI) to get a broader view of market dynamics.

3. Test Each Indicator's Contribution

Evaluate the unique value of each indicator in your strategy. Remove indicators that don't significantly improve your ability to make decisions.

- Use backtesting or paper trading to assess the impact of removing redundant indicators on your performance.

4. Keep Your Chart Clean

Limit the number of indicators displayed on your chart to maintain visual clarity. Use overlays and separate panes strategically to organize your analysis.

- **Example:** Display a Moving Average as an overlay on the price chart and keep the RSI in a separate pane below.

Common Redundant Indicator Combinations

1. **MACD and Moving Averages:** Both are trend-following indicators. Instead, use one and pair it with a complementary momentum or volume indicator.
2. **RSI and Stochastic Oscillator:** Both measure momentum and overbought/oversold conditions. Choose one based on your trading style.
3. **Bollinger Bands and ATR:** Both assess volatility. Use Bollinger Bands for breakout opportunities and ATR for stop-loss placement.

Example of a Non-Redundant Indicator Setup

For a trend-following strategy:

- Use a **50-day Moving Average** to confirm the trend.
- Add **RSI** to identify potential overbought or oversold conditions.
- Include **Volume Price Analysis (VPA)** to confirm the strength of price moves.

This combination ensures that each indicator provides unique insights without overlap.

Actionable Insights for Traders

- Review your current chart setup and identify overlapping indicators. Replace redundant indicators with complementary ones.
- Regularly evaluate the effectiveness of your indicators to ensure they continue adding value to your strategy.
- Keep your chart clean and focused, prioritizing actionable signals over visual complexity.

By avoiding indicator redundancy, traders can achieve a clearer, more effective trading strategy. This disciplined approach simplifies analysis, reduces decision fatigue, and enhances the ability to act decisively in dynamic markets.

13.4 BUILDING AN INDICATOR FRAMEWORK

An indicator framework is a systematic approach to using technical indicators in your trading strategy. It involves selecting a balanced set of indicators that complement each other, organizing their application, and interpreting their signals effectively. A well-constructed framework provides structure, reduces noise, and increases confidence in decision-making, helping traders navigate complex markets with precision.

Why Build an Indicator Framework?

Without a clear framework, traders may fall into the trap of inconsistent analysis, overreliance on a single indicator, or misinterpretation of conflicting signals. A framework:

- Ensures consistency in decision-making.
- Simplifies analysis by focusing on essential insights.
- Reduces the risk of redundant or conflicting indicators.
- Helps adapt strategies to different market conditions.

Key Components of an Indicator Framework

1. Define Your Trading Goals

The first step in building an indicator framework is understanding your trading objectives.

- Are you aiming for short-term gains through day trading or swing trading?

Chapter 13:
Understanding Technical Indicators

- Do you focus on long-term trends for position trading? Your goals will influence the type and combination of indicators you use. For example, day traders might prioritize momentum and volume indicators, while trend-following investors rely on moving averages.

2. Choose Complementary Indicators

Select indicators from different categories to provide a comprehensive view of market dynamics.

- **Trend Indicators:** Identify the overall market direction (e.g., Moving Averages, MACD).
- **Momentum Indicators:** Highlight overbought or oversold conditions (e.g., RSI, Stochastic Oscillator).
- **Volume Indicators:** Confirm price action strength (e.g., OBV, Accumulation/Distribution Line).
- **Volatility Indicators:** Measure price fluctuations (e.g., Bollinger Bands, ATR).

Example Framework

- A **50-day Moving Average** to identify the trend.
- **RSI** to gauge momentum.
- **OBV** to confirm trend strength.
- **ATR** to set stop-loss levels based on volatility.

3. Organize Indicators by Function

Structure your framework so that each indicator has a specific role. This prevents overlap and ensures each tool contributes unique insights.

- **Primary Indicators:** Provide the main signals for entry and exit.
- **Confirming Indicators:** Validate the primary signals.
- **Contextual Indicators:** Offer additional information, such as market volatility or volume trends.

4. Adapt to Different Market Conditions

Markets can range, trend, or experience high volatility. Your framework should be flexible enough to adapt to these conditions.

- In trending markets, rely on trend-following indicators like MACD or Moving Averages.
- In ranging markets, use oscillators like RSI or Stochastic Oscillator.
- During high volatility, incorporate ATR or Bollinger Bands for better risk management.

5. Test and Optimize

Before deploying your framework in live trading, test it thoroughly:

- **Backtesting:** Evaluate how the framework performs on historical data to identify strengths and weaknesses.

- **Forward Testing:** Use paper trading to see how it performs in real-time conditions without risking capital.
- **Refinement:** Adjust indicators, timeframes, or settings based on testing results to improve performance.

Common Pitfalls to Avoid

- **Overcomplicating the Framework:** Using too many indicators can lead to conflicting signals and analysis paralysis. Focus on simplicity and clarity.
- **Ignoring Market Context:** Indicators are tools, not guarantees. Always consider broader market conditions when interpreting signals.
- **Failing to Test:** Implementing an untested framework can lead to unreliable results and unnecessary losses.

Practical Example of an Indicator Framework in Action

A swing trader looking for opportunities in an uptrending market might use:

- **Trend Indicator:** A 20-day Moving Average to confirm the trend.
- **Momentum Indicator:** RSI to identify pullbacks during the trend.
- **Volume Indicator:** OBV to ensure strong buying interest supports the trend.
- **Volatility Indicator:** ATR to set dynamic stop-loss levels, accounting for market fluctuations.

When the RSI drops below 30 during an uptrend confirmed by the Moving Average, and OBV shows increasing volume, the trader enters a long position. They use ATR to place a stop-loss that adapts to current volatility.

Key Takeaways

- Building an indicator framework ensures consistency, clarity, and efficiency in trading decisions.
- Select complementary indicators from different categories to cover all aspects of market analysis.
- Test and refine your framework regularly to adapt to changing market conditions and improve performance.

A well-constructed indicator framework is not just a set of tools—it's a strategy for disciplined and informed trading. By following a structured approach, traders can better navigate the markets and achieve their financial goals with confidence.

Chapter 14:
Trend-Following Indicators

Chapter 14: Trend-Following Indicators

14.1 Moving Averages and Their Variations

Moving averages (MAs) are one of the most popular and versatile tools in technical analysis. They simplify price data by creating a smoothed line that tracks the overall trend, helping traders identify direction, momentum, and potential reversals. Understanding the various types of moving averages and how to use them effectively is essential for trend-following strategies.

What Are Moving Averages?

A moving average calculates the average price of an asset over a specified number of periods, smoothing out short-term fluctuations to reveal the underlying trend. The result is a dynamic line that adjusts with price changes, making it easier to identify trend direction and strength.

- **Purpose:** Moving averages help filter market noise, highlight trends, and provide dynamic support and resistance levels.
- **Common Applications:** Identifying trends, generating entry and exit signals, and confirming price action.

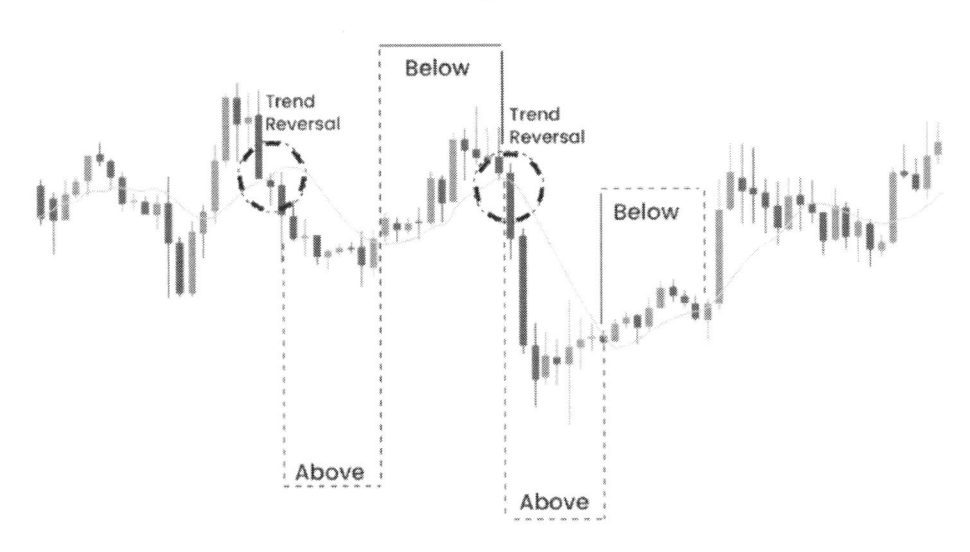

Moving Average

Types of Moving Averages

1. Simple Moving Average (SMA):

The SMA calculates the average price over a set number of periods. Each price point is given equal weight, making it easy to understand and widely used.

- **Example:** A 20-day SMA calculates the average closing price of the last 20 days and updates daily as new prices are added.
- **Best Use:** Ideal for identifying long-term trends and smoothing out price data in less volatile markets.

2. Exponential Moving Average (EMA):

The EMA gives more weight to recent prices, making it more responsive to current price action compared to the SMA.

- **Example:** A 20-day EMA reacts more quickly to recent price changes, making it suitable for shorter-term trading.
- **Best Use:** Effective in fast-moving markets where timely signals are crucial.

3. Weighted Moving Average (WMA):

The WMA assigns weights to prices based on their recency, with the most recent prices receiving the highest weight.

- **Example:** A 10-day WMA prioritizes the most recent data more significantly than the SMA or EMA.
- **Best Use:** Useful for traders who want to focus heavily on the latest price action.

4. Hull Moving Average (HMA):

The HMA uses a weighted average formula to reduce lag while maintaining smoothness. It is highly responsive to price changes, making it a favorite for advanced traders.

- **Best Use:** Effective for detecting trend changes early with minimal lag.

How to Use Moving Averages in Trading

1. Identifying Trend Direction:

- When the price is above the moving average, it indicates an uptrend.
- When the price is below the moving average, it signals a downtrend.

2. Dynamic Support and Resistance Levels:

Moving averages often act as dynamic support or resistance levels where price tends to bounce or reverse.

- **Example:** A 50-day SMA in an uptrend might act as support during pullbacks, offering an entry opportunity.

Chapter 14:
Trend-Following Indicators

3. Crossover Strategies:

- A **Golden Cross** occurs when a shorter-term moving average (e.g., 50-day) crosses above a longer-term moving average (e.g., 200-day), signaling a bullish trend.

- A **Death Cross** occurs when a shorter-term moving average crosses below a longer-term one, signaling a bearish trend.

4. Multi-Timeframe Analysis:

Use different moving averages for different timeframes to confirm trends and fine-tune entries and exits.

- **Example:** A trader might use a 50-day SMA for the daily chart to confirm the overall trend and a 10-day EMA for intraday entries.

Common Moving Average Combinations

- **Short-Term Trading:** Pair a 10-day EMA with a 20-day EMA for faster signals.
- **Swing Trading:** Combine a 20-day SMA with a 50-day SMA for medium-term analysis.
- **Position Trading:** Use a 50-day SMA and a 200-day SMA for long-term trends.

Practical Example: Moving Averages in Action

Imagine a stock trending upward with the price consistently bouncing off the 50-day SMA. A trader identifies a pullback toward the SMA as an entry opportunity. Once the price confirms support at the SMA, the trader enters a long position, setting a stop-loss slightly below the moving average and targeting the next resistance level.

Tips for Using Moving Averages Effectively

- Use longer-period moving averages for trend confirmation and shorter-period ones for precision entries.
- Combine moving averages with other indicators like RSI or MACD to validate signals.
- Be cautious of whipsaws in choppy markets; moving averages work best in trending environments.

Moving averages are foundational tools for trend-following traders. By understanding their variations and applications, you can tailor them to suit your trading style, improve your timing, and gain a clearer perspective on market trends. Mastering these tools ensures you're well-equipped to navigate the markets with confidence and precision.

14.2 MACD Analysis and Trading

The **Moving Average Convergence Divergence (MACD)** is a versatile and powerful trend-following indicator that also serves as a momentum oscillator. Its ability to highlight trend direction, strength, and potential reversals makes it a cornerstone tool for traders of all levels. By mastering MACD analysis and trading techniques, you can significantly enhance your ability to navigate the markets.

What Is the MACD?

The MACD calculates the difference between two moving averages of different time periods, typically the **12-day EMA** (faster moving average) and the **26-day EMA** (slower moving average). This difference is plotted as the MACD line, which oscillates above and below a zero line. The indicator also features a **Signal Line**, which is a 9-day EMA of the MACD line, and a histogram that visualizes the distance between the two lines.

Key Components of the MACD

1. **MACD Line:** The difference between the 12-day EMA and 26-day EMA, reflecting momentum and trend strength.

2. **Signal Line:** A 9-day EMA of the MACD line, used to generate trading signals.

3. **Histogram:** Represents the distance between the MACD line and the Signal Line, offering a visual cue for momentum shifts.

Moving Average Convergence Divergence (MACD)

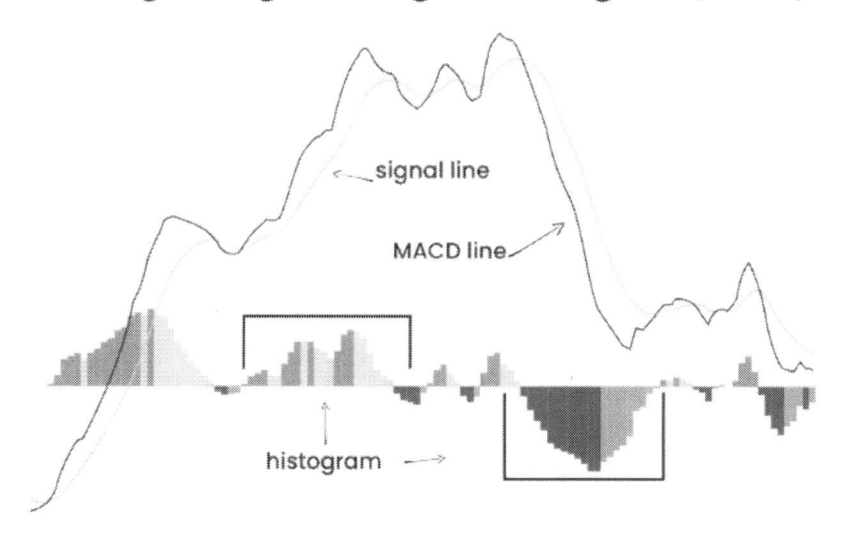

How to Interpret the MACD

1. **Zero Line Crossovers:**

    o When the MACD line crosses above the zero line, it indicates bullish momentum and the start of an uptrend.

Chapter 14:
Trend-Following Indicators

- o When the MACD line crosses below the zero line, it signals bearish momentum and the start of a downtrend.

2. **MACD and Signal Line Crossovers:**
   - o A **Bullish Crossover** occurs when the MACD line crosses above the Signal Line, indicating upward momentum and a potential buy signal.
   - o A **Bearish Crossover** occurs when the MACD line crosses below the Signal Line, signaling downward momentum and a potential sell signal.

3. **Divergences:**
   - o **Bullish Divergence:** The price makes lower lows while the MACD makes higher lows, suggesting weakening bearish momentum and a potential reversal upward.
   - o **Bearish Divergence:** The price makes higher highs while the MACD makes lower highs, indicating weakening bullish momentum and a potential reversal downward.

4. **Histogram Dynamics:**
   - o A growing histogram indicates strengthening momentum in the direction of the MACD line.
   - o A shrinking histogram signals weakening momentum and a potential trend shift.

Using the MACD in Trading

1. Trend Confirmation

The MACD is highly effective for confirming the strength and direction of a trend. Traders often use zero line crossovers as confirmation of a new trend aligning with the prevailing market conditions.

Example:
If a stock is trading above its 200-day SMA and the MACD crosses above the zero line, it confirms the uptrend, providing confidence to enter a long position.

2. Entry and Exit Signals

Use MACD and Signal Line crossovers to time entries and exits.

- **Bullish Entry:** Enter a long position when the MACD line crosses above the Signal Line and the histogram starts expanding.
- **Bearish Entry:** Enter a short position when the MACD line crosses below the Signal Line and the histogram begins to shrink.

3. Divergences for Reversals

Spot divergences between the MACD and price action to anticipate trend reversals.

- **Bullish Divergence Example:** A stock is making new lows, but the MACD shows higher lows. This signals that bearish momentum is weakening, and a reversal upward may occur.

4. Combining MACD with Other Tools

For improved accuracy, combine MACD with trendlines, moving averages, or support/resistance levels.

- Example: Use MACD crossovers to confirm breakout signals from a triangle pattern.

Common MACD Settings

While the default MACD settings (12, 26, 9) work well for many scenarios, traders can adjust them based on their trading style:

- **Short-Term Trading:** Use faster settings like (6, 13, 5) for quicker signals.
- **Long-Term Trading:** Use slower settings like (24, 52, 18) to filter out noise and focus on major trends.

Practical Example: Trading with MACD

Imagine a stock trending upward with the MACD line crossing above the Signal Line at -2 on the histogram, accompanied by a breakout above $100.

- **Entry Point:** Enter the trade as the histogram begins to expand and confirms the breakout.
- **Exit Point:** Exit the trade when the MACD line crosses below the Signal Line or when the histogram begins shrinking near $120, a major resistance level.

Tips for Trading with the MACD

- Always confirm MACD signals with price action and other indicators to avoid false signals.
- Be cautious of lag in the MACD, especially in highly volatile or choppy markets.
- Monitor the histogram closely; its dynamics often signal shifts before the MACD line crosses the Signal Line.

The MACD is an invaluable tool for identifying trends, timing entries and exits, and spotting reversals. By integrating MACD analysis into your trading framework, you can gain a deeper understanding of market dynamics and enhance your decision-making precision.

Chapter 14:
Trend-Following Indicators

14.3 ADX AND TREND STRENGTH

The **Average Directional Index (ADX)** is a powerful indicator designed to measure the strength of a trend, rather than its direction. Developed by J. Welles Wilder, the ADX is widely used to assess whether a market is trending and to determine the strength of that trend. Understanding how to interpret and use the ADX effectively can help traders identify high-probability opportunities and avoid markets with weak or choppy movements.

What Is the ADX?

The ADX is part of the **Directional Movement System**, which includes three lines:

1. **ADX Line:** Measures the overall strength of the trend.
2. **+DI (Positive Directional Indicator):** Represents upward price movement.
3. **-DI (Negative Directional Indicator):** Represents downward price movement.

The ADX line ranges from 0 to 100, with higher values indicating stronger trends. Unlike other indicators, the ADX does not specify whether the trend is bullish or bearish—it only measures its strength.

Average Directional Index (ADX)

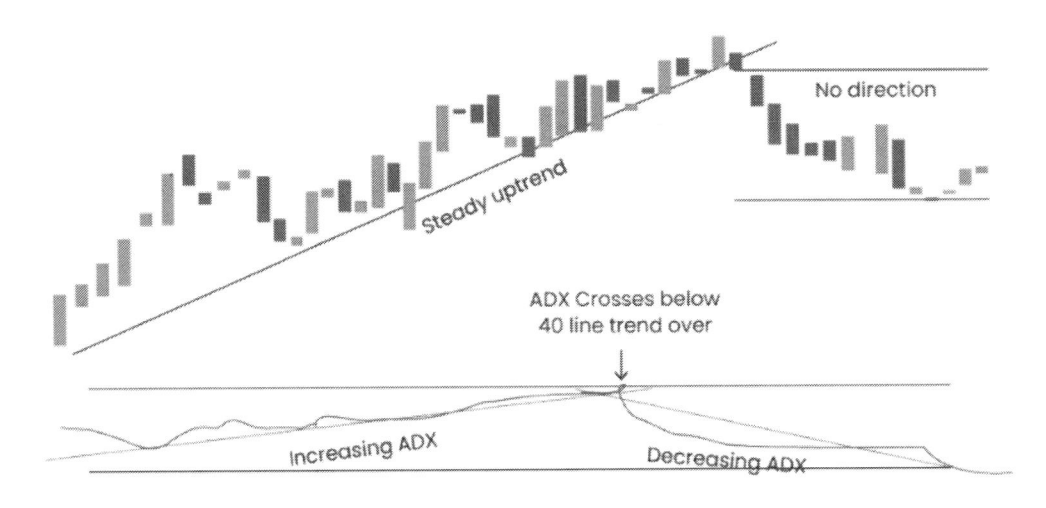

How to Interpret the ADX

1. **Trend Strength Levels:**
    - **0-25:** Weak or no trend. The market is likely consolidating or range-bound.
    - **25-50:** Strong trend. The market is trending significantly in either direction.
    - **50-75:** Very strong trend. Momentum is high, often accompanied by increased volatility.

-○ **75-100:** Extremely strong trend. Rare and typically associated with parabolic price moves.
2. **Directional Indicators (+DI and -DI):**
   - ○ When the +DI line is above the -DI line, it suggests a bullish trend.
   - ○ When the -DI line is above the +DI line, it indicates a bearish trend.
   - ○ The ADX line confirms the strength of the trend, regardless of direction.

Using the ADX in Trading

1. Identifying Trending Markets

The ADX is highly effective in distinguishing trending markets from range-bound ones.

- A rising ADX above 25 signals the start of a trend.
- A falling ADX below 25 indicates a weakening trend or transition to consolidation.

Example:

If the ADX rises above 25 while the +DI line is above the -DI line, it signals the beginning of a strong bullish trend, prompting traders to look for long opportunities.

2. Confirming Breakouts

The ADX can validate breakouts from consolidation patterns like triangles or rectangles. A rising ADX during the breakout confirms that the move is supported by strong trend momentum.

- Use the ADX in combination with price action to ensure the breakout is genuine.

3. Filtering Trades

Avoid entering trades in weak or choppy markets by checking the ADX. If the ADX is below 20-25, focus on range-based strategies instead of trend-following ones.

4. Measuring Trend Strength for Stop-Loss Placement

In strong trends (ADX above 30), traders may use wider stop-loss levels to account for increased volatility. In weaker trends (ADX below 25), tighter stops are advisable as price movements are less decisive.

Practical Example: Trading with the ADX

Imagine a stock breaking out of a symmetrical triangle pattern, with the ADX rising from 20 to 30 and the +DI line crossing above the -DI line.

- **Entry Point:** Enter a long position as the ADX rises above 25, confirming the trend's strength.
- **Stop-Loss Placement:** Set the stop-loss below the breakout level, accounting for potential volatility.
- **Exit Strategy:** Monitor the ADX; if it peaks and begins to decline, consider exiting the trade as trend strength wanes.

Chapter 14:
Trend-Following Indicators

Combining ADX with Other Indicators

The ADX works best when combined with other tools for context and confirmation:

- **Trend Indicators:** Use Moving Averages to confirm the trend direction.
- **Momentum Indicators:** Pair with RSI or MACD to validate entry points.
- **Chart Patterns:** Combine with breakout patterns to ensure trend continuation.

Example Strategy:

A trader notices an ascending triangle breakout. The ADX rises above 25 during the breakout, and the +DI line is above the -DI line. The trader enters a long position, using RSI to ensure the market is not overbought.

Tips for Using the ADX Effectively

- Avoid using the ADX alone; always pair it with directional indicators or price action for context.
- Monitor the ADX line's slope; a rising ADX signals strengthening trends, while a falling ADX suggests weakening trends.
- In choppy or sideways markets, consider switching to range-based strategies or waiting for the ADX to rise above 25.

The ADX is an invaluable tool for assessing trend strength, filtering trades, and validating breakouts. By incorporating it into your trading framework, you can enhance your ability to focus on strong trends and avoid wasting time and capital in low-probability environments.

14.4 Ichimoku Cloud Analysis

The **Ichimoku Kinko Hyo**, or "Ichimoku Cloud," is a comprehensive technical analysis tool that combines trend-following, momentum, and support/resistance indicators into a single system. Developed by Japanese journalist Goichi Hosoda, it provides a complete view of market dynamics at a glance. By mastering Ichimoku Cloud analysis, traders can identify trends, forecast potential reversals, and refine their entry and exit strategies.

Components of the Ichimoku Cloud

The Ichimoku system consists of five lines, each offering unique insights into market behavior:

1. **Tenkan-sen (Conversion Line):**
    - A 9-period average calculated as $\text{Tenkan-sen (Conversion Line)} = \frac{\text{High} + \text{Low}}{2}$
    - Represents short-term momentum and acts as a faster-moving average.
2. **Kijun-sen (Base Line):**

- A 26-period average calculated as Kijun-sen (Base Line) $= \frac{\text{High}+\text{Low}}{2}$
- Represents medium-term momentum and serves as a baseline for trend analysis.

3. **Senkou Span A (Leading Span A):**
   - The midpoint between the Tenkan-sen and Kijun-sen, plotted 26 periods ahead.
   - Forms one boundary of the "cloud" and reflects short-to-medium-term trends.

4. **Senkou Span B (Leading Span B):**
   - A 52-period average of the high and low, plotted 26 periods ahead.
   - Represents long-term support/resistance and forms the second boundary of the cloud.

5. **Chikou Span (Lagging Span):**
   - The current closing price plotted 26 periods behind.
   - Provides a perspective on how current prices compare to historical price action.

The **Cloud (Kumo)** is the shaded area between Senkou Span A and Senkou Span B. Its shape and position relative to price provide valuable insights into trend direction, strength, and potential reversals.

How to Interpret the Ichimoku Cloud

1. **Trend Direction:**
   - Price above the cloud indicates a bullish trend.
   - Price below the cloud indicates a bearish trend.
   - Price within the cloud suggests consolidation or indecision.

2. **Cloud Thickness:**
   - A thick cloud represents strong support/resistance and indicates a robust trend.
   - A thin cloud suggests weak support/resistance and potential vulnerability to reversals.

3. **Future Cloud (Leading Spans A and B):**
   - A bullish cloud has Leading Span A above Leading Span B.
   - A bearish cloud has Leading Span A below Leading Span B.
   - The future cloud's slope provides early signals of potential trend continuation or reversal.

4. **Lagging Span Confirmation:**
   - The Chikou Span above the price line confirms bullish momentum.
   - The Chikou Span below the price line confirms bearish momentum.

Chapter 14:
Trend-Following Indicators

Using the Ichimoku Cloud in Trading

1. Identifying Trends:

- In a bullish trend, look for price above the cloud, with the Tenkan-sen crossing above the Kijun-sen and the future cloud bullishly sloping.

- In a bearish trend, look for price below the cloud, with the Tenkan-sen crossing below the Kijun-sen and the future cloud bearish.

Example: A stock trading at $150 shows price above a thick bullish cloud, with the Tenkan-sen crossing above the Kijun-sen. This confirms a strong uptrend, making it an ideal candidate for a long position.

2. Entry and Exit Strategies:

- **Bullish Entry:** Enter a long position when price breaks above the cloud with the Tenkan-sen above the Kijun-sen.

- **Bearish Entry:** Enter a short position when price breaks below the cloud with the Tenkan-sen below the Kijun-sen.

- **Exit Strategy:** Exit when the price re-enters the cloud or when the Tenkan-sen crosses below the Kijun-sen in a bullish trend.

3. Support and Resistance:

- Use the cloud as dynamic support or resistance. For instance, in a bullish trend, the top of the cloud (Senkou Span A) often acts as support during pullbacks.

4. Trading Breakouts:

- Monitor the slope of the future cloud. A steep bullish slope after a breakout above the cloud confirms strong momentum.

Practical Example: Trading with the Ichimoku Cloud

A stock breaks above a bearish cloud at $100, with the Tenkan-sen crossing above the Kijun-sen. The future cloud turns bullish, and the Chikou Span rises above the price line.

- **Entry Point:** Enter at $101 as the breakout is confirmed.

- **Stop-Loss Placement:** Set a stop-loss below the cloud at $95, accounting for volatility.

- **Exit Strategy:** Exit at $120 when the price re-enters the cloud, signaling potential trend weakness.

Tips for Mastering Ichimoku Cloud Analysis

- Avoid trading solely based on a single Ichimoku component; always consider the entire system.

- The Ichimoku Cloud works best in trending markets and may produce false signals in choppy conditions.

- Combine the Ichimoku system with other indicators like RSI or MACD for added confirmation.

The Ichimoku Cloud is a comprehensive tool that provides unparalleled clarity in trend analysis and trading strategy development. By mastering its components and interpretations, traders can gain a decisive edge in navigating dynamic markets.

Chapter 15: Momentum Indicators

15.1 RELATIVE STRENGTH INDEX (RSI)

The **Relative Strength Index (RSI)** is a momentum oscillator that measures the speed and change of price movements. Developed by J. Welles Wilder, the RSI is widely used to identify overbought and oversold market conditions, helping traders anticipate potential reversals and refine their entry and exit strategies. Its simplicity and effectiveness make it a staple in both beginner and advanced trading toolkits.

Understanding RSI

The RSI oscillates between 0 and 100, providing a relative strength measurement of recent price gains to losses over a specified period, typically 14 periods. Traders interpret the RSI based on key levels and its position within the range.

- **Overbought Conditions:** RSI above 70 suggests that the market is overbought, potentially signaling a reversal or pullback.

- **Oversold Conditions:** RSI below 30 indicates that the market is oversold, suggesting a potential upward reversal.

- **Neutral Zone:** RSI between 30 and 70 reflects balanced conditions, where price movements are neither overextended nor exhausted.

RSI Range Shifts

RSI Levels	Zone
70–100	Bullish
30–70	Sideways
0–30	Bearish

How to Use RSI in Trading

1. Identify Overbought and Oversold Levels

- **Overbought Zone:** When the RSI rises above 70, it indicates that the asset may be overvalued and due for a correction.
- **Oversold Zone:** When the RSI drops below 30, it suggests undervaluation and the potential for a rebound.

Example:
A stock with an RSI of 80 has been in a prolonged uptrend. A trader interprets this as an overbought condition and prepares for a potential reversal by either exiting a long position or looking for short opportunities.

2. Detect Divergences

Divergences occur when the RSI moves in the opposite direction of price action, signaling potential trend reversals:

- **Bullish Divergence:** Price makes lower lows, but the RSI forms higher lows, indicating weakening bearish momentum and a potential upward reversal.
- **Bearish Divergence:** Price makes higher highs, but the RSI forms lower highs, suggesting waning bullish momentum and a potential downward reversal.

3. Identify Trend Confirmation

During strong trends, the RSI often remains in extended zones:

- In an uptrend, RSI may hover between 40 and 90, with pullbacks finding support around 40-50.
- In a downtrend, RSI typically ranges between 10 and 60, with resistance near 50-60.

4. Use RSI for Entry and Exit Timing

RSI can help fine-tune entry and exit points:

- Enter long positions when the RSI exits oversold territory (e.g., crosses above 30).
- Exit long positions or enter short positions when the RSI exits overbought territory (e.g., crosses below 70).

RSI Settings for Different Trading Styles

While the standard RSI setting is 14 periods, it can be adjusted to suit various trading styles:

- **Short-Term Trading:** Use a 7 or 9-period RSI for quicker signals, suitable for day trading or scalping.
- **Long-Term Trading:** Use a 21 or 28-period RSI for smoother, more reliable signals in position trading.

Practical Example: RSI in Action

Chapter 15:
Momentum Indicators

A trader observes a stock with the RSI falling below 30, signaling an oversold condition. At the same time, the price forms a bullish hammer candlestick at a key support level. The trader enters a long position, setting a stop-loss just below the support. When the RSI rises above 50, indicating strengthening momentum, the trader adds to the position. The trade is exited when the RSI approaches 70, signaling a potential overbought condition.

Combining RSI with Other Indicators

The RSI works best when combined with other tools for confirmation and context:

- **Moving Averages:** Use RSI to time entries and exits within a trend confirmed by moving averages.
- **MACD:** Pair RSI with MACD crossovers to validate momentum shifts.
- **Support and Resistance Levels:** Align RSI signals with key price levels for higher-probability trades.

Tips for Effective RSI Use

- Avoid acting on RSI signals in isolation; confirm with other indicators or price action.
- During strong trends, RSI may remain in overbought or oversold zones for extended periods. Use trend analysis to contextualize signals.
- Adjust RSI settings based on your preferred timeframe and trading style for optimal results.

The RSI is a versatile and reliable momentum indicator that provides valuable insights into market conditions and potential reversals. By incorporating RSI into your trading strategy, you can enhance your timing and precision, navigating both trending and range-bound markets with greater confidence.

15.2 STOCHASTIC OSCILLATOR

The **Stochastic Oscillator** is a momentum indicator designed to compare a security's closing price to its price range over a specified period. Developed by George Lane, this tool is particularly effective for identifying overbought and oversold conditions, timing entries and exits, and detecting potential trend reversals. Its simplicity and adaptability make it a favorite among traders seeking to refine their strategies.

Understanding the Stochastic Oscillator

The Stochastic Oscillator generates two lines plotted on a scale of 0 to 100:

1. **%K Line:** The primary line that tracks the current closing price relative to the high-low range over a given period (typically 14).

2. **%D Line:** A 3-period moving average of the %K line, acting as a signal line for smoothing.

Key levels on the scale include:

- **Above 80:** Indicates overbought conditions, suggesting the price may be due for a pullback.

- **Below 20:** Indicates oversold conditions, signaling the potential for an upward reversal.

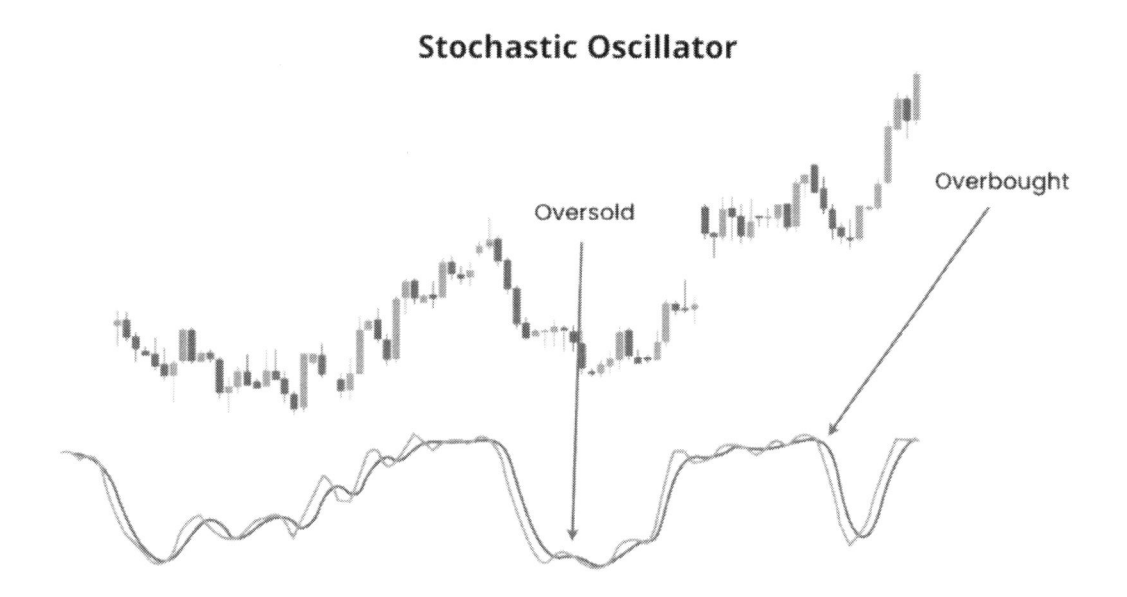

Stochastic Oscillator

How to Interpret the Stochastic Oscillator

1. Overbought and Oversold Levels

- **Overbought Zone (Above 80):** Suggests the market may be overextended to the upside and is likely to correct or consolidate.

- **Oversold Zone (Below 20):** Indicates the market may be overextended to the downside, with a potential rebound on the horizon.

2. Crossovers

The interaction between the %K and %D lines generates trading signals:

- **Bullish Crossover:** The %K line crosses above the %D line in the oversold zone, indicating a potential buying opportunity.

- **Bearish Crossover:** The %K line crosses below the %D line in the overbought zone, signaling a potential selling opportunity.

3. Divergences

Divergences between the Stochastic Oscillator and price action can signal weakening momentum:

Chapter 15:
Momentum Indicators

- **Bullish Divergence:** The price forms lower lows, while the oscillator forms higher lows, indicating weakening bearish momentum and a possible reversal upward.
- **Bearish Divergence:** The price forms higher highs, while the oscillator forms lower highs, suggesting weakening bullish momentum and a potential reversal downward.

Using the Stochastic Oscillator in Trading

1. Identifying Trend Reversals

The Stochastic Oscillator is highly effective in spotting turning points in range-bound markets.

- **Example:** A stock trading near a key support level shows the Stochastic Oscillator crossing above 20 with a bullish crossover. This signals a reversal, prompting the trader to consider a long position.

2. Timing Entries and Exits

The oscillator's crossovers provide actionable entry and exit signals:

- Enter long positions when the %K line crosses above the %D line in oversold territory.
- Exit or enter short positions when the %K line crosses below the %D line in overbought territory.

3. Trend Confirmation

While the Stochastic Oscillator is most effective in sideways markets, it can also confirm trends.

- In an uptrend, the oscillator often oscillates between 20 and 80, with pullbacks finding support near 20-40.
- In a downtrend, it oscillates between 20 and 80, with rallies encountering resistance near 60-80.

4. Filtering False Signals

To reduce the risk of false signals, combine the oscillator with other tools, such as trendlines or moving averages, for context.

- **Example:** A bullish crossover in the oversold zone is more reliable when confirmed by a breakout above a descending trendline.

Practical Example: Trading with the Stochastic Oscillator

Imagine a stock in a consolidating range between $50 and $60. The Stochastic Oscillator falls below 20, then forms a bullish crossover while the price approaches $50. The trader enters a long position at $51, targeting $60 as the resistance level. A stop-loss is set at $49, just below the support zone. The trade is exited when the price nears $60 and the oscillator enters overbought territory above 80.

Combining the Stochastic Oscillator with Other Indicators

The Stochastic Oscillator works best when used alongside complementary indicators:

- **Volume Indicators:** Confirm the validity of signals by analyzing market participation.

- **RSI:** Use the RSI to validate overbought or oversold conditions for additional confidence.
- **Trend Indicators:** Combine with moving averages to align oscillator signals with the prevailing trend.

Tips for Effective Stochastic Oscillator Use

- Use the Stochastic Oscillator primarily in range-bound or moderately trending markets to avoid misleading signals in highly volatile conditions.
- Adjust the oscillator's settings to suit your trading timeframe. For short-term trading, consider faster settings like 9-periods for %K. For longer-term strategies, use 14-periods or higher.
- Combine crossovers with price action analysis, such as candlestick patterns or support/resistance levels, for more robust trade setups.

The Stochastic Oscillator is a versatile tool that provides insights into market momentum and potential turning points. By integrating it into your trading strategy, you can enhance your timing, capitalize on reversals, and navigate market cycles with greater precision.

Chapter 16:
Volume-Based Indicators

16.1 On-Balance Volume (OBV)

The **On-Balance Volume (OBV)** is a powerful volume-based indicator that measures the cumulative flow of volume relative to price movements. Developed by Joseph Granville, OBV serves as a leading indicator, helping traders identify potential price trends, confirm reversals, and anticipate breakouts by analyzing the relationship between volume and price.

Understanding OBV

The OBV is calculated by adding or subtracting the day's volume to a running total, depending on whether the price closes higher or lower than the previous close:

- **If the close is higher than the previous close:** Add the volume to the OBV.
- **If the close is lower than the previous close:** Subtract the volume from the OBV.
- **If the close is unchanged:** The OBV remains the same.

The concept behind OBV is straightforward: volume often precedes price. When OBV rises, it indicates that buying pressure is increasing, which may signal an upcoming price rally. Conversely, when OBV falls, it reflects increasing selling pressure, which could precede a price decline.

How to Interpret OBV

1. Confirming Trends

OBV can confirm the strength and direction of a trend:

- **Rising OBV in an Uptrend:** Confirms that the uptrend is supported by strong buying volume.
- **Falling OBV in a Downtrend:** Indicates that the downtrend is supported by strong selling volume.

2. Spotting Divergences

Divergences between OBV and price action often signal potential reversals:

- **Bullish Divergence:** Price makes lower lows, but OBV makes higher lows, suggesting that buying pressure is building despite the price decline.
- **Bearish Divergence:** Price makes higher highs, but OBV makes lower highs, indicating weakening buying momentum and a potential reversal downward.

3. Anticipating Breakouts

A sudden surge in OBV without a corresponding price movement can indicate an imminent breakout. If OBV rises sharply while the price consolidates, it suggests accumulation and a likely bullish breakout. Similarly, a drop in OBV during consolidation signals distribution and a potential bearish breakout.

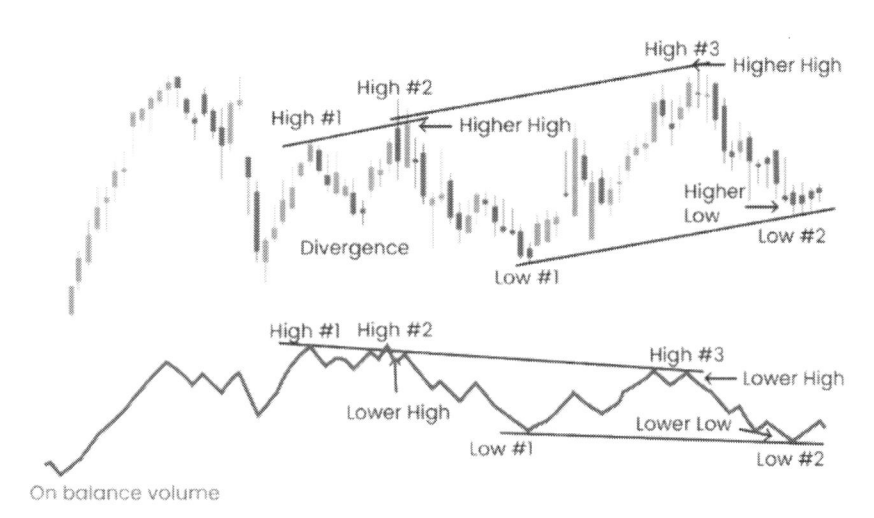

Using OBV in Trading

1. Trend Confirmation

Use OBV to confirm the validity of a trend.

- **Example:** A stock in an uptrend shows rising OBV, indicating strong buying pressure. This reinforces the likelihood that the trend will continue.

2. Entry and Exit Points

Combine OBV signals with price action to refine entry and exit points:

- **Entry:** Enter long positions when OBV makes higher highs alongside price.
- **Exit:** Exit long positions when OBV begins to diverge negatively from price, signaling potential weakness.

3. Supporting Other Indicators

OBV can act as a complement to trend or momentum indicators, providing additional context to confirm signals. For example, use OBV to validate Moving Average crossovers or RSI overbought/oversold conditions.

Practical Example: Trading with OBV

Chapter 16:
Volume-Based Indicators

Imagine a stock trading in a tight range between $50 and $60. While the price appears flat, OBV steadily rises, indicating accumulation. The trader anticipates a bullish breakout above $60 and enters a long position as the price breaks out with OBV continuing to rise.

- **Stop-Loss Placement:** Place a stop-loss below the breakout level at $58.
- **Exit Strategy:** Exit the trade if OBV begins to decline sharply, signaling distribution.

Combining OBV with Other Tools

To maximize effectiveness, combine OBV with additional technical tools:

- **Trendlines:** Use OBV trends to confirm price trendlines.
- **Volume Indicators:** Pair OBV with Volume Price Analysis (VPA) to gain deeper insights into volume dynamics.
- **Support and Resistance:** Align OBV movements with key levels to confirm breakout or reversal strength.

Example Strategy: A trader notices a bullish flag pattern on the price chart. OBV rises steadily during the consolidation phase, confirming accumulation. When the price breaks out, the trader enters a long position, confident in the breakout's strength.

Tips for Using OBV Effectively

- Use OBV primarily for trend confirmation and breakout anticipation rather than standalone signals.
- Monitor OBV divergence as an early warning of potential reversals.
- Be cautious in low-volume markets, as OBV signals may be less reliable in thinly traded assets.

The On-Balance Volume indicator provides traders with invaluable insights into the relationship between volume and price, helping to confirm trends, spot divergences, and anticipate significant price moves. Incorporating OBV into your trading strategy can enhance your ability to make informed, high-probability decisions.

16.2 VOLUME PRICE ANALYSIS (VPA)

Volume Price Analysis (VPA) is a method of interpreting market movements by analyzing the relationship between price action and trading volume. The idea behind VPA is that volume reflects the true intentions of market participants, making it a crucial component for confirming trends, identifying reversals, and spotting key breakout or breakdown points. By mastering VPA, traders can gain deeper insights into the underlying dynamics of market movements.

The Core Principles of Volume Price Analysis

Volume Price Analysis revolves around understanding how volume interacts with price behavior. Key principles include:

1. Volume Confirms Price Trends

In a healthy trend, volume typically moves in the same direction as the price. For example:

- In an uptrend, rising volume during price increases confirms strong buying interest.
- In a downtrend, rising volume during price decreases indicates strong selling pressure.

2. Divergences Between Volume and Price

When volume and price move in opposite directions, it signals potential weakening of the current trend:

- **Bullish Divergence:** Volume rises as price falls, suggesting accumulation and a potential reversal upward.
- **Bearish Divergence:** Volume falls as price rises, signaling weak buying interest and a potential reversal downward.

3. Volume Precedes Price

Sharp increases in volume often precede significant price moves. For instance, a spike in volume during a consolidation phase can indicate accumulation or distribution, leading to an eventual breakout or breakdown.

How to Apply VPA in Trading

1. Confirming Trends

VPA helps validate the strength of trends:

- A price rally accompanied by increasing volume suggests sustained buying interest, reinforcing the uptrend.
- A price drop on high volume confirms strong selling pressure, validating the downtrend.

2. Identifying Reversals

VPA can provide early warnings of trend reversals:

- A reversal may occur when price reaches a significant support or resistance level with a noticeable volume spike, indicating a shift in supply and demand dynamics.
- Look for "climactic volume" at the end of prolonged trends, often signaling exhaustion and potential reversal.

3. Spotting Breakouts and Breakdowns

Volume is a critical factor in confirming breakouts or breakdowns:

- A breakout above resistance with high volume signals strong conviction and increases the likelihood of sustained movement.

- A breakdown below support with rising volume indicates strong selling interest and confirms the bearish move.

Practical Examples of Volume Price Analysis

Example 1: Confirming a Trend: A stock is in an uptrend, with each price rally accompanied by increasing volume. During pullbacks, volume decreases, suggesting weak selling pressure. This pattern confirms the strength of the uptrend and provides confidence to stay in the trade or add to positions.

Example 2: Detecting a Reversal: After a prolonged downtrend, a stock forms a bullish engulfing candlestick at a key support level. The day's volume spikes significantly, signaling strong buying interest. The trader interprets this as a reversal and enters a long position.

Example 3: Validating a Breakout: A stock has been consolidating between $50 and $55 for weeks. On a particular day, the price breaks above $55 with a sharp increase in volume. This confirms the breakout, prompting the trader to enter a long position with a target at the next resistance level.

Key Volume Patterns to Watch

- **Climactic Volume:** A sudden spike in volume at the end of a trend often indicates a reversal.
- **Volume Dry-Up:** Decreasing volume during a consolidation phase may precede a breakout or breakdown.
- **Volume Surges on Breakouts:** High volume on a breakout signals conviction and potential continuation.
- **Volume Divergences:** Diverging volume and price patterns suggest weakening momentum.

Combining VPA with Other Tools

Volume Price Analysis is most effective when used in conjunction with other indicators and chart patterns:

- **Support and Resistance Levels:** Align volume spikes with key levels to identify potential reversals or breakouts.
- **Candlestick Patterns:** Combine VPA with candlestick analysis for stronger confirmation of signals.
- **Moving Averages:** Use moving averages to identify the overall trend and validate volume-driven price moves.

Tips for Mastering VPA

- Focus on significant volume changes rather than minor fluctuations.
- Be cautious in thinly traded markets, where volume may be less reliable as a signal.

- Use VPA to confirm other technical tools rather than relying on it in isolation.

Volume Price Analysis offers an invaluable perspective on the interplay between price and market activity. By incorporating VPA into your trading framework, you can uncover hidden opportunities, enhance your timing, and build a more comprehensive understanding of market dynamics.

16.3 ACCUMULATION/DISTRIBUTION LINE

The **Accumulation/Distribution Line (A/D Line)** is a volume-based indicator designed to measure the flow of money into and out of a security. Developed by Marc Chaikin, the A/D Line helps traders identify whether a security is being accumulated (bought) or distributed (sold) by comparing price movements to volume. By integrating this indicator into your analysis, you can gain valuable insights into the underlying strength of trends and potential reversals.

Understanding the Accumulation/Distribution Line

The A/D Line considers both price and volume to calculate a **Money Flow Multiplier (MFM)** for each period:

$$\text{Money Flow Multiplier (MFM)} = \frac{(\text{Close - Low}) - (\text{High - Close})}{\text{High - Low}}$$

The result is multiplied by the period's volume to derive the **Money Flow Volume (MFV)**:

$$\text{Money Flow Volume (MFV)} = \text{MFM} \times \text{Volume}$$

The A/D Line is a cumulative indicator that adds the current period's MFV to the previous period's A/D Line value. A rising A/D Line suggests accumulation (buying pressure), while a declining A/D Line indicates distribution (selling pressure).

How to Interpret the Accumulation/Distribution Line

1. Confirming Trends

The A/D Line can validate the strength of price trends:

- **Rising A/D Line:** Indicates sustained buying interest, confirming an uptrend.
- **Falling A/D Line:** Suggests sustained selling pressure, confirming a downtrend.

2. Spotting Divergences

Divergences between the A/D Line and price action often signal potential reversals:

- **Bullish Divergence:** Price forms lower lows while the A/D Line forms higher lows, suggesting accumulation and a possible upward reversal.

Chapter 16:
Volume-Based Indicators

- **Bearish Divergence:** Price forms higher highs while the A/D Line forms lower highs, indicating distribution and a potential downward reversal.

3. Identifying Breakouts and Breakdowns

The A/D Line can highlight potential breakouts or breakdowns by showing changes in buying or selling pressure ahead of price movements:

- A rising A/D Line during price consolidation suggests accumulation and a likely bullish breakout.
- A falling A/D Line during consolidation signals distribution and a likely bearish breakdown.

Using the A/D Line in Trading

1. Confirming Price Trends

The A/D Line serves as a tool to confirm the legitimacy of price trends:

- In an uptrend, a rising A/D Line confirms that the trend is supported by strong buying volume.
- In a downtrend, a falling A/D Line confirms that the trend is supported by strong selling volume.

Example:
A stock in an uptrend shows a rising A/D Line, confirming that institutional investors are accumulating shares. This reinforces confidence in the trend's strength.

2. Spotting Reversals with Divergences

Divergences between the A/D Line and price action can alert traders to potential trend changes:

- **Bullish Example:** A stock makes a new low, but the A/D Line forms a higher low, signaling that selling pressure is decreasing. The trader anticipates a reversal and enters a long position.
- **Bearish Example:** A stock makes a new high, but the A/D Line forms a lower high, indicating weakening buying interest. The trader prepares for a potential short opportunity.

3. Anticipating Breakouts or Breakdowns

Monitor the A/D Line during consolidation phases:

- If the A/D Line rises while the price remains flat, it suggests accumulation and a likely bullish breakout.
- If the A/D Line falls while the price consolidates, it signals distribution and a possible bearish breakdown.

Practical Example: Trading with the A/D Line

A stock is consolidating near $100, with its price trading in a tight range. During this phase, the A/D Line rises steadily, suggesting accumulation by institutional traders. The trader enters a long position at $101 as the price breaks above the consolidation range, setting a stop-loss at $98. The trade is exited at $110 when the price nears a major resistance level.

Combining the A/D Line with Other Tools

To maximize its effectiveness, use the A/D Line in conjunction with other indicators:

- **Volume Indicators:** Pair the A/D Line with On-Balance Volume (OBV) to validate volume trends.
- **Trend Indicators:** Combine with Moving Averages or MACD to confirm trend direction.
- **Support and Resistance Levels:** Align A/D Line movements with price levels to identify potential breakouts or reversals.

Example Strategy: A trader notices a bullish divergence between the A/D Line and price. The price is near a long-term support level, and the MACD shows a bullish crossover. The trader enters a long position, confident in the alignment of signals.

Tips for Effective Use of the A/D Line

- Use the A/D Line as a confirmation tool rather than a standalone signal generator.
- Pay attention to divergences for early warnings of potential reversals.
- Be cautious of false signals in low-volume markets, where the A/D Line may be less reliable.

The Accumulation/Distribution Line provides deep insights into the interplay between price and volume, helping traders identify accumulation, distribution, and potential trend shifts. By incorporating the A/D Line into your analysis, you can enhance your ability to anticipate market moves and make more informed trading decisions.

16.4 MONEY FLOW INDEX

The **Money Flow Index (MFI)** is a momentum indicator that incorporates both price and volume data to measure buying and selling pressure. Often referred to as the "volume-weighted RSI," the MFI operates on a scale of 0 to 100 and helps traders identify overbought and oversold conditions, spot divergences, and confirm trends. By combining price action with volume analysis, the MFI provides a comprehensive view of market dynamics.

Understanding the Money Flow Index

The MFI uses the **Typical Price** and volume to calculate **Money Flow**:

1. **Typical Price (TP):**

$$\text{Typical Price (TP):} \quad TP = \frac{\text{High} + \text{Low} + \text{Close}}{3}$$

Chapter 16:
Volume-Based Indicators

2. **Raw Money Flow (RMF):**

$$\text{Raw Money Flow (RMF):} \quad \text{RMF} = \text{TP} \times \text{Volume}$$

3. **Money Flow Ratio (MFR):**

$$\text{Money Flow Ratio (MFR):} \quad \text{MFR} = \frac{\text{Positive Money Flow (PMF)}}{\text{Negative Money Flow (NMF)}}$$

4. **Money Flow Index (MFI):**

$$\text{Money Flow Index (MFI):} \quad \text{MFI} = 100 - \left(\frac{100}{1 + \text{MFR}}\right)$$

Positive Money Flow occurs when the current Typical Price is greater than the previous Typical Price, while Negative Money Flow occurs when the current Typical Price is lower than the previous Typical Price.

How to Interpret the Money Flow Index

1. Overbought and Oversold Conditions

- **Above 80:** Indicates overbought conditions and potential reversal or consolidation.
- **Below 20:** Indicates oversold conditions and potential upward reversal.

2. Divergences

Divergences between the MFI and price can signal trend reversals:

- **Bullish Divergence:** Price makes lower lows, but the MFI forms higher lows, indicating weakening selling pressure.
- **Bearish Divergence:** Price makes higher highs, but the MFI forms lower highs, signaling weakening buying momentum.

3. Confirming Trends

The MFI can validate the strength of trends:

- In an uptrend, the MFI often stays above 50, with pullbacks finding support around this level.
- In a downtrend, the MFI typically remains below 50, with rallies encountering resistance near this level.

Using the Money Flow Index in Trading

1. Spotting Reversals

The MFI is particularly effective in identifying turning points in the market:

- Enter long positions when the MFI rises above 20 after a bullish divergence.
- Enter short positions when the MFI falls below 80 after a bearish divergence.

Example:

A stock with an MFI reading of 85 near a resistance level shows a bearish divergence as the MFI begins to decline. The trader enters a short position, anticipating a reversal.

2. Timing Entries and Exits

The MFI helps refine entry and exit points:

- Enter long positions when the MFI exits oversold territory.
- Exit long positions or enter short positions when the MFI exits overbought territory.

3. Confirming Breakouts

A rising MFI during a price breakout confirms strong buying momentum, increasing the likelihood of sustained movement. Conversely, a falling MFI during a breakdown signals strong selling pressure.

Practical Example: Trading with MFI

A stock consolidates near $100, with the MFI dipping below 20, signaling oversold conditions. As the price holds support and the MFI rises above 20, the trader enters a long position at $101.

- **Stop-Loss Placement:** Below the support level at $98.
- **Exit Strategy:** Exit at $110 when the MFI approaches 80, indicating overbought conditions.

Combining MFI with Other Indicators

The MFI is most effective when used alongside complementary tools:

- **Volume Indicators:** Pair MFI with On-Balance Volume (OBV) or Accumulation/Distribution Line for deeper volume insights.
- **Trend Indicators:** Use Moving Averages or MACD to align MFI signals with broader trend analysis.
- **Support and Resistance Levels:** Combine MFI with price levels to validate breakout or reversal signals.

Tips for Effective Use of the MFI

- Adjust the MFI's period setting to suit your trading style. Shorter periods (e.g., 10) provide quicker signals, while longer periods (e.g., 20) offer smoother readings.
- Use the MFI to confirm other indicators rather than relying on it in isolation.
- Be cautious in low-volume markets, as the MFI's reliability depends on accurate volume data.

The Money Flow Index provides a unique perspective by combining price and volume data to gauge market momentum and confirm trends. By incorporating MFI into your trading strategy, you can gain a deeper understanding of market dynamics and improve your ability to identify high-probability opportunities.

Chapter 16:
Volume-Based Indicators

PART 5:
Building Your Trading System

Chapter 17: Strategy Development

17.1 DEFINING YOUR TRADING STYLE

Building a successful trading system begins with understanding and defining your unique **trading style**. Your trading style reflects not only your goals and time availability but also your personality, risk tolerance, and decision-making approach. By clearly identifying your style, you can align your strategies, tools, and resources to create a system that complements your strengths and mitigates your weaknesses.

What Are Trading Styles?

There are several primary trading styles, each with distinct characteristics. Choosing the right one involves assessing how you interact with the market and what you aim to achieve:

1. **Scalping:**
    - **Characteristics:** Involves very short-term trades, often lasting seconds to minutes, to capture small price changes.
    - **Personality Fit:** Suitable for traders who thrive under pressure, make quick decisions, and can monitor the market constantly.
    - **Example:** A scalper might use 1-minute charts and execute multiple trades in a single session to capitalize on intraday volatility.

2. **Day Trading:**
    - **Characteristics:** Positions are opened and closed within the same trading day to avoid overnight risk.
    - **Personality Fit:** Best for those with time to actively monitor markets and a tolerance for fast-paced decision-making.
    - **Example:** A day trader may focus on breakout patterns during high-volume market hours, targeting predictable intraday trends.

3. **Swing Trading:**
    - **Characteristics:** Trades are held for several days to weeks, aiming to capture medium-term price swings.
    - **Personality Fit:** Ideal for traders who prefer a balance between active trading and less frequent decision-making.

- Example: A swing trader might use daily charts to identify bullish flag patterns, holding positions until the price nears resistance.

4. **Position Trading:**
   - **Characteristics:** Long-term trading style where positions are held for weeks to months, focusing on major trends.
   - **Personality Fit:** Suitable for patient individuals who prefer thorough analysis over frequent trading.
   - **Example:** A position trader could hold a long position in a stock after identifying a sustained uptrend on weekly charts.

5. **Algorithmic or Quantitative Trading:**
   - **Characteristics:** Involves using automated systems or algorithms to execute trades based on predefined criteria.
   - **Personality Fit:** Appeals to tech-savvy traders comfortable with programming or using software to manage strategies.
   - **Example:** A trader might deploy a bot that buys when the RSI crosses 30 and sells when it crosses 70.

Factors to Consider When Choosing Your Style

1. Time Commitment: Your availability to monitor the markets dictates your style. Scalping and day trading require constant attention, while swing and position trading are more flexible.

2. Risk Tolerance: Different styles come with varying levels of risk. Scalping involves frequent trades with smaller risks per trade, whereas position trading exposes you to broader market movements.

3. Financial Goals: Consider whether you seek consistent small gains (scalping, day trading) or larger, infrequent profits (swing and position trading).

4. Emotional Suitability: Your trading style should align with your emotional strengths. If fast decisions cause stress, avoid scalping. If patience is a challenge, shorter-term styles may be better suited.

How to Define Your Trading Style

1. **Self-Assessment:**
   - Reflect on your personality traits, risk tolerance, and available time.
   - Ask yourself: "Do I prefer rapid decisions, or do I thrive with methodical planning?"

2. **Experimentation:**
   - Test different styles using a demo account.
   - Evaluate which approach feels natural and delivers consistent results.

Chapter 17:
Strategy Development

3. **Documentation:**
   - Write down your preferred trading style in your system documentation.
   - Include details about the timeframes, risk parameters, and tools you'll use.
4. **Adjust as Needed:**
   - Your trading style may evolve as you gain experience. Stay flexible and willing to adapt to changing market conditions or personal circumstances.

Example: Aligning Style with Strategy

A trader who works a full-time job might choose swing trading, focusing on setups identified on daily charts. They analyze potential trades during the evening and set orders to execute during market hours. This style aligns with their time constraints and preference for thoughtful decision-making.

Conclusion

Defining your trading style is the foundation for building a system that works for you. By aligning your approach with your personal and financial goals, you can create a framework that enhances your strengths and minimizes stress. Remember, there is no single "best" trading style—only the one that fits you best. Take the time to explore, refine, and document your style to set yourself up for long-term success.

17.2 CREATING ENTRY RULES

Clear and well-defined **entry rules** are a cornerstone of any successful trading system. Your entry rules determine the conditions under which you open a trade, ensuring your decisions are systematic, repeatable, and grounded in market analysis rather than emotion. By establishing precise criteria, you can eliminate guesswork, increase consistency, and align your trades with your overall strategy.

The Importance of Entry Rules

Every entry decision should have a strong rationale, rooted in the interplay of price action, technical indicators, and market context. A trade entry without clear justification increases the likelihood of losses. Effective entry rules ensure that:

- **You trade only high-probability setups.**
- **Your actions align with your trading goals and style.**
- **You maintain discipline and avoid emotional decisions.**

Key Components of Entry Rules

1. Signal Confirmation

Your entry should be based on specific signals that align with your strategy. These signals could come from:

- **Technical Indicators:** Such as RSI, MACD, or Moving Averages.
- **Chart Patterns:** Like triangles, flags, or head-and-shoulders patterns.
- **Candlestick Patterns:** For example, bullish engulfing or hammer patterns.

2. Market Context

Evaluate the broader market conditions to ensure your entry aligns with the prevailing trend or market sentiment:

- **Trend Identification:** Use tools like Moving Averages or the ADX to confirm the trend.
- **Support and Resistance Levels:** Ensure the price is near a key level that supports your setup.

3. Entry Trigger

An entry trigger is the precise event that signals you to enter a trade. Triggers are often based on price action or indicator behavior, such as:

- A moving average crossover.
- A breakout above resistance or below support with high volume.
- An RSI reading exiting oversold territory.

Chapter 17:
Strategy Development

4. Timeframe Alignment

Ensure your entry signals are consistent across multiple timeframes:

- Use a higher timeframe to confirm the overall trend.
- Use a lower timeframe to refine the exact entry point.

Types of Entry Strategies

1. Breakout Entries

- Enter when the price breaks above resistance or below support, confirmed by increased volume.
- **Example:** A stock trading in a range between $100 and $110 breaks above $110 with a sharp rise in volume. This breakout signals a potential long entry.

2. Pullback Entries

- Wait for a retracement within a trend to enter at a better price.
- **Example:** In an uptrend, enter when the price pulls back to a rising moving average or a Fibonacci retracement level.

3. Reversal Entries

- Look for signs of exhaustion at the end of a trend, such as divergence, candlestick patterns, or climactic volume.
- **Example:** A bullish hammer forms at a strong support level, indicating a potential reversal and a long entry.

Establishing Entry Rules

To create effective entry rules, follow these steps:

1. Define Your Signal Criteria

Identify the specific conditions under which you will enter a trade. For example:

- "Enter a long position when the 20-day moving average crosses above the 50-day moving average and RSI rises above 50."

2. Incorporate Context

Ensure your entry rules account for the broader market context. For example:

- "Enter long only if the price is above the 200-day moving average and the trend is confirmed by the ADX."

3. Use a Checklist

Before entering a trade, review a checklist of your entry criteria. For example:

- Is the trend direction confirmed?
- Has the entry signal triggered?

- Is volume supporting the setup?

4. Test and Refine

Backtest your entry rules to evaluate their effectiveness. Adjust based on performance data while maintaining consistency.

Practical Example: A Defined Entry Rule

A swing trader focusing on breakout setups defines their entry rules as follows:

- "Enter a long position when the price closes above resistance with volume 50% higher than the 20-day average. The RSI must be above 60, and the ADX must indicate a trend strength above 25. Place a buy-stop order $0.50 above the breakout level to confirm momentum."

Common Mistakes to Avoid

- **Chasing Trades:** Entering late after the move has already started can reduce your risk-to-reward ratio.
- **Ignoring Market Context:** Focusing solely on signals without evaluating the broader trend can lead to false entries.
- **Overcomplicating Rules:** Too many conditions can result in missed opportunities.

Tips for Effective Entry Rules

- Use objective criteria to reduce emotional decision-making.
- Ensure your rules are consistent with your trading style and strategy.
- Backtest and forward-test your entry rules to build confidence and refine performance.

Effective entry rules are the foundation of a disciplined trading approach. By clearly defining your conditions, you can confidently enter trades that align with your strategy, increasing your chances of long-term success.

Chapter 17:
Strategy Development

17.3 ESTABLISHING EXIT CRITERIA

Defining **exit criteria** is just as critical as determining your entries. Knowing when and how to close a trade ensures you lock in profits, minimize losses, and maintain control over your trading strategy. Without clear exit rules, emotional decisions can lead to premature exits or holding losing trades too long, undermining your overall profitability.

Why Exit Criteria Matter

A well-structured exit strategy ensures that:

- **You secure gains before the market reverses.**
- **Losses are contained to manageable levels.**
- **Your trading decisions remain disciplined and consistent.**

Key Types of Exit Criteria

1. Profit Targets

Profit targets are predetermined levels where you close a trade to lock in gains. These targets are often based on:

- **Support and Resistance Levels:** Exit near a key resistance in an uptrend or a key support in a downtrend.
- **Risk-Reward Ratio:** Set a target that offers a favorable ratio, such as 3:1, relative to your stop-loss distance.
- **Technical Indicators:** Use tools like Fibonacci extensions, Bollinger Bands, or moving averages to determine price targets.

Example: A swing trader enters a long position at $50 with a stop-loss at $48. The trader sets a profit target at $56, achieving a 3:1 reward-to-risk ratio.

2. Stop-Loss Orders

Stop-loss orders protect against excessive losses by automatically closing a trade when the price moves against you. Types of stop-loss strategies include:

- **Fixed Stop-Loss:** A set price level below your entry point for long trades or above for short trades.
- **Trailing Stop-Loss:** Adjusts as the price moves in your favor, locking in profits while allowing for further gains.
- **Volatility-Based Stop-Loss:** Uses an indicator like Average True Range (ATR) to set stops based on the asset's typical price movement.

Example: A day trader uses a trailing stop set at 2% below the current price. As the price rises from $100 to $110, the stop-loss adjusts to $107, securing profits if the price reverses.

3. Time-Based Exits

Time-based exits close trades after a predetermined period, regardless of price action. This approach is often used in:

- **Day Trading:** Close all positions before the market closes to avoid overnight risk.
- **Swing Trading:** Exit trades if they fail to hit targets within a specified timeframe.

4. Technical Exit Signals

Exit signals can be based on specific technical conditions, such as:

- **Indicator Crossovers:** For example, exiting when the MACD line crosses below the signal line.
- **Candlestick Patterns:** Closing a trade when a bearish engulfing pattern forms near a resistance level.
- **Breakdowns of Support or Resistance:** Exiting a long position if the price falls below a key support level.

Balancing Risk and Reward

When establishing exit criteria, always consider the **risk-to-reward ratio**:

- **Reward-to-Risk Ratio:** Aim for trades that offer a ratio of at least 2:1 or higher. This ensures that your winning trades compensate for potential losses.
- **Position Sizing:** Use your exit criteria to determine the size of your position, ensuring that your risk per trade aligns with your overall risk management strategy.

Example: Combining Exit Strategies

A swing trader enters a long position at $100, with the following exit rules:

- **Profit Target:** Exit at $120, near a key resistance level.
- **Stop-Loss:** Set at $95, below the recent swing low, ensuring a 4:1 reward-to-risk ratio.
- **Trailing Stop-Loss:** Adjust to $5 below the current price if the price rises above $110.
- **Time Limit:** Exit after 10 trading days if neither the profit target nor stop-loss is triggered.

Avoiding Common Exit Mistakes

- **Exiting Too Early:** Fear can lead to closing trades prematurely before reaching the full profit potential.
- **Holding Too Long:** Hope can cause traders to hold onto trades past their profit targets, risking reversals.
- **Ignoring Market Context:** Exit decisions should consider market conditions, such as trends and volatility, to avoid unnecessary losses.

Tips for Effective Exit Rules

- Define exits before entering the trade to ensure discipline and consistency.

Chapter 17:
Strategy Development

- Use a combination of exit criteria (e.g., stop-loss and profit targets) to adapt to varying market conditions.

- Backtest your exit strategies to validate their effectiveness in historical scenarios.

- Keep your rules flexible enough to adjust to significant changes in market conditions.

Establishing clear and precise exit criteria allows you to protect your capital and maximize profits, ensuring long-term trading success. By balancing risk and reward and adhering to your rules, you can confidently navigate the markets and avoid emotional decision-making.

17.4 Position Sizing Methodology

Effective **position sizing** is a fundamental aspect of risk management that determines how much capital you allocate to each trade. By carefully calculating position size, you can manage your exposure to risk, protect your trading capital, and maintain consistent results over time. Position sizing ensures that no single trade can significantly harm your account, regardless of market conditions.

The Importance of Position Sizing

Position sizing is critical for achieving long-term success in trading. Without proper sizing:

- **Over-leveraged trades can wipe out your account in a single loss.**
- **Under-sized trades may lead to missed profit opportunities.**

A robust position sizing methodology helps:

- Limit your risk per trade.
- Maintain emotional discipline by reducing stress associated with losses.
- Achieve a balanced portfolio and consistent results.

Key Factors in Position Sizing

1. Account Size

Your total account balance serves as the foundation for determining the appropriate position size.

- Example: If your account size is $10,000 and you aim to risk 1% per trade, your maximum risk per trade would be $100.

2. Risk Per Trade

Define a fixed percentage of your account that you are willing to risk on any single trade. A common guideline is between **1% and 2%** of your total account balance.

- **Example:** With a $50,000 account and a 1% risk tolerance, the maximum loss you should accept per trade is $500.

3. Stop-Loss Distance

The distance between your entry price and stop-loss level, expressed in dollars or points, determines the size of your risk.

- **Example:** If your entry price is $100 and your stop-loss is set at $95, your stop-loss distance is $5 per share.

4. Trade Setup and Volatility

Consider the market conditions and volatility of the asset you're trading. Higher volatility assets may require smaller position sizes to account for larger price swings.

Chapter 17:
Strategy Development

How to Calculate Position Size

The formula for position size is straightforward:

$$\text{Position Size} = \frac{\text{Risk Per Trade}}{\text{Stop-Loss Distance}}$$

Example Calculation

- Account Size: $20,000
- Risk Per Trade: 1% ($200)
- Stop-Loss Distance: $2

$$\text{Position Size} = \frac{200}{2} = 100 \text{ shares}$$

You would trade 100 shares, risking $200 if the stop-loss is triggered.

Position Sizing Techniques

1. Fixed Dollar Risk

Allocate a fixed dollar amount to each trade based on your risk tolerance.

- **Example:** Always risk $200 per trade, regardless of the asset.

2. Fixed Percentage Risk

Risk a fixed percentage of your account balance on each trade, allowing your position size to scale with your account growth or drawdowns.

- **Example:** Risk 1% of your account per trade.

3. Volatility-Based Position Sizing

Adjust position size based on market volatility, using tools like the Average True Range (ATR) to set appropriate stop-loss levels.

- **Example:** If the ATR of a stock is $3, your stop-loss distance should accommodate this volatility, resulting in a smaller position size.

4. Kelly Criterion

A mathematical formula that calculates optimal position size based on win rate and reward-to-risk ratio.

- While effective, this method can result in aggressive sizing, so consider scaling it down for practical use.

Practical Example: Position Sizing in Action

A swing trader with a $50,000 account wants to risk 1.5% per trade:

- **Risk Per Trade:** 1.5% of $50,000 = $750.
- **Stop-Loss Distance:** $5.

- **Position Size:** Position Size $= \frac{750}{5} = 150$ shares

The trader buys 150 shares and sets a stop-loss to limit their risk to $750. If the trade moves in their favor, they can adjust the stop-loss to secure profits.

Common Position Sizing Mistakes

- **Ignoring Volatility:** Using the same position size across all trades without accounting for volatility can lead to excessive risk.

- **Over-Leveraging:** Allocating too much capital to a single trade can result in significant losses.

- **Underestimating Stop-Loss Distance:** Placing stops too close to the entry price can result in frequent, unnecessary losses.

Tips for Effective Position Sizing

- Stick to your risk tolerance. Even a well-planned trade can fail, so never risk more than you can afford to lose.

- Use smaller position sizes in highly volatile markets to protect against unpredictable swings.

- Review and adjust your position sizing methodology as your account grows or market conditions change.

Position sizing is the backbone of disciplined trading. By implementing a systematic approach, you can manage risk effectively, build confidence in your strategy, and achieve consistent results over the long term.

Chapter 18: Risk Management Framework

18.1 Risk per Trade Calculation

One of the foundational pillars of effective trading is managing your **risk per trade**. Calculating risk per trade ensures that no single position can significantly harm your account, allowing you to weather inevitable losses and sustain long-term success. By implementing this calculation, you create a structured framework that minimizes emotional decision-making and reinforces disciplined trading.

What Is Risk per Trade?

Risk per trade refers to the specific dollar amount or percentage of your total account equity that you are willing to lose on a single trade. This value is determined before entering the trade and serves as the basis for calculating your position size.

- **Fixed Dollar Risk:** A predetermined amount you are comfortable losing on each trade.
- **Percentage Risk:** A fixed percentage of your account equity, often ranging between **1% and 2%** for most traders.

Why Risk per Trade Matters

1. **Protects Capital:** Prevents overexposure to a single trade, reducing the risk of catastrophic losses.
2. **Encourages Consistency:** Enforces discipline by standardizing your approach to risk.
3. **Supports Emotional Stability:** Knowing your risk is controlled helps reduce stress and impulsive decisions during trading.
4. **Facilitates Scalability:** A consistent risk framework can be adjusted as your account grows or shrinks.

The Formula for Risk per Trade

The formula for calculating your position size based on risk per trade is:

$$\text{Position Size} = \frac{\text{Risk per Trade}}{\text{Stop-Loss Distance}}$$

Where:

- **Risk per Trade:** The dollar amount or percentage of account equity you are willing to lose.
- **Stop-Loss Distance:** The difference between the entry price and the stop-loss level.

Steps to Calculate Risk per Trade

1. Define Your Risk Tolerance

Determine the percentage of your account you are willing to risk on each trade. A common range is **1% to 2%** of your account equity.

- **Example:** For a $50,000 account, risking 1% means a maximum loss of $500 per trade.

2. Identify Stop-Loss Level

Set a stop-loss level based on technical analysis or volatility. The stop-loss distance is the difference between your entry price and stop-loss price.

- **Example:** If you plan to buy a stock at $100 and set a stop-loss at $95, your stop-loss distance is $5.

3. Calculate Position Size

Use the formula to determine how many shares or contracts to trade:

$$\text{Position Size} = \frac{500}{5} = 100 \text{ shares}$$

You would trade 100 shares, ensuring that a $5 move against your position results in a maximum loss of $500.

Examples of Risk per Trade in Action

Example 1: Day Trading Scenario

A day trader with a $10,000 account risks 1% per trade ($100). They identify a setup with a $2 stop-loss distance.

- **Position Size:** $\text{Position Size} = \frac{100}{2} = 50 \text{ shares}$

   This ensures the trader sticks to their risk tolerance even in a volatile intraday environment.

Example 2: Swing Trading Scenario

A swing trader with a $75,000 account risks 1.5% per trade ($1,125). They identify a bullish flag pattern and set a $3 stop-loss distance.

- **Position Size:**

$$\frac{1,125}{3} = 375 \text{ shares}$$

   This allows the trader to take a meaningful position while adhering to their risk management plan.

Adjusting Risk Based on Market Conditions

- **Volatile Markets:** Use smaller position sizes or wider stop-loss levels to account for larger price swings.

Chapter 18:
Risk Management Framework

- **Low-Volatility Markets:** Use tighter stop-loss levels and adjust position size accordingly.

Common Mistakes to Avoid

- **Over-Risking:** Risking more than your predefined amount can lead to significant drawdowns and emotional stress.

- **Underestimating Stop-Loss Distance:** Setting stops too close can result in premature exits from trades that would have been profitable.

- **Ignoring Account Changes:** Failing to adjust risk as your account grows or shrinks can disrupt your long-term strategy.

Tips for Effective Risk per Trade Management

- Start with conservative risk levels (e.g., 1%) and increase only after consistent performance.

- Backtest your risk strategy to ensure it aligns with your trading system.

- Reassess your risk tolerance periodically and adjust based on experience or changing market conditions.

Calculating risk per trade is a non-negotiable element of a disciplined trading approach. By understanding and applying this concept, you can protect your capital, build confidence in your strategy, and ensure steady progress toward your financial goals.

18.2 PORTFOLIO RISK MANAGEMENT

Portfolio risk management focuses on controlling your total exposure across all active trades to ensure the sustainability and growth of your trading capital. While managing individual trades is essential, overlooking the broader portfolio risk can lead to overexposure and significant drawdowns during volatile market conditions. A sound portfolio risk management strategy helps balance potential rewards against acceptable levels of risk, fostering long-term success.

The Importance of Portfolio Risk Management

1. **Preserves Capital:** By capping total portfolio risk, you protect against catastrophic losses during periods of unfavorable market conditions.

2. **Balances Diversification and Concentration:** Ensures you spread risk across multiple positions while avoiding over-diversification.

3. **Adapts to Market Volatility:** Maintains flexibility to adjust risk exposure as market conditions change.

Core Principles of Portfolio Risk Management

1. Total Risk Exposure Limit

Establish a maximum percentage of your total account equity to risk across all open trades. A common guideline is to limit total portfolio risk to **5%–10%** of your account balance.

- **Example:** With a $50,000 account, risking 2% per trade and capping total portfolio risk at 10%, you could safely manage up to five active trades simultaneously.

2. Diversification

Diversification reduces risk by spreading exposure across different assets, sectors, or markets. Avoid overloading your portfolio with positions that are highly correlated.

- **Good Diversification:** Trading a mix of equities, forex pairs, and commodities.
- **Poor Diversification:** Holding multiple positions in the same sector or currency pair.

3. Position Correlation

Assess the correlation between positions to ensure your portfolio isn't overly exposed to similar risks.

- **Example:** Avoid holding multiple long positions in tech stocks, as they are likely to react similarly to market events.

4. Dynamic Adjustment Based on Volatility

Allocate risk dynamically by reducing position sizes during high-volatility periods and increasing them in calmer markets.

- **Example:** In a volatile market, reduce individual position risk to 1% or lower, while in stable markets, increase to 2%.

How to Implement Portfolio Risk Management

Step 1: Define Your Total Risk Tolerance

Set a clear limit on how much of your account equity you're willing to risk across all trades. This should be a small, manageable percentage, typically between **5% and 10%**.

Step 2: Allocate Risk to Individual Positions

Divide your total portfolio risk across active trades, ensuring no single trade exceeds your predetermined risk per trade.

- **Example:** With a 10% portfolio risk cap and five trades, each trade would risk 2% of the account equity.

Step 3: Monitor Correlations

Use correlation analysis tools or manually assess the relationships between assets. Reduce exposure to highly correlated positions to avoid compounding risk.

Step 4: Adjust for Changing Market Conditions

Reevaluate portfolio risk based on market volatility, macroeconomic events, or shifts in your trading system.

Chapter 18:
Risk Management Framework

- **Example:** During earnings season, reduce position sizes in equities to account for increased volatility.

Step 5: Rebalance Regularly

Periodically review and rebalance your portfolio to ensure risk levels remain within acceptable limits. Exit underperforming trades and adjust positions to maintain alignment with your overall strategy.

Practical Examples of Portfolio Risk Management

Example 1: Diversified Portfolio

A trader with a $100,000 account risks 10% of the portfolio across five trades. Each trade is allocated 2%, and the positions include:

- A long position in tech stocks.
- A short position in an energy ETF.
- A forex pair (EUR/USD).
- A commodity (gold).
- An index fund (S&P 500).

This diversification reduces the risk of portfolio drawdown from sector-specific or market-specific events.

Example 2: High Correlation Adjustment

A trader holds three long positions in the tech sector during a volatile market. To reduce risk, they close one position and allocate the risk to a less correlated asset, such as a bond ETF or a defensive stock.

Common Mistakes to Avoid

- **Overexposure to One Asset:** Concentrating too much risk in a single position or sector.
- **Ignoring Correlations:** Holding multiple positions that are highly correlated, increasing portfolio vulnerability.
- **Exceeding Total Risk Limits:** Allowing portfolio risk to creep above predefined limits during periods of overconfidence.
- **Failing to Adapt to Market Conditions:** Sticking to static risk allocations without accounting for changing volatility.

Tips for Effective Portfolio Risk Management

- Limit total risk exposure to protect against unexpected market events.
- Regularly assess correlations between positions to maintain a balanced portfolio.
- Adjust risk dynamically to suit prevailing market conditions.

- Reevaluate and rebalance your portfolio periodically to ensure alignment with your strategy.

Portfolio risk management is about seeing the bigger picture. By setting clear limits and ensuring diversification, you can protect your trading account while maintaining opportunities for growth. A disciplined approach to portfolio risk management is essential for achieving long-term success in the markets.

18.3 DRAWDOWN MANAGEMENT

Drawdown management is the practice of controlling and recovering from losses during periods of unfavorable trading performance. A drawdown represents the decline from a portfolio's peak value to its lowest point and is an inevitable part of trading. Effective drawdown management ensures that you maintain emotional and financial stability, allowing you to recover and thrive in the long run.

Understanding Drawdowns

- **What Is a Drawdown?:** A drawdown is the percentage decrease in your trading account from its peak value due to a series of losses.

$$\text{Drawdown } (\%) = \frac{\text{Peak Value} - \text{Trough Value}}{\text{Peak Value}} \times 100$$

- **Example:**
  If your account grows to $100,000 but declines to $90,000 during a series of losing trades, your drawdown is:

$$\text{Drawdown} = \frac{100{,}000 - 90{,}000}{100{,}000} \times 100 = 10\%$$

- **Maximum Drawdown (MDD):** The largest drawdown recorded in a trading period, used to measure overall risk.

The Impact of Drawdowns

Drawdowns affect both your financial and emotional well-being.

- **Financial Impact:** Larger drawdowns require disproportionately higher returns to recover. For example:
  - A 10% drawdown requires an 11% return to recover.
  - A 50% drawdown requires a 100% return to recover.
- **Emotional Impact:** Significant drawdowns can lead to stress, fear, and impulsive decisions, often exacerbating losses.

Key Principles of Drawdown Management

Chapter 18:
Risk Management Framework

1. Set a Maximum Acceptable Drawdown

Define the maximum drawdown percentage you're willing to tolerate. A common threshold is **20%** or less for most traders.

2. Monitor Drawdowns Actively

Track your account equity regularly to identify drawdowns early. Use performance metrics or trading software to measure drawdown in real time.

3. Reduce Risk During Drawdowns

As your account experiences a drawdown, reduce your position sizes and risk per trade.

- **Example:** If you typically risk 2% per trade, lower it to 1% during a 10% drawdown.

4. Avoid Chasing Losses

Do not increase position sizes or take impulsive trades to recover losses quickly. Instead, focus on disciplined execution and stick to your strategy.

5. Implement a Stop-Loss on Drawdowns

Set a personal rule to pause trading if your account reaches a specific drawdown threshold, such as 15%. Use this time to evaluate and adjust your strategy.

Strategies for Managing and Recovering from Drawdowns

1. Conduct a Performance Review

Analyze your trading performance to identify the cause of the drawdown:

- Were trades entered according to your system?
- Were market conditions outside your strategy's scope?
- Did emotions influence your decisions?

2. Adjust Risk Parameters

Reduce risk per trade during drawdowns to protect capital. For example:

- If you're in a 10% drawdown, cut your risk from 2% to 1% or less.
- Consider trading smaller position sizes or focusing on high-probability setups only.

3. Refocus on High-Quality Trades

Avoid overtrading and concentrate on setups that strictly meet your criteria. Patience and discipline are key to recovering losses.

4. Diversify Your Trading Approach

If your drawdown is linked to a specific market or strategy, diversify by exploring uncorrelated markets or complementary strategies.

5. Take a Break

If emotions are affecting your decision-making, step away from the market. Use the time to reassess your goals and refine your system.

6. Backtest and Optimize Your Strategy

Backtest your trading system using historical data to identify potential weaknesses. Make refinements to improve performance without deviating from your core principles.

Practical Example: Managing a 15% Drawdown

A trader with a $50,000 account experiences a 15% drawdown, reducing their account to $42,500. To manage and recover:

- **Step 1:** Pause trading and review recent performance to identify mistakes or strategy flaws.
- **Step 2:** Lower risk per trade from 2% ($1,000) to 1% ($425) until the account recovers to $47,500.
- **Step 3:** Focus exclusively on trades with a 3:1 risk-to-reward ratio to rebuild the account efficiently.

Common Mistakes in Drawdown Management

- **Overtrading During Drawdowns:** Attempting to recover losses quickly often leads to deeper drawdowns.
- **Ignoring Risk Adjustments:** Maintaining the same risk per trade despite a reduced account balance increases the likelihood of further losses.
- **Abandoning the Trading Plan:** Deviating from your strategy in an attempt to "win back" losses leads to inconsistent results.

Tips for Effective Drawdown Management

- Establish a clear maximum drawdown threshold and stick to it.
- Lower position sizes and risk per trade during drawdowns to protect your capital.
- Take regular breaks to avoid emotional decision-making when performance declines.
- Use drawdowns as an opportunity to evaluate and improve your trading system.

Drawdowns are an unavoidable part of trading, but with a solid management plan, they become a temporary setback rather than a permanent obstacle. By implementing disciplined practices and focusing on long-term growth, you can navigate drawdowns effectively and emerge as a stronger, more resilient trader.

18.4 RISK ADJUSTMENT IN VOLATILE MARKETS

Chapter 18:
Risk Management Framework

Volatile markets present both opportunities and challenges for traders. Rapid price fluctuations can lead to increased profit potential, but they also heighten risk. **Adjusting your risk management strategies during volatile periods** is essential to safeguard your trading capital while capitalizing on favorable setups. By proactively adapting your approach, you can navigate market turbulence with confidence and discipline.

Understanding Volatile Markets

Volatility refers to the degree of price variation over a given period. It often arises from major news events, economic data releases, geopolitical tensions, or sudden shifts in market sentiment. While heightened volatility can create large trading opportunities, it can also amplify losses if not managed correctly.

- **Example of Volatile Markets:** Sudden price swings in forex pairs after central bank announcements or stock market fluctuations during earnings season.

Why Adjust Risk in Volatile Markets?

1. **Increased Stop-Loss Distance:** Wider price swings require larger stop-loss levels to avoid premature exits. This increases your risk per trade if position sizes remain unchanged.

2. **Rapid Position Reversals:** High volatility can lead to unexpected reversals, making it crucial to reduce exposure.

3. **Emotional Impact:** Volatile markets often trigger emotional decision-making, amplifying the need for controlled risk.

Key Strategies for Risk Adjustment

1. Reduce Position Sizes

In volatile markets, smaller position sizes help mitigate risk when price swings are larger.

- **Example:** If you usually risk 2% of your account on each trade, reduce it to 1% or lower during periods of high volatility.

- **Why It Works:** Smaller positions allow for wider stop-loss levels without exceeding your risk tolerance.

2. Use Volatility Indicators

Incorporate tools like the **Average True Range (ATR)** or **Bollinger Bands** to gauge market volatility and adjust your strategy accordingly.

- **Example:** If the ATR value increases, indicating higher volatility, adjust your stop-loss distance and position size based on the new conditions.

3. Tighten Entry and Exit Criteria

Demand higher-quality setups to reduce the likelihood of being caught in erratic price movements.

- Focus on trades with strong confluence of signals, such as support/resistance levels aligning with candlestick patterns and technical indicators.

4. Implement Trailing Stops

Use trailing stop-loss orders to lock in profits while allowing trades to benefit from extended moves.

- **Example:** Set a trailing stop 1.5 times the ATR value to dynamically adjust to market fluctuations.

5. Avoid Overexposure

Increased volatility often leads to correlated movements across assets. Limit the number of open positions to avoid overexposure.

- **Example:** If forex volatility spikes, hold no more than two active trades in related currency pairs, such as EUR/USD and GBP/USD.

Adapting Your Trading Plan

During volatile periods, update your trading plan to reflect the following adjustments:

1. **Risk Per Trade:** Lower your risk allocation per trade to accommodate wider stop-loss levels.
2. **Stop-Loss Placement:** Place stops beyond significant support/resistance levels to reduce the likelihood of being stopped out prematurely.
3. **Timeframe Adjustments:** Use higher timeframes to filter out noise and focus on broader trends.
4. **Position Scaling:** Enter trades incrementally rather than committing full positions at once, allowing for more flexibility as the market evolves.

Practical Example: Risk Adjustment in Action

A trader with a $50,000 account typically risks 2% ($1,000) per trade. During a period of high volatility, they observe the following:

- The ATR of their chosen stock doubles from $2 to $4, indicating wider price swings.
- To maintain their 2% risk limit, the trader adjusts their position size:

$$\text{New Position Size} = \frac{\text{Risk Per Trade}}{\text{Stop-Loss Distance}} = \frac{1{,}000}{4} = 250 \text{ shares}$$

- They reduce their position size from 500 shares (at $2 stop-loss) to 250 shares, accommodating the increased volatility while keeping their risk controlled.

Common Mistakes to Avoid

- **Ignoring Volatility Changes:** Trading with standard position sizes and stop-loss distances during high volatility increases risk.
- **Overtrading:** Attempting to capitalize on every price swing often leads to poor decision-making and excessive losses.

- **Neglecting Correlations:** Failing to account for correlated assets can result in compounded losses.

Tips for Effective Risk Adjustment in Volatile Markets

- Monitor volatility indicators like ATR or implied volatility metrics for consistent insights.
- Lower position sizes and set wider stop-loss levels to account for increased price swings.
- Focus on high-probability setups with strong confluence of signals.
- Maintain emotional discipline by sticking to your predefined risk management rules.

Volatile markets require flexibility and heightened discipline. By adapting your risk management approach to account for larger price movements, you can protect your capital while taking advantage of the opportunities that volatility offers.

18.5 POSITION SCALING TECHNIQUES

Position scaling involves adjusting your trade size incrementally, either by adding to or reducing your position based on market conditions. This technique allows you to maximize gains in favorable scenarios while limiting losses or exposure during periods of uncertainty. Effective position scaling requires careful planning and discipline, ensuring your adjustments align with your risk management framework.

Why Use Position Scaling?

1. **Maximizing Profits:** Adding to winning trades capitalizes on strong trends.
2. **Reducing Risk:** Scaling out of positions locks in profits or minimizes exposure in uncertain markets.
3. **Flexibility:** Enables traders to adapt to changing market conditions without overcommitting capital upfront.
4. **Improved Risk Control:** Ensures that your position size is appropriate at every stage of the trade.

Types of Position Scaling

1. Scaling In

Scaling into a position involves entering a trade incrementally rather than committing the full position size at once.

- **Advantages:** Reduces risk by allowing confirmation of the trade's direction before fully committing capital.
- **Methods:**
    - Entering partial positions at key levels (e.g., breakout, pullback).
    - Using dollar-cost averaging during accumulation phases.

Example of Scaling In: A trader plans to buy 1,000 shares of a stock. Instead of purchasing all at $100, they enter 500 shares at $100 and add another 500 at $102, once the breakout is confirmed.

2. Scaling Out

Scaling out involves reducing your position size as the trade progresses, locking in profits or minimizing exposure.

- **Advantages:** Secures gains while leaving part of the position open for further upside.
- **Methods:**
    - Selling portions of the position at predetermined price levels (e.g., partial profit targets).
    - Exiting incrementally as the trend weakens or volatility increases.

Chapter 18:
Risk Management Framework

Example of Scaling Out: A trader holds 1,000 shares and sets profit targets at $110 and $115. They sell 500 shares at $110 to lock in some gains and let the remaining shares run to $115.

Implementing Position Scaling Techniques

Step 1: Define Your Entry Plan

For scaling in, identify key levels where you'll add to your position. These levels should align with support/resistance zones, trendlines, or breakout points.

- **Example:** Add 50% of your position at a breakout and the remaining 50% on a retest of the breakout level.

Step 2: Establish Profit Targets and Exit Criteria

For scaling out, determine profit targets based on technical analysis or predefined risk-reward ratios.

- **Example:** Sell one-third of the position when the trade reaches 2:1 reward-to-risk, another third at 3:1, and hold the final third as a runner with a trailing stop.

Step 3: Adjust Stop-Loss Levels

As you scale in or out, adjust your stop-loss levels to manage risk effectively:

- **Scaling In:** Tighten stops on initial entries as new positions are added to protect against increased exposure.
- **Scaling Out:** Use trailing stops to protect profits on the remaining position.

Step 4: Use Risk-Based Position Sizing

Ensure that your scaling plan adheres to your overall risk tolerance. Avoid overexposing your portfolio by capping the total position size relative to your account balance.

- **Example:** Limit the total risk per trade to 2% of your account, regardless of scaling.

Practical Examples of Position Scaling

Example 1: Swing Trading with Scaling In

A trader identifies a bullish flag pattern with an entry point at $50 and a stop-loss at $47. They plan to buy 300 shares but enter as follows:

- 150 shares at $50 when the price breaks above the flag.
- 150 shares at $51 when the breakout is confirmed by increased volume.

By scaling in, the trader minimizes initial risk while building a full position once the setup proves reliable.

Example 2: Day Trading with Scaling Out

A day trader enters 1,000 shares of a stock at $100 with a profit target of $110 and a stop-loss at $95. They scale out as follows:

- Sell 500 shares at $105 to lock in partial profits.

- Sell another 300 shares at $108 as momentum slows.
- Exit the remaining 200 shares at $110 or when the trailing stop is hit.

Common Mistakes to Avoid

- **Over-Scaling:** Adding too aggressively to a position can exceed your risk tolerance, exposing your account to large losses.
- **Scaling Without Confirmation:** Adding to losing trades ("averaging down") without clear technical justification often leads to amplified losses.
- **Neglecting Exit Plans:** Failing to define scaling-out criteria may result in missed opportunities to lock in profits.

Tips for Effective Position Scaling

- Align scaling strategies with your trading style and system.
- Use technical confirmation before scaling in to avoid overexposure.
- Set realistic profit targets and stick to your scaling-out plan.
- Review your scaling approach periodically to ensure it complements your overall strategy.

Position scaling is a powerful tool for managing risk and maximizing returns. By adding to winners and strategically reducing exposure, you can navigate the markets with greater confidence and precision, ensuring your trades align with your financial goals and risk tolerance.

Chapter 19:
Trade Execution

19.1 Entry Techniques

Executing a trade effectively begins with mastering **entry techniques**. An entry is more than just opening a position; it's the culmination of your analysis, strategy, and preparation. A well-timed entry can significantly improve your risk-to-reward ratio and set the stage for a successful trade. However, entering the market without a clear plan can lead to costly mistakes and missed opportunities.

The Importance of Precise Entries

A precise entry ensures you:

- Capitalize on high-probability setups.
- Minimize the risk of adverse price movements immediately after entering the trade.
- Create a structured foundation for managing the position as it evolves.

Effective entry techniques blend technical signals, market context, and execution strategy, offering a balanced approach to initiating trades.

Timing Your Entry

Timing is critical in trading. Entering too early exposes you to unnecessary risk, while entering too late can diminish profit potential. The key is to align your entry with a confluence of signals, increasing the probability of success.

For example, if you are trading a bullish breakout, wait for confirmation, such as a close above resistance accompanied by increased volume. This reduces the likelihood of a false breakout and provides a stronger basis for your entry.

Types of Entry Techniques

1. Breakout Entries

Breakout entries involve entering a position when the price moves decisively beyond a key level, such as support, resistance, or a consolidation pattern.

- **Example:** If a stock breaks above a resistance level at $50 with a surge in volume, this indicates bullish momentum, making it an ideal point to enter a long position.

2. Pullback Entries

Pullback entries allow you to join a trend at a more favorable price after a brief retracement. This approach ensures you don't chase the market while also confirming the trend's strength.

- **Example:** In an uptrend, wait for the price to retrace to a rising moving average or a Fibonacci level before entering.

3. Reversal Entries

Reversal entries capitalize on price turning points, such as trend changes or exhaustion. This technique requires strong confirmation to avoid entering against the prevailing trend prematurely.

- **Example:** A bullish hammer candlestick forming at a key support level indicates potential reversal, signaling a long entry.

Tools to Refine Your Entries

Several tools can help refine your entry points, ensuring higher precision:

- **Technical Indicators:** Moving averages, RSI, and Bollinger Bands can provide confirmation for entries aligned with your strategy.
- **Candlestick Patterns:** Patterns like engulfing candles or morning stars add confidence to your entry decision.
- **Volume Analysis:** Increased volume during a breakout or reversal adds credibility to the move, signaling a stronger entry.

Aligning Entry with Market Context

Always evaluate the broader market context before entering a trade. This involves analyzing:

- **Trend Direction:** Ensure your entry aligns with the prevailing trend to increase the likelihood of success.
- **Key Levels:** Confirm that the entry is near significant support or resistance to improve the risk-to-reward ratio.
- **Timeframes:** Use multiple timeframes to validate your entry signal. For instance, a bullish setup on a lower timeframe is more reliable if it aligns with a broader uptrend on a higher timeframe.

Example of a Well-Planned Entry

Suppose you're analyzing a stock trading in a consolidation range between $100 and $110. After weeks of oscillating within this range, the price breaks above $110 with a long bullish candle and a volume spike. This breakout confirms buyer strength, providing a clear signal for a long entry. To refine the entry further, you place a buy-stop order slightly above $110.50 to confirm momentum continuation.

Chapter 19:
Trade Execution

Avoiding Common Entry Mistakes

One of the most frequent errors traders make is entering trades impulsively, driven by fear of missing out (FOMO). Another mistake is relying on a single indicator or signal without considering the broader context. For example, entering based solely on an RSI reading without analyzing trend direction or support levels can lead to premature or poorly timed trades.

Tips for Effective Entries

- Always wait for confirmation of your signal before entering a trade.
- Use pending orders like buy-stop or sell-stop to avoid emotional execution errors.
- Start with partial positions when uncertain, adding more as the trade confirms your analysis.

Final Thought

A strong entry is the first step toward a successful trade. By combining technical signals, market context, and disciplined execution, you can improve the quality of your trades and enhance your overall performance. Mastering entry techniques requires practice, but the effort pays off in the form of more consistent and profitable outcomes.

19.2 Exit Management

Effective **exit management** is a cornerstone of successful trading. While entering a trade requires precise timing and analysis, the ability to manage exits strategically determines your overall profitability. Exiting a trade is not just about taking profits—it's also about minimizing losses, adapting to market conditions, and ensuring discipline.

The Importance of Exit Management

Exits can make or break your trade. A poorly managed exit might result in leaving money on the table or incurring unnecessary losses. Proper exit strategies help you:

- Lock in profits at optimal levels.
- Avoid emotional decisions that undermine your trading plan.
- Protect your capital during adverse market moves.

Types of Exit Strategies

1. Profit-Target Exits

Profit-target exits involve closing a trade when the price reaches a predefined level, ensuring you capture gains while avoiding the risk of reversal.

- **Example:** Set a profit target at a resistance level or based on a specific risk-to-reward ratio, such as 3:1.

- **When to Use:** In trending markets or with trades based on technical patterns, such as breakouts or continuation patterns.

2. Stop-Loss Exits

Stop-loss exits are predefined levels at which you close a trade to limit losses. A stop-loss ensures you don't hold onto losing positions beyond your risk tolerance.

- **Example:** Place a stop-loss just below a support level in a long trade.
- **When to Use:** On every trade—stop-loss orders are a non-negotiable part of disciplined trading.

3. Trailing Stop Exits

Trailing stops adjust dynamically as the price moves in your favor, locking in profits while allowing for further upside.

- **Example:** If the price rises by $5, the trailing stop moves up by $5, staying a fixed distance from the current price.
- **When to Use:** In trending markets where the price is likely to continue moving in your favor.

4. Time-Based Exits

Time-based exits involve closing a trade after a predetermined period, regardless of price action.

- **Example:** Exit a day trade before the market closes to avoid overnight risk.
- **When to Use:** In day trading or when holding positions for extended periods carries significant risks.

Combining Exit Strategies

Many traders use a combination of exit strategies to balance risk and reward. For instance:

- Use a **profit target** to close part of the position at a 3:1 reward-to-risk ratio.
- Apply a **trailing stop** to the remaining position to capture additional gains.
- Set a **time-based exit** to close any remaining position by the end of the trading day.

This multi-pronged approach ensures you maximize profits while maintaining control over risk.

Adapting Exits to Market Conditions

Exits should be flexible to adapt to varying market conditions:

- In **volatile markets**, use wider stops and trailing stops to accommodate larger price swings.
- In **sideways markets**, focus on tighter stops and shorter time frames to avoid prolonged stagnation.

Chapter 19:
Trade Execution

Example of Exit Management in Action

Suppose you enter a long trade at $50 with the following exit plan:

- Profit target: $60, based on resistance at a prior high.
- Stop-loss: $47, below a key support level.
- Trailing stop: Moves up $1 for every $2 the price rises, locking in gains as the trade progresses.

As the price moves to $55, your trailing stop adjusts to $53, securing profits even if the price reverses. If the price reaches $60, you close part of the position at the profit target and let the rest run with the trailing stop.

Common Exit Management Mistakes

1. **Premature Exits:** Exiting trades too early due to fear or impatience, often before the trade reaches its potential.
2. **Holding Too Long:** Staying in a trade past logical exit points due to greed or hope, risking reversal and loss of profits.
3. **Ignoring Market Signals:** Failing to adjust exits based on changing market conditions, such as increased volatility or trend reversals.

Best Practices for Exit Management

- **Define Exits Before Entry:** Plan your profit targets and stop-loss levels before opening a trade to avoid emotional decision-making.
- **Use Technical Analysis:** Base your exits on key levels, such as support/resistance, Fibonacci extensions, or moving averages.
- **Stick to Your Plan:** Avoid the temptation to adjust your exit rules mid-trade unless market conditions change significantly.
- **Log and Review Exits:** Maintain a trading journal to analyze your exit strategies and refine them over time.

Final Thought

Exit management is where profits are realized, and losses are controlled. By planning your exits with the same precision as your entries, you can ensure disciplined, consistent trading that aligns with your financial goals. Remember, mastering exits is not just about timing the market perfectly—it's about managing risk and securing rewards efficiently and effectively.

19.3 PARTIAL PROFIT TAKING

Partial profit taking is a trading technique that involves closing a portion of your position to secure gains while allowing the remainder to benefit from potential further price movement. This strategy strikes a balance between locking in profits and maintaining exposure to favorable trends. By systematically scaling out of positions, traders can reduce risk and optimize returns, especially in volatile markets.

The Purpose of Partial Profit Taking

Securing partial profits provides multiple advantages:

- **Reduces Emotional Stress:** Locking in gains early alleviates the pressure of deciding when to exit entirely.

- **Improves Risk Management:** Lowering your position size decreases overall exposure, making it easier to tolerate volatility.

- **Maximizes Profit Potential:** Retaining a portion of the position allows you to capture additional gains if the trend continues.

For example, imagine you enter a long trade on a stock at $50, targeting $60 with a stop-loss at $45. When the price reaches $55, you sell half your position to lock in profits, adjust your stop-loss on the remaining shares to $52, and let the rest run toward your target. This approach ensures you benefit from the trade regardless of whether the trend continues or reverses.

How to Implement Partial Profit Taking

1. **Set Multiple Profit Targets:** Define incremental levels where you'll take partial profits, such as at key support/resistance levels or Fibonacci extensions. For instance:
   - Close 50% of your position at a 2:1 reward-to-risk ratio.
   - Close another 25% at a higher resistance level.
   - Hold the remaining 25% to capture extended moves.

2. **Adjust Stop-Loss Levels:** As you take partial profits, tighten your stop-loss on the remaining position to protect gains. Trailing stops are especially effective in managing residual exposure while allowing the trade to continue.

3. **Base Decisions on Market Context:** Use technical analysis to identify optimal levels for partial exits. For example, if a stock is approaching a major resistance level, consider taking partial profits to hedge against a potential reversal.

Examples of Partial Profit Taking

Scenario 1: Swing Trading

A swing trader enters a trade on a stock at $100, targeting $120. They sell:

- 50% of their position at $110 to secure initial profits.
- 25% at $115 to capitalize on continued momentum.
- The remaining 25% is closed at $118 after the price reverses slightly, just shy of the $120 target.

Chapter 19:
Trade Execution

By scaling out incrementally, the trader locks in consistent gains while still benefiting from the majority of the price movement.

Scenario 2: Day Trading

A day trader buys a forex pair at 1.2000, targeting 1.2100. As the price approaches 1.2050, they sell half the position to secure profits and move the stop-loss to breakeven on the remaining half. If the price reverses, the trade ends with minimal risk and partial profits secured. If the trend continues, the remaining position generates additional gains.

Adapting to Market Conditions

The effectiveness of partial profit taking depends on market conditions:

- **In Trending Markets:** Take smaller partial profits and let the majority of your position ride the trend.
- **In Range-Bound Markets:** Take larger partial profits near the top of the range, as the probability of reversal increases.

Common Mistakes to Avoid

- **Taking Profits Too Early:** Selling too much of the position too quickly can limit overall returns, especially in trending markets.
- **Holding Without a Plan:** Failing to define clear exit criteria for the remaining position can lead to emotional decision-making.
- **Ignoring Volatility:** In volatile markets, adjusting profit targets and stop-loss levels dynamically is crucial to account for sudden price swings.

Tips for Successful Partial Profit Taking

- Set clear profit targets aligned with technical levels to avoid impulsive decisions.
- Adjust stop-loss levels incrementally to protect gains while allowing for further upside.
- Combine partial exits with trailing stops for a balanced approach to locking in profits and managing risk.
- Review your profit-taking strategy regularly to ensure it complements your overall trading plan.

Conclusion

Partial profit taking is a versatile tool that allows you to manage risk effectively while maximizing profit potential. By scaling out of positions strategically, you create a structured approach to exits that reduces emotional pressure and ensures disciplined execution. Incorporate this technique into your trading plan, and you'll be better equipped to navigate the complexities of dynamic market conditions.

19.4 STOP LOSS PLACEMENT

Stop-loss placement is a critical component of risk management that protects your capital from excessive losses. By predefining the maximum amount you are willing to lose on a trade, you can trade with greater confidence and discipline. Proper stop-loss placement not only safeguards your account but also ensures that your trading decisions are based on logic and strategy rather than emotion.

Why Stop Losses Are Essential

A stop-loss order automatically closes a position when the price reaches a predetermined level. This serves several purposes:

- **Limits Losses:** Protects your account from catastrophic drawdowns.
- **Promotes Discipline:** Prevents emotional decision-making during volatile market moves.
- **Supports Consistent Trading:** Aligns your risk per trade with your overall trading strategy.

Without a stop-loss, even a single trade can lead to significant losses, undermining your long-term profitability.

Types of Stop Losses

1. Fixed Stop Loss

A fixed stop-loss is set at a specific price level based on a predetermined dollar amount or percentage.

- **Example:** Risking 2% of a $50,000 account on a trade means a maximum loss of $1,000. If you buy a stock at $100 with a stop-loss at $95, your position size is calculated to ensure the loss does not exceed $1,000.

2. Technical Stop Loss

A technical stop-loss is based on chart patterns, support/resistance levels, or other technical indicators.

- **Example:** Place a stop-loss below a key support level or just beyond the low of a bullish candlestick pattern.

3. Volatility-Based Stop Loss

This stop-loss adapts to market volatility, often using indicators like the Average True Range (ATR) to determine an appropriate buffer.

- **Example:** If the ATR of a stock is $2, set your stop-loss $2 below your entry price for a long position.

Chapter 19:
Trade Execution

4. Trailing Stop Loss

A trailing stop-loss moves with the market price, locking in profits as the trade moves in your favor.

- **Example:** For every $1 the stock price rises, the trailing stop adjusts upward by $1, maintaining a fixed distance.

Factors to Consider When Placing Stop Losses

1. Market Structure

Evaluate key support and resistance levels, trendlines, or Fibonacci retracement levels to determine logical stop-loss placement. Placing stops too close to these levels increases the risk of being stopped out prematurely.

2. Time Frame

The time frame of your trade influences stop-loss placement. Intraday trades often require tighter stops, while swing or position trades demand wider stops to accommodate larger price movements.

3. Trade Setup and Strategy

Align your stop-loss with the specific trade setup. For example:

- In a breakout trade, place the stop-loss below the breakout level.
- In a pullback trade, place the stop-loss below the retracement low.

4. Risk-to-Reward Ratio

Ensure your stop-loss placement supports a favorable risk-to-reward ratio. A minimum ratio of **1:2** (risking $1 to gain $2) is recommended.

Examples of Stop-Loss Placement

Example 1: Support and Resistance-Based Stop

You buy a stock at $100 after it bounces off a support level at $95. To protect your trade, place the stop-loss slightly below the support level, such as at $94, to allow for minor price fluctuations.

Example 2: ATR-Based Stop

You enter a forex trade at 1.2000, and the ATR is 0.0050. Set your stop-loss 1.5 times the ATR below the entry price:

$1.2000 - (0.0050 \times 1.5) = 1.1925$

Example 3: Chart Pattern-Based Stop

In a bullish flag pattern, place the stop-loss below the flag's low to protect against a breakdown. If the flag's low is $50, set your stop at $49.50.

Common Mistakes to Avoid

- **Placing Stops Too Close:** Tight stops often lead to premature exits due to normal market fluctuations.
- **Ignoring Volatility:** Failing to account for market volatility can result in poorly placed stops.
- **Over-Widening Stops:** Stops placed too far away can lead to significant losses if the trade goes against you.
- **Not Using Stops:** Trading without a stop-loss exposes your account to unlimited risk.

Adjusting Stop Losses

Stop-loss levels can be adjusted as the trade progresses, but only under specific conditions:

- **Trailing Stops:** Use trailing stops to secure profits as the trade moves in your favor.
- **Break-Even Stops:** Move the stop-loss to your entry price once the trade has gained sufficient ground to eliminate risk.

Practical Tips for Effective Stop Losses

- Align your stop-loss with market context, avoiding arbitrary levels.
- Backtest your stop-loss strategy to ensure it complements your overall trading system.
- Use pending orders to set stop-losses automatically, reducing the likelihood of errors during execution.
- Combine stop-loss placement with position sizing to ensure you adhere to your risk management plan.

Conclusion

Stop-loss placement is not about avoiding losses entirely—it's about managing them effectively to protect your capital and keep you in the game. By combining technical analysis, risk management principles, and market context, you can place stop-losses that align with your strategy and trading objectives. Mastering this skill is essential for building a sustainable and disciplined approach to trading.

19.5 ORDER TYPES AND USAGE

Understanding and effectively using **order types** is fundamental to executing trades efficiently and managing risk in real-time. The right order type allows you to control entry, exit, and risk parameters, ensuring that your trading strategy aligns with market dynamics. Each order type serves a specific purpose, and knowing when and how to use them can significantly enhance your trading performance.

Chapter 19:
Trade Execution

Types of Orders and Their Applications

1. Market Orders

A market order executes your trade immediately at the best available price.

- **Advantages:** Guarantees execution, ideal for fast-moving markets.
- **Disadvantages:** May result in slippage during volatile conditions, leading to less favorable prices.
- **When to Use:** Entering or exiting positions where immediate execution is critical, such as during a breakout.

Example: A trader identifies a breakout above $50 and uses a market order to enter the trade instantly, ensuring participation in the move.

2. Limit Orders

A limit order executes a trade only at a specified price or better.

- **Advantages:** Offers price control, avoids unfavorable execution.
- **Disadvantages:** May not execute if the price doesn't reach the limit level.
- **When to Use:** Placing entries at support/resistance levels or setting profit targets.

Example: You set a limit order to buy at $48, anticipating a pullback to a support level, or sell at $55 as a profit target.

3. Stop Orders

A stop order becomes a market order when the price reaches the stop level.

- **Advantages:** Automates entries and exits based on predefined levels.
- **Disadvantages:** May experience slippage when triggered.
- **When to Use:** Protecting against losses with stop-loss orders or entering trades during breakouts.

Example: Place a stop-loss at $95 for a long position entered at $100 to cap potential losses.

4. Stop-Limit Orders

A stop-limit order combines the features of a stop order and a limit order. Once the stop price is reached, the order becomes a limit order rather than a market order.

- **Advantages:** Controls execution price while automating trade management.
- **Disadvantages:** May not execute in fast-moving markets if the limit price is skipped.
- **When to Use:** For traders requiring precise control over execution price during volatile conditions.

Example: Set a stop-limit order with a stop price at $100 and a limit price at $99. This ensures execution only if the price stays above $99 after reaching $100.

5. Trailing Stop Orders

A trailing stop dynamically adjusts as the price moves in your favor, maintaining a fixed percentage or dollar distance from the current price.

- **Advantages:** Locks in profits while allowing for continued upside.
- **Disadvantages:** May trigger prematurely in choppy markets.
- **When to Use:** Managing exits for trending trades without constant monitoring.

Example: A trailing stop set at $2 below the market price adjusts upward as the price rises, protecting gains while staying in the trade.

Integrating Order Types into Your Strategy

To maximize the effectiveness of your trading system, combine different order types based on your strategy's objectives:

- **Breakout Traders:** Use stop orders for entries and trailing stops for exits to ride momentum.
- **Range Traders:** Use limit orders to enter near support/resistance and stop-loss orders to protect against breakouts.
- **Trend Followers:** Combine trailing stops with stop-limit orders to secure profits while allowing the trend to continue.

Order Management Best Practices

1. **Plan Ahead:** Define your entry, exit, and stop-loss levels before placing any orders to avoid emotional decisions.
2. **Test in Simulations:** Practice using different order types in demo accounts to understand their behavior in real-time conditions.
3. **Monitor Execution:** Even with automated orders, regularly review your trades to ensure proper execution and refine your approach.

Common Mistakes to Avoid

- **Using Market Orders Without Context:** Avoid market orders in illiquid or volatile markets where slippage can be significant.
- **Neglecting Stop-Loss Orders:** Trading without stop-losses exposes you to unlimited risk.
- **Overcomplicating Orders:** Using overly complex order setups without understanding them can lead to execution errors.

Practical Example of Combining Order Types

Suppose you're trading a stock currently priced at $100, targeting $120 with a stop-loss at $95:

- Use a **limit order** to enter at $100.

Chapter 19:
Trade Execution

- Set a **stop-loss order** at $95 to cap losses.
- Place a **profit-taking limit order** at $120.
- Add a **trailing stop order** to dynamically protect gains if the stock surpasses $110.

PART 6:
Trading Psychology

Chapter 20:
Psychological Foundations

20.1 Understanding Trading Psychology

Trading psychology is the mental and emotional framework that influences a trader's decisions and actions in the market. While technical analysis, strategies, and indicators form the foundation of trading, it's the psychological aspect that often separates successful traders from those who struggle. At its core, trading psychology is about mastering yourself—your emotions, reactions, and mindset—to execute your strategy consistently and effectively.

Trading is a game of probabilities, not certainties. This reality often clashes with human instincts, which are wired to seek control and avoid loss. Fear, greed, hope, and regret frequently cloud judgment, leading to impulsive decisions that deviate from well-thought-out plans. Even the most technically sound strategy can falter if a trader succumbs to emotional biases.

Think of trading as a journey that requires discipline and self-awareness. It's not just about analyzing charts or crunching numbers but also about understanding your internal drivers. How do you react when a trade moves against you? Do you hold on to losing positions, hoping they'll turn around, or do you exit as planned? Conversely, do you close winning trades prematurely out of fear of losing unrealized profits? These behaviors often stem from psychological tendencies rather than logical reasoning.

The good news is that trading psychology isn't an inherent trait you either possess or lack—it's a skill you can develop. It begins with awareness. Recognizing the emotions and thought patterns that influence your trading decisions is the first step toward managing them. For example, the fear of loss might make you hesitant to take a valid trade setup, while greed might push you to overtrade in search of quick profits.

A practical way to understand your trading psychology is to reflect on your experiences. Consider keeping a trading journal not just for recording trades but also for noting your emotions during those trades. Were you anxious, overconfident, or calm? Did you follow your strategy, or did emotions lead you astray? Over time, patterns will emerge, offering valuable insights into your psychological strengths and weaknesses.

Another critical element of trading psychology is accepting losses as a natural part of trading. No strategy is foolproof, and losing trades are inevitable. Successful traders view losses not as failures but as part of the process. They focus on the bigger picture, knowing that consistency over time, not the outcome of a single trade, determines profitability.

The financial markets are unforgiving, and developing mental resilience is essential to navigate their unpredictability. Unlike traditional careers, where effort often correlates directly with results, trading can be disheartening when hard work doesn't immediately pay off. This is where cultivating a long-term perspective becomes invaluable. The ability to stick to your plan, even during drawdowns, sets the foundation for enduring success.

Ultimately, trading psychology is about aligning your mindset with the realities of the market. It's about replacing emotional reactions with logical responses and building a mental framework that supports consistent decision-making. As you delve deeper into this chapter, you'll uncover the common psychological challenges traders face and strategies to overcome them, paving the way for a more disciplined and profitable trading journey.

20.2 COMMON PSYCHOLOGICAL CHALLENGES

Trading is as much a psychological endeavor as it is a technical one. Even with a sound strategy, traders often find themselves battling internal conflicts that can undermine their success. These psychological challenges are universal, affecting traders at all levels of experience. By recognizing and addressing them, you can develop the mental fortitude needed to stay disciplined and consistent in the face of market uncertainty.

Fear: The Paralyzing Force

Fear is perhaps the most common psychological hurdle in trading. It manifests in various ways:

- **Fear of Loss:** The apprehension of losing money can prevent traders from entering valid setups, even when the odds are in their favor. This fear is often amplified after experiencing a string of losing trades.

- **Fear of Missing Out (FOMO):** Seeing others profit from a market move can lead to impulsive decisions, such as chasing trades after the opportunity has passed. These late entries often result in losses, reinforcing the cycle of fear.

- **Fear of Being Wrong:** Trading involves probabilities, not certainties. Yet, many traders struggle with the idea of being "wrong," leading them to hold on to losing positions longer than they should.

To overcome fear, it's essential to shift your perspective. Losses are not failures; they are an inevitable part of trading. A single trade doesn't define your success—your ability to execute your plan consistently does.

Greed: The Endless Pursuit

Greed is the flipside of fear and can be equally destructive. It pushes traders to:

- Take on excessive risk in pursuit of quick profits.
- Ignore their trading plans and let winning trades run beyond logical targets, often leading to reversals and reduced gains.

Chapter 20:
Psychological Foundations

- Overtrade, believing that more trades will equate to more profits.

While the allure of quick riches is strong, trading is not a get-rich-quick endeavor. Greed often clouds judgment, leading to decisions that deviate from your strategy and increase risk. The key to managing greed lies in setting realistic expectations and adhering to your plan.

Impatience: The Need for Instant Results

Impatience can lead traders to force trades or abandon strategies prematurely. The markets don't move on your schedule, and waiting for the right setup requires discipline. Impatience often results in:

- Taking suboptimal trades that don't meet your criteria.
- Closing positions too early, cutting profits short.

The solution lies in embracing the process. Trading is a long-term endeavor, and patience is rewarded over time. Remind yourself that the goal is consistent profitability, not immediate gratification.

Overconfidence: The Silent Threat

After a streak of successful trades, overconfidence can creep in, leading to reckless behavior such as increasing position sizes or ignoring risk management rules. Overconfidence blinds traders to potential pitfalls and fosters complacency. The market is a humbling environment, and a single misstep can erase gains accumulated over weeks or months.

The antidote to overconfidence is humility. Always respect the market's unpredictability and adhere to your rules, regardless of recent success.

Revenge Trading: The Emotional Trap

Revenge trading occurs when traders try to recover losses quickly by taking impulsive, high-risk trades. This behavior is driven by frustration and the desire to "win back" what was lost, often leading to even greater losses. Revenge trading is a vicious cycle that can spiral out of control.

To break free from this trap, take a step back after a loss. Review your strategy, evaluate what went wrong, and approach the next trade with a clear mind. Remember, trading is a marathon, not a sprint.

Analysis Paralysis: The Danger of Overthinking

With the wealth of information available, traders can fall into the trap of overanalyzing, leading to indecision. This phenomenon, known as analysis paralysis, often results in missed opportunities or hesitation at critical moments.

Simplifying your strategy and focusing on key indicators can help. Trust the work you've put into developing your system and execute trades with conviction.

Dealing with Psychological Challenges

The first step in overcoming these challenges is awareness. By acknowledging your psychological tendencies, you can actively work to counter them. Keeping a **trading journal** is invaluable for identifying recurring patterns in your behavior. Note not only the technical details of your trades but also your emotional state during execution.

Develop routines that support emotional stability. This could include:

- Taking regular breaks to avoid burnout.
- Practicing mindfulness or meditation to manage stress.
- Setting predefined limits on daily or weekly losses to prevent emotional trading.

Psychological challenges are an inevitable part of trading, but they don't have to dictate your success. By recognizing and addressing fear, greed, impatience, and other emotional pitfalls, you can cultivate the discipline and resilience required to trade effectively. The journey to mastering your trading psychology is ongoing, but every step you take brings you closer to consistent profitability.

20.3 DEVELOPING MENTAL RESILIENCE

Mental resilience is the ability to remain calm, focused, and disciplined in the face of challenges, setbacks, and uncertainty. In trading, where losses are inevitable and the markets are unpredictable, resilience is the trait that separates successful traders from those who struggle. Developing mental resilience is not just about enduring tough times; it's about thriving through them and using each experience to grow stronger and more confident.

The Importance of Resilience in Trading

The financial markets are volatile by nature. Even the most robust trading strategies will experience losing streaks, sudden market shifts, or unexpected drawdowns. Without resilience, these challenges can lead to emotional decision-making, such as revenge trading or abandoning a proven system prematurely. Resilient traders, on the other hand, understand that setbacks are temporary and focus on the bigger picture.

Imagine encountering a series of losing trades despite following your strategy perfectly. A resilient trader views this as part of the probability game, maintaining confidence in their system and continuing to execute trades with discipline. They understand that consistency over time—not the outcome of any single trade—determines success.

Chapter 20:
Psychological Foundations

Building Blocks of Mental Resilience

1. Acceptance of Losses

Losses are an inherent part of trading. Resilient traders accept this reality and avoid personalizing their setbacks. Instead of viewing a loss as a failure, they see it as an opportunity to learn and improve. This mindset shift reduces emotional distress and promotes rational decision-making.

2. Long-Term Perspective

Trading is a marathon, not a sprint. Resilient traders focus on the cumulative results of hundreds of trades rather than obsessing over individual wins or losses. This long-term perspective helps them stay grounded during both profitable streaks and drawdowns.

3. Emotional Regulation

Developing the ability to manage emotions like fear, greed, and frustration is critical for resilience. Emotional regulation doesn't mean suppressing feelings; it means acknowledging them without letting them dictate your actions. Techniques like mindfulness meditation or deep breathing exercises can help maintain emotional balance during volatile market conditions.

4. Confidence in Your Strategy

Resilience stems from trust in your trading system. When you have thoroughly backtested, forward tested, and refined your strategy, you can trade with the confidence that it is designed to perform over time. This trust minimizes self-doubt, even when the strategy encounters temporary setbacks.

Practical Steps to Build Mental Resilience

1. Develop a Resilience Routine

Create habits that strengthen your mental fortitude, such as:

- Starting your day with a clear plan and realistic goals for your trading session.
- Reviewing past trades to reinforce lessons learned and celebrate progress.
- Taking breaks during trading to prevent burnout and maintain focus.

2. Embrace a Growth Mindset

A growth mindset sees challenges as opportunities to learn and improve. Instead of dwelling on losses, ask yourself:

- What did I do right?
- What could I have done better?
- How can I apply these insights to future trades?

This approach transforms setbacks into steppingstones for growth.

3. Practice Self-Compassion

Trading can be a lonely and demanding endeavor. Resilient traders treat themselves with kindness, understanding that mistakes are part of the learning process. Self-compassion fosters a positive mindset, reducing the tendency to spiral into negative self-talk after a poor trade.

4. Build a Support Network

Connect with other traders who understand the emotional challenges of the profession. Sharing experiences and learning from others can provide valuable perspectives and motivation during tough times.

5. Set Realistic Expectations

Unrealistic goals, such as expecting to double your account in a month, can lead to frustration and impulsive trading. Resilient traders set achievable targets, understanding that consistent, incremental gains are more sustainable than chasing large, immediate profits.

Examples of Resilience in Action

Scenario 1: A Losing Streak

A trader experiences five consecutive losing trades. Instead of panicking, they review their journal to confirm that all trades adhered to their strategy. Confident in their system, they continue trading with discipline, knowing that probabilities will eventually work in their favor.

Scenario 2: Market Uncertainty

During a sudden market downturn, a trader resists the urge to make impulsive decisions. Instead, they stick to their plan, adjusting risk parameters as needed while maintaining focus on long-term goals.

The Role of Resilience in Decision-Making

Resilience enables traders to approach each decision with clarity and confidence. Instead of reacting emotionally to market movements, resilient traders respond logically, grounded in their preparation and experience. This steadiness allows them to seize opportunities while minimizing mistakes.

Mental resilience is not a fixed trait—it's a skill that can be cultivated over time with intention and practice. By accepting losses, maintaining a long-term perspective, regulating emotions, and building confidence in your strategy, you develop the capacity to navigate the ups and downs of trading with composure. Resilience transforms challenges into opportunities, enabling you to achieve consistent success in an unpredictable market.

20.4 BUILDING TRADING CONFIDENCE

Chapter 20:
Psychological Foundations

Confidence is the cornerstone of successful trading. It's the belief in your ability to execute your strategy consistently and make informed decisions, even in the face of uncertainty. Unlike arrogance, which leads to recklessness, confidence is built on a foundation of preparation, practice, and a deep understanding of both yourself and the markets. When confidence is strong, it becomes a guiding force that enables you to act decisively and maintain discipline, regardless of market conditions.

The Importance of Trading Confidence

In trading, doubt can be as damaging as overconfidence. Hesitation may cause you to miss valid setups, while second-guessing your strategy can lead to emotional decisions and deviation from your plan. Building and maintaining confidence allows you to:

- Execute trades with precision and conviction.
- Stay committed to your system during periods of drawdowns or market volatility.
- Recover quickly from losses without compromising your discipline.

Confident traders understand that no single trade defines their success. Instead, they focus on the bigger picture—consistent execution over the long term.

How to Build Trading Confidence

1. Master Your Strategy

Confidence begins with preparation. The more you understand your trading strategy, the more comfortable you'll feel executing it.

- Conduct thorough **backtesting** and **forward testing** to ensure your system is robust.
- Know your strategy's strengths, weaknesses, and expected performance metrics.
- Practice executing trades in a demo or paper trading environment until it becomes second nature.

When you trust your system, you'll find it easier to stay disciplined, even when faced with uncertainty.

2. Start Small and Build Gradually

Begin with smaller position sizes to minimize the emotional impact of losses while you build confidence. As your comfort level grows and your results validate your approach, gradually increase your risk within the limits of your trading plan.

3. Keep a Detailed Journal

Document every trade, including your thought process, emotions, and the outcome. Regularly review your journal to:

- Identify patterns in your decision-making.
- Celebrate successful trades that followed your plan.
- Learn from mistakes without self-criticism.

A journal serves as a powerful tool for reinforcing confidence by showing tangible evidence of your growth and improvement.

4. Focus on Process, Not Outcomes

Confidence should be rooted in your ability to follow your plan, not the results of individual trades. Even the best setups can result in losses due to the probabilistic nature of trading. Instead of fixating on winning or losing, ask yourself:

- Did I follow my rules?
- Was my risk management sound?
- Did I remain disciplined?

When you focus on the process, the results will take care of themselves over time.

5. Manage Your Environment

Surround yourself with supportive influences that encourage confidence:

- Engage with a community of traders who share your values and goals.
- Avoid overly negative or overly optimistic sources of information that can skew your perspective.
- Create a calm and focused workspace that promotes clear thinking.

Overcoming Confidence Killers

Fear of Failure: Understand that losses are part of trading and don't reflect on your capabilities. Treat each trade as one step in a larger journey.

Overanalysis: Constantly doubting your decisions can erode confidence. Simplify your approach by trusting your preparation and focusing on execution.

Comparisons: Comparing your results to others can undermine your confidence. Focus on your own progress and goals, not someone else's performance.

The Feedback Loop of Confidence

Confidence grows through a positive feedback loop:

- Preparation leads to successful execution.
- Successful execution reinforces your belief in your abilities.
- Increased belief encourages disciplined behavior, leading to more consistent results.

This cycle strengthens over time, creating a solid foundation for long-term success.

Practical Example: Building Confidence After a Loss

Imagine you've experienced a string of losing trades despite following your strategy. Instead of doubting yourself, you review your journal and confirm that each trade adhered to your plan. This

Chapter 20:
Psychological Foundations

reflection reinforces that the losses were within the system's expected probabilities and not a result of poor decision-making. By staying committed to the process, you regain confidence and approach the next trade without hesitation.

Conclusion

Building trading confidence is an ongoing process that requires preparation, self-awareness, and discipline. By mastering your strategy, focusing on the process, and cultivating a supportive environment, you can trade with conviction and resilience. Confidence doesn't eliminate challenges—it equips you to face them head-on, ensuring that you stay on the path to consistent success. As you continue to develop this essential trait, you'll find that the markets become less daunting and your ability to navigate them grows stronger with every trade.

Chapter 21: Emotional Management

21.1 Dealing with Fear

Fear is a natural and instinctive emotion that can have a significant impact on trading decisions. In the financial markets, fear often arises from the possibility of loss, uncertainty, or a lack of confidence in one's strategy. While it's impossible to eliminate fear entirely, successful traders learn to manage it effectively, ensuring that it doesn't cloud their judgment or lead to impulsive actions.

Fear in trading manifests in various ways. It might prevent you from taking a trade even when your setup meets all the criteria, or it might cause you to exit a winning position prematurely to avoid the risk of losing unrealized profits. This hesitation and over-caution can erode profitability and undermine the effectiveness of even the best strategies.

The root of trading fear often lies in a misunderstanding of risk and a lack of trust in your system. If you haven't fully embraced the reality that losses are part of trading, fear can dominate your mindset. Similarly, if your strategy hasn't been rigorously tested, or if you lack the discipline to follow it consistently, doubt will creep in, fueling fear and hesitation.

To address fear, start by reframing how you perceive losses. Losses are not failures; they are the cost of doing business in the trading world. Just as a retailer expects some level of overhead expenses, traders should anticipate and accept occasional losing trades. The key is to ensure that losses are manageable and within the parameters of your risk management plan.

Another powerful way to combat fear is through preparation. When you've thoroughly backtested and forward-tested your strategy, you build confidence in its ability to deliver long-term results. This preparation provides a sense of control, even in volatile market conditions. Knowing that you've accounted for various scenarios reduces the uncertainty that feeds fear.

Mindfulness techniques can also play a significant role in managing fear. Practicing deep breathing, meditation, or visualization exercises can help you stay grounded during stressful trading moments. By calming your nervous system, you can approach decisions with greater clarity and logic, rather than being driven by fear-based reactions.

A practical approach to dealing with fear is to start small. If the thought of risking significant capital causes anxiety, reduce your position size until you feel comfortable. Gradually increase your risk as your confidence grows. This incremental approach allows you to build resilience without overwhelming yourself.

Chapter 21:
Emotional Management

Lastly, remind yourself that trading is a long-term endeavor. Fear often arises from a fixation on short-term outcomes, such as the result of a single trade. Shift your focus to the bigger picture. A single loss is inconsequential in the context of hundreds of trades executed over time. The ultimate goal is consistent execution of your strategy, not perfection in every trade.

Dealing with fear requires both mental and practical adjustments. By redefining your relationship with losses, trusting your preparation, and staying present in the moment, you can transform fear from a debilitating obstacle into a manageable part of the trading process. Over time, you'll find that fear loses its grip, allowing you to trade with greater confidence and clarity.

21.2 Controlling Greed

Greed is one of the most pervasive and insidious emotions in trading. While the desire for profit drives every trader to the markets, unchecked greed can lead to impulsive decisions, excessive risk-taking, and ultimately, significant losses. Controlling greed is essential for maintaining discipline, sticking to your trading plan, and preserving both your capital and long-term profitability.

Greed in trading often manifests as overtrading, holding onto winning positions too long in hopes of greater gains, or risking more than your plan allows to chase larger profits. For example, after a few successful trades, a trader may feel invincible and double their position size without considering the increased risk. Similarly, a trader might ignore their profit targets, only to watch the market reverse and erode their gains.

At its core, greed stems from unrealistic expectations. Many traders enter the market with the hope of quick riches, expecting to double their account in weeks or turn every trade into a massive windfall. These expectations not only fuel greed but also set traders up for disappointment and poor decision-making when reality doesn't align with their aspirations.

To control greed, the first step is to establish **realistic goals**. Instead of focusing on making a fortune overnight, aim for consistent, incremental gains. A target of a small percentage growth per month, compounded over time, can lead to significant wealth without the stress or risks associated with aggressive trading.

Another effective strategy is to adhere strictly to your **trading plan**. Your plan should include predefined rules for entry, exit, position sizing, and risk management. By committing to these rules, you remove the temptation to chase profits or hold positions beyond their logical targets. When the market tempts you to deviate, remind yourself of the discipline and effort that went into creating your plan.

Taking profits systematically is another way to keep greed in check. Define clear profit targets for each trade based on your strategy, and stick to them. If your system allows for scaling out of positions, lock in partial profits as the market moves in your favor. This approach ensures you realize gains while leaving room for potential upside, balancing ambition with prudence.

Mindfulness practices can also help you recognize and manage the emotional triggers of greed. For instance, when you notice the impulse to overtrade or chase profits, take a moment to pause and reflect. Ask yourself: "Is this decision aligned with my plan, or is it driven by emotion?" This simple act of self-awareness can prevent impulsive actions and reinforce disciplined behavior.

Maintaining a long-term perspective is crucial. Greed often arises from a fixation on immediate results, such as making a large profit in a single trade. Shift your focus to the bigger picture: building wealth consistently over years. This mindset not only reduces the pressure to maximize every trade but also fosters a sustainable approach to trading.

Finally, remember that the market operates on probabilities, not guarantees. Chasing profits or taking excessive risks doesn't increase your chances of success; it merely exposes you to greater losses. By managing greed, you align your actions with the market's realities, increasing your likelihood of achieving consistent results.

Controlling greed is an ongoing process that requires self-awareness, discipline, and a commitment to your trading plan. With practice, you can transform greed from a destructive force into a motivating factor that drives you to approach the markets thoughtfully and strategically. This shift will not only protect your capital but also set you on the path to sustainable trading success.

21.3 Managing Trading Stress

Trading is inherently stressful. The financial markets are unpredictable, decisions must often be made quickly, and real money is at stake. Add to this the pressure of achieving consistent results, and it's no wonder that many traders experience high levels of stress. While some stress can enhance focus and performance, excessive stress can cloud judgment, lead to emotional decision-making, and ultimately derail your trading success. Managing trading stress is therefore critical to maintaining clarity, discipline, and long-term profitability.

Stress in trading often stems from uncertainty. Unlike other professions where effort directly correlates with results, trading involves probabilities, and even well-planned trades can lead to losses. This lack of control over outcomes can create anxiety, particularly for those who are risk-averse or new to the markets. Stress is also amplified during volatile market conditions, losing streaks, or periods of personal financial pressure.

To manage trading stress, it's important to start with **realistic expectations**. Trading is not a guaranteed path to instant wealth, and losses are a natural part of the process. Accepting this reality reduces the fear of failure and the stress associated with unrealistic goals. Approach trading as a long-term endeavor, focusing on consistent execution rather than short-term results.

Building a **structured routine** can also help reduce stress. Having a clear plan for your trading day—including set times for analysis, decision-making, and breaks—creates a sense of order and control. By following a routine, you minimize impulsive actions and make more deliberate, thoughtful decisions. For example, reviewing your trading plan each morning and journaling your trades at the end of the day can provide a grounding framework.

One of the most effective ways to manage stress is to focus on **risk management**. When you trade within your predefined risk limits, you reduce the emotional weight of each decision. Knowing that no single trade can significantly harm your account provides peace of mind and allows you to trade with confidence. For instance, setting a maximum percentage of your capital to risk per trade ensures that even a string of losses won't jeopardize your overall financial health.

Taking regular **breaks** during trading is essential. Prolonged periods of screen time can lead to mental fatigue, which increases stress and the likelihood of errors. Step away from your desk periodically to recharge. Engaging in activities that relax your mind—such as going for a walk, practicing mindfulness, or even exercising—can help you return to the market with a fresh perspective.

Practicing **mindfulness and emotional awareness** is another powerful tool for managing stress. Pay attention to your emotional state during trading. Are you feeling tense, frustrated, or overwhelmed? Recognizing these emotions allows you to address them before they influence your decisions. Techniques like deep breathing, meditation, or journaling can help you stay centered and reduce stress in the moment.

It's also important to maintain a healthy **work-life balance**. Trading can be all-consuming, but dedicating time to hobbies, family, and physical activity keeps stress levels in check. A balanced life enhances your mental clarity, emotional resilience, and overall performance in the markets.

Finally, learn to view setbacks as opportunities for growth rather than sources of stress. Every trader experiences losing trades and challenging periods, but these moments often hold the greatest lessons. Reflecting on what went wrong, adjusting your approach, and moving forward with renewed focus transforms stress into a steppingstone for improvement.

Managing trading stress requires a combination of mindset, preparation, and self-care. By adopting realistic expectations, sticking to a structured routine, prioritizing risk management, and maintaining balance, you can trade with a clear mind and steady hand. Over time, these habits will not only reduce stress but also enhance your ability to navigate the markets effectively and achieve your trading goals.

21.4 MAINTAINING DISCIPLINE

Discipline is the backbone of successful trading. It's the ability to stick to your strategy, follow your rules, and execute your plan consistently, regardless of market conditions or emotional temptations. While having a well-constructed trading plan is essential, its effectiveness depends entirely on your ability to maintain discipline. Without it, even the best strategies can falter.

Trading discipline is tested in many ways. You might be tempted to skip a trade that aligns perfectly with your strategy because of fear, or you might enter a position impulsively without proper analysis due to excitement or impatience. Overconfidence after a winning streak or frustration after a series of losses can also lead to deviations from your plan. Each of these moments of weakness undermines the foundation of consistent, profitable trading.

The first step in maintaining discipline is recognizing that trading is a probabilistic endeavor, not a game of certainties. Even a high-probability setup can result in a loss, and that's okay. What matters is your adherence to the process, not the outcome of any single trade. By focusing on the process, you eliminate the emotional highs and lows that often lead to impulsive decisions.

A critical component of discipline is having a **well-defined trading plan**. Your plan should outline your entry and exit criteria, position sizing rules, risk management parameters, and guidelines for when to avoid trading. When every decision is preplanned, there's less room for emotional interference. For example, if your plan dictates that you risk no more than 1% of your account per trade, you avoid the temptation to increase position size after a few wins.

Another tool for building discipline is maintaining a **trading journal**. Writing down the reasons behind every trade, along with the outcomes and your emotional state, creates accountability. When you review your journal, patterns of discipline—or the lack thereof—become evident. For instance, you might notice a tendency to overtrade after a loss or to exit trades prematurely. Identifying these habits allows you to address and correct them.

It's also important to develop a **pre-trading routine**. This routine can include reviewing your plan, analyzing the markets, and mentally preparing for the session. A structured approach sets a disciplined tone for the day and minimizes the likelihood of impulsive actions. Similarly, having an end-of-day routine to review trades and reflect on your performance reinforces good habits.

Emotional management plays a significant role in maintaining discipline. Emotions like fear, greed, frustration, and overconfidence often drive traders to deviate from their plans. Techniques such as mindfulness, deep breathing, or taking short breaks during trading can help you stay composed and focused. For example, if you feel the urge to enter a trade that doesn't meet your criteria, pause and ask yourself, "Am I acting on logic or emotion?"

Discipline also requires patience. Markets don't always present clear opportunities, and sitting on the sidelines during uncertain conditions is often the best decision. Resisting the urge to trade for the sake of action is a hallmark of disciplined traders. They understand that not trading is a valid and often profitable choice.

Finally, cultivate a long-term perspective. Discipline isn't about perfection in every trade; it's about consistency over hundreds of trades. Viewing each decision as part of a broader journey reduces the pressure to get every trade "right" and helps you stay committed to your plan.

Maintaining discipline is an ongoing effort that requires self-awareness, accountability, and a commitment to your goals. By prioritizing process over outcomes, creating structured routines, and managing your emotions, you can develop the discipline needed to navigate the markets with confidence. Over time, this discipline becomes second nature, enabling you to approach trading with the clarity and consistency required for sustained success.

Chapter 21:
Emotional Management

21.5 Recovery from Losses

Losses are an inevitable part of trading, no matter how skilled or experienced you are. They are not a reflection of failure but a normal aspect of working within a probabilistic environment. What defines successful traders is not the absence of losses but their ability to recover from them—mentally, emotionally, and strategically—without letting setbacks derail their progress.

Recovering from losses begins with a shift in mindset. Many traders view losses as personal failures, leading to frustration, self-doubt, or even revenge trading in an attempt to quickly recoup their losses. This emotional reaction often exacerbates the situation, resulting in further losses and a vicious cycle of poor decision-making. The key is to recognize that losses are a cost of doing business in the markets and to focus on learning from them.

The first step in recovery is **acceptance**. Acknowledge the loss without judgment or blame. Resist the urge to dwell on what could have been; instead, focus on what you can control moving forward. Losses are only damaging if they lead to emotional decision-making or deviations from your trading plan. Treat each loss as an opportunity to improve your strategy and refine your approach.

Analyze the cause of the loss with a clear and objective mind. Was it due to a failure to follow your plan, an error in execution, or simply the result of market conditions beyond your control? For example:

- If you ignored your stop-loss, the issue may lie in discipline.
- If your strategy failed to perform in a specific market environment, it might need refinement.
- If the loss was within the expected probabilities of your system, it's simply part of trading and doesn't require any adjustment.

This analysis helps you distinguish between avoidable mistakes and unavoidable outcomes, allowing you to address the root cause effectively.

A **trading journal** is invaluable in this process. Documenting the details of losing trades—including your thought process, emotional state, and deviations from your plan—provides insights that can prevent similar mistakes in the future. For instance, if your journal reveals a pattern of overtrading after losses, you can implement rules to limit trading during emotionally charged periods.

Take a break if needed. Emotional recovery is as important as financial recovery. Stepping away from the markets for a day or two allows you to regain composure and approach your next trades with a clear mind. Use this time to reflect, recalibrate, and reaffirm your commitment to disciplined trading.

Once you've addressed the emotional and strategic aspects of the loss, **create a plan for moving forward**. This plan should include:

- Reaffirming your adherence to your trading rules.
- Adjusting risk parameters if necessary, such as reducing position sizes temporarily to rebuild confidence.

- Setting realistic goals that focus on process rather than immediate recovery of lost capital.

It's essential to **avoid revenge trading**, the impulse to take aggressive or impulsive trades to recover losses quickly. Revenge trading often leads to further mistakes and exacerbates the drawdown. Instead, focus on executing your strategy with precision and discipline, knowing that consistent application of your plan will eventually lead to recovery.

Maintaining a **long-term perspective** is also crucial. A single loss—or even a string of losses—does not define your trading career. Focus on the bigger picture, recognizing that trading success is measured over hundreds of trades, not individual outcomes. Remind yourself that losses are a normal part of the journey and that resilience is a key trait of all successful traders.

Finally, cultivate **self-compassion**. Be kind to yourself and recognize that mistakes are part of the learning process. Harsh self-criticism only adds to the emotional burden, making it harder to recover. Instead, focus on what you've learned and how you can grow from the experience.

Recovering from losses requires patience, self-awareness, and a commitment to disciplined trading. By accepting losses, analyzing their causes, and taking deliberate steps to move forward, you not only restore your confidence but also strengthen your resilience. Over time, these experiences become invaluable lessons that contribute to your growth as a trader, enabling you to navigate the markets with clarity and composure.

PART 7:
Practical Application

Chapter 22: Case Studies

22.1 SUCCESSFUL TRADE ANALYSIS

Case studies of successful trades are invaluable for bridging the gap between theory and practice. They provide concrete examples of how to apply trading strategies, interpret market conditions, and execute plans with discipline. Analyzing successful trades helps traders understand what went right, reinforcing confidence and offering a blueprint for replicating similar results in the future.

Overview of a Successful Trade

Let's consider a real-world example to illustrate the application of key trading principles. This case study involves a **bullish engulfing pattern** on a daily candlestick chart, complemented by additional technical indicators and sound risk management.

Market Context:

The trade occurred in a trending market where the price had been steadily rising for weeks. After a brief pullback, a bullish engulfing pattern formed near a key support level, indicating potential reversal and continuation of the trend.

Trade Setup:

- **Pattern Recognized:** Bullish engulfing pattern on the daily chart.

- **Additional Confirmation:** The RSI (Relative Strength Index) was approaching oversold territory but hadn't yet crossed the threshold, signaling potential upward momentum. Additionally, the price was bouncing off the 50-day moving average, a widely respected dynamic support level.

- **Risk-Reward Assessment:** The stop-loss was placed below the low of the engulfing candlestick, and the profit target was set at the next major resistance level, providing a risk-to-reward ratio of 1:3.

Trade Execution:

After confirming the pattern during the market's close, the trade was initiated at the opening price of the next day. The position size was calculated to ensure no more than 1% of the account balance was at risk.

Key Aspects of the Trade

1. **Pattern Recognition:**

Chapter 22:
Case Studies

> The bullish engulfing pattern was clear and well-defined, meeting all criteria discussed earlier in the book. The larger green candlestick completely engulfed the prior smaller red candlestick, signaling strong buyer interest.
>
> 2. **Confluence of Factors:**
>
> The presence of the RSI near oversold levels and the bounce off the 50-day moving average added confidence to the setup. These elements demonstrated the power of combining candlestick patterns with technical indicators to validate trade ideas.
>
> 3. **Risk Management:**
>
> A tight stop-loss was placed below the support level, minimizing potential loss if the trade didn't work out. The defined risk-to-reward ratio ensured that the trade was worth taking from a probabilistic standpoint.
>
> 4. **Patience and Execution:**
>
> The trader waited for the candlestick pattern to complete and confirm the setup, avoiding the temptation to act prematurely. The entry, stop-loss, and target levels were adhered to without deviation.

Outcome and Analysis

The trade moved in favor of the setup within two days, quickly reaching the predefined profit target. By sticking to the plan and following the strategy, the trader capitalized on a high-probability setup while maintaining disciplined risk management.

Key Lessons from the Successful Trade:

- Combining candlestick patterns with technical indicators strengthens trade reliability.
- Setting realistic targets and adhering to a risk-to-reward ratio ensures sustainable profitability.
- Patience in waiting for confirmation is crucial to avoid false signals.

Successful trades are the result of preparation, discipline, and adherence to a plan. By analyzing these trades, you gain insight into the principles and practices that lead to consistent performance. Each successful trade reinforces the importance of combining technical analysis, risk management, and emotional control, setting the foundation for long-term success.

22.2 FAILED TRADE ANALYSIS

While successful trades provide valuable lessons, failed trades often offer even greater insights. Analyzing trades that didn't go as planned helps identify mistakes, refine strategies, and improve decision-making. Importantly, failed trades remind us that losses are part of trading, even when a strategy is executed flawlessly. The key lies in learning from these experiences to prevent repeating errors and building resilience.

Overview of a Failed Trade

Let's examine a case study involving a **bearish engulfing pattern** that didn't result in the anticipated price movement. This trade demonstrates the importance of context, discipline, and flexibility when trading candlestick patterns.

Market Context:

The trade took place in a consolidating market where price action was oscillating within a range. A bearish engulfing pattern appeared near the upper boundary of the range, suggesting a potential reversal to the downside.

Trade Setup:

- **Pattern Recognized:** A bearish engulfing pattern on a 4-hour chart.
- **Additional Confirmation:** The MACD showed a bearish crossover, reinforcing the potential for downward momentum.
- **Risk-Reward Assessment:** The stop-loss was placed above the high of the engulfing candlestick, with a profit target at the range's lower boundary, yielding a risk-to-reward ratio of 1:2.

Trade Execution:

The trade was initiated shortly after the engulfing pattern completed. The position size adhered to the trader's rule of risking no more than 1% of the account balance on a single trade.

What Went Wrong

1. **Ignoring Market Context:**

    The bearish engulfing pattern formed within a consolidating range, where price action often lacks clear direction. Trading patterns in a range-bound market without confirming a breakout can lead to false signals.

2. **Overreliance on a Single Timeframe:**

    The trade relied solely on the 4-hour chart without considering higher timeframes. On the daily chart, the market was showing bullish pressure, which conflicted with the short-term bearish signal.

3. **Premature Entry:**

    The trader entered the trade immediately after the pattern formed without waiting for additional confirmation, such as a close below the range's upper boundary or an increase in bearish volume.

4. **Emotional Attachment to the Setup:**

Chapter 22:
Case Studies

When the price briefly moved in favor of the trade, the trader decided to hold the position longer than planned, hoping for larger gains. This deviation from the plan led to increased exposure when the market reversed.

Outcome and Analysis

The price initially moved slightly lower but then reversed and broke above the range's upper boundary, hitting the stop-loss. The loss was within acceptable limits due to proper risk management, but the trader's decision to deviate from the plan amplified the frustration.

Key Lessons from the Failed Trade

- **Respect Market Context:** Patterns should always be analyzed within the broader context of the market's behavior. In this case, the consolidating range and conflicting signals on the daily chart reduced the reliability of the bearish engulfing pattern.

- **Use Multiple Timeframes:** Cross-referencing setups on higher and lower timeframes can provide a clearer picture of market dynamics and prevent acting on isolated signals.

- **Wait for Confirmation:** Additional confirmation, such as a breakout or increased volume, can filter out false signals in range-bound markets.

- **Stick to the Plan:** Deviating from the original trade plan by holding for larger gains introduces unnecessary risk. Discipline in following your strategy is paramount, especially in uncertain conditions.

Steps for Improvement

To prevent similar outcomes in the future:

- Incorporate market context analysis into your routine to identify whether the market is trending or consolidating.

- Include a confirmation checklist to ensure setups align across multiple timeframes.

- Reinforce discipline by reviewing your trading plan regularly and documenting instances where you deviated from it.

Conclusion

Failed trades are an invaluable part of the learning process. By analyzing what went wrong, traders can identify gaps in their strategy, refine their approach, and strengthen their discipline. Losses are not failures; they are opportunities to grow and adapt. Embrace them as steppingstones toward becoming a more skilled and confident trader.

22.3 MARKET CONDITION ANALYSIS

Understanding market conditions is a critical aspect of successful trading. The financial markets are dynamic, constantly transitioning between phases of trending, consolidating, and volatile behavior. Each condition requires a different approach, and failing to adapt can lead to suboptimal trades, unnecessary risks, and missed opportunities. Market condition analysis allows traders to tailor their strategies to align with the prevailing environment, increasing the likelihood of consistent success.

Types of Market Conditions

1. **Trending Markets**

    Trending markets exhibit a clear directional movement, either upward (bullish) or downward (bearish). These conditions are characterized by higher highs and higher lows in an uptrend or lower highs and lower lows in a downtrend.

    - **Key Opportunities:** Trend-following strategies, such as using moving averages or trendlines, work best in these conditions.
    - **Challenges:** Overtrading during temporary pullbacks or corrections can lead to losses if the trend resumes.

2. **Range-Bound Markets**

    In range-bound or consolidating markets, prices oscillate between well-defined support and resistance levels without a clear directional bias.

    - **Key Opportunities:** Traders can focus on buying near support and selling near resistance, often using oscillators like RSI to identify overbought and oversold conditions.
    - **Challenges:** Breakouts from the range can occur unexpectedly, leading to losses for traders who fail to adjust.

3. **Volatile Markets**

    Volatile markets are marked by sharp, unpredictable price swings, often caused by significant news events or economic data releases.

    - **Key Opportunities:** Volatility provides opportunities for quick profits using shorter timeframes and tight risk management.
    - **Challenges:** Increased risk of stop-loss triggers due to larger price movements.

Identifying Market Conditions

Successful market condition analysis begins with a comprehensive assessment of price action and technical indicators. Here are some tools and techniques to identify and classify market conditions:

- **Moving Averages:** The slope and alignment of moving averages can indicate trending markets. For example, a bullish trend is often confirmed when shorter-term moving averages are above longer-term ones, both sloping upward.
- **Trendlines and Channels:** Drawing trendlines or identifying price channels helps visualize trends and key levels in range-bound markets.
- **Volatility Indicators:** Tools like Bollinger Bands or the Average True Range (ATR) measure volatility, providing clues about the market's behavior.

Chapter 22: Case Studies

- **Support and Resistance Levels:** Recognizing key levels helps determine whether the market is consolidating within a range or preparing for a breakout.

Adapting Strategies to Market Conditions

1. **In Trending Markets:**

- Use trend-following strategies like **moving average crossovers**, **breakout trades**, or **pullback entries**.
- Avoid countertrend trades unless there are strong reversal signals confirmed by candlestick patterns or divergence on indicators like RSI.

2. **In Range-Bound Markets:**

- Focus on **mean-reversion strategies**, buying near support and selling near resistance.
- Use oscillators to identify overbought and oversold conditions, ensuring trades align with the range boundaries.

3. **In Volatile Markets:**

- Adopt **short-term strategies** with smaller position sizes and wider stop-losses to account for larger price swings.
- Avoid overleveraging and ensure proper risk management to withstand sudden, unpredictable moves.

Case Study: Applying Market Condition Analysis

Scenario:
You observe a bullish trend in a stock that has been climbing steadily for several weeks. A candlestick pattern, such as a bullish engulfing, forms at a key moving average, signaling a continuation of the trend.

Action:
You identify the trend using the slope of the 50-day moving average and confirm it with higher highs and higher lows on the daily chart. Recognizing that the market is trending, you use a trend-following strategy, entering on a pullback to the moving average and setting a stop-loss below the recent swing low.

Outcome:
The market resumes its upward trajectory, and your disciplined approach to analyzing and aligning with the trending condition leads to a profitable trade.

Key Takeaways

- Market conditions dictate the effectiveness of trading strategies. Adapting to these conditions is critical for consistent performance.
- Tools like moving averages, trendlines, and volatility indicators provide insights into market behavior.

- Avoid applying the same strategy universally. What works in a trending market may fail in a range-bound or volatile environment.

Conclusion

Market condition analysis is the cornerstone of strategic trading. By identifying whether the market is trending, range-bound, or volatile, you can adapt your approach to maximize opportunities and minimize risks. Mastering this skill allows you to navigate the markets with confidence, ensuring your strategies remain effective across varying conditions.

22.4 PATTERN RECOGNITION IN PRACTICE

Recognizing and applying patterns in real-time trading is where theory meets action. While understanding patterns conceptually is essential, the ability to spot them amidst live market fluctuations and use them effectively is a skill honed through practice and discipline. Pattern recognition in practice involves identifying high-probability setups, confirming signals with supporting analysis, and executing trades with precision.

The first step in practical pattern recognition is to develop an intuitive familiarity with patterns through repetition. By consistently reviewing historical charts, traders train their eyes to spot common formations such as engulfing patterns, head and shoulders, or triangles. This familiarity allows for faster recognition during live trading, where decisions often need to be made quickly.

In live market conditions, context is critical. A pattern does not exist in isolation; its reliability depends on the surrounding market structure. For example, a bullish engulfing pattern at a major support level in a trending market is more reliable than the same pattern in a choppy, range-bound market. Combining patterns with other forms of analysis, such as trendlines, moving averages, or volume, helps validate the setup and increases its probability of success.

Let's consider an example of a **morning star pattern** in practice. Suppose you're analyzing a stock that has been in a downtrend but approaches a significant support level. Over three days, the candles form a morning star—a long bearish candle followed by a small-bodied candle and then a large bullish candle that closes above the midpoint of the first. Recognizing this as a potential reversal signal, you confirm the setup with additional analysis: the RSI indicates oversold conditions, and the support level aligns with a key Fibonacci retracement level.

Execution of such a trade involves adhering to pre-established rules. You enter the trade at the close of the bullish candle, set a stop-loss below the support level to protect against a false breakout, and define a target based on the next resistance level. This disciplined approach ensures that pattern recognition translates into actionable and risk-managed trades.

Another practical consideration is the role of **timeframes**. Patterns that appear on higher timeframes, such as daily or weekly charts, tend to be more reliable due to reduced market noise. However, intraday traders can still capitalize on patterns by ensuring that setups align across

Chapter 22:
Case Studies

multiple timeframes. For instance, a bullish flag on a 15-minute chart that aligns with a larger uptrend on the daily chart carries more weight than the same pattern appearing in isolation.

While recognizing patterns is essential, avoiding over-reliance on them is equally important. Not all patterns lead to successful trades, and false signals are part of the trading landscape. To mitigate this risk, traders should develop a checklist to confirm patterns before taking action. This checklist might include factors like volume, the presence of supporting indicators, and the broader market context.

Journaling is a valuable tool for refining pattern recognition skills. Documenting each trade, including the identified pattern, the context in which it appeared, and the trade's outcome, helps highlight strengths and areas for improvement. Over time, this practice builds confidence and sharpens a trader's ability to discern high-quality setups from less reliable ones.

Pattern recognition in practice is as much about discipline and context as it is about technical knowledge. By combining a strong understanding of patterns with rigorous analysis, traders can identify high-probability setups and execute them with confidence. This process transforms theoretical knowledge into actionable strategies, paving the way for consistent success in the markets.

22.5 RISK MANAGEMENT EXAMPLES

Risk management is the cornerstone of successful trading. Even the most accurate analysis and well-timed trades can falter without proper risk control. In this section, we will explore practical examples that demonstrate how effective risk management safeguards capital, enhances confidence, and ensures long-term profitability. By applying these principles to real-world scenarios, you can understand how to integrate risk management into every aspect of your trading.

Example 1: Setting a Stop-Loss for a Bullish Trade

Scenario:
A trader identifies a bullish engulfing pattern near a strong support level on the daily chart of a stock. The setup aligns with the prevailing uptrend and is further validated by rising volume and an RSI reading near the oversold zone.

Actionable Risk Management:

- The trader enters the trade at $100.

- The stop-loss is set at $95, just below the support level and slightly below the low of the engulfing pattern. This placement protects against a false breakout while allowing room for natural price fluctuations.

- The target is set at $110, near the next resistance level, yielding a risk-to-reward ratio of 1:2.

Outcome:

The price initially consolidates but eventually rises to $110, hitting the target. The stop-loss placement ensured the trader was protected in case the support failed, while the 1:2 risk-to-reward ratio justified the trade.

Example 2: Adjusting Position Size Based on Risk

Scenario:

A trader identifies a breakout above a descending triangle on the 4-hour chart of a currency pair. The entry price is $1.2000, and the stop-loss is placed at $1.1900.

Actionable Risk Management:

- The trader's account balance is $10,000, and their rule is to risk no more than 1% of their account on a single trade.
- The risk per trade is calculated as $100 (1% of $10,000).
- The dollar risk per unit (entry price minus stop-loss) is $1.2000 - $1.1900 = $0.0100.
- The position size is calculated as $100 ÷ $0.0100 = 10,000 units.

Outcome:

The position size ensures that even if the trade hits the stop-loss, the loss will not exceed $100, preserving capital for future trades. This approach allows the trader to remain consistent in managing risk across various setups.

Example 3: Scaling Out of a Winning Trade

Scenario:

A trader enters a bullish flag pattern on a stock at $50, with an initial target of $60. As the price rises to $55, the trader notices that momentum is slowing and decides to secure some profits while keeping part of the position open for further gains.

Actionable Risk Management:

- The trader sells half of the position at $55, locking in a partial profit.
- The stop-loss for the remaining position is moved to the breakeven price of $50, eliminating the risk of loss on the trade.

Outcome:

If the price continues to $60, the trader benefits from additional profits on the remaining position. If the price reverses, the trader still retains the profits secured at $55, minimizing the emotional and financial impact of the reversal.

Example 4: Avoiding Overexposure Through Correlation Awareness

Scenario:

A trader spots bullish setups in two correlated assets, such as gold and silver. Entering both trades simultaneously increases exposure to the same market movement.

Actionable Risk Management:

Chapter 22:
Case Studies

- Instead of taking full positions in both assets, the trader halves the position size for each. This adjustment reduces the overall risk while still participating in both setups.

Outcome:

If the market moves unfavorably, the reduced exposure limits the total loss. If both trades succeed, the trader achieves a balanced profit without overleveraging.

Example 5: Managing Risk During High Volatility

Scenario:

A major economic announcement is expected, and the markets are highly volatile. The trader identifies a setup but is aware that price swings could exceed normal ranges.

Actionable Risk Management:

- The trader reduces the position size to account for the increased volatility and widens the stop-loss to avoid being stopped out prematurely.

- Alternatively, the trader waits for the announcement to pass before entering the trade, reducing exposure to unpredictable movements.

Outcome:

By adjusting the approach to suit the volatility, the trader minimizes the risk of large, unexpected losses while maintaining discipline and control.

Key Takeaways from Risk Management Examples

- Always calculate position size based on predefined risk parameters, ensuring no single trade jeopardizes your capital.

- Use stop-loss orders strategically to protect against adverse movements while allowing the trade room to develop.

- Adjust risk and position size according to market conditions, such as increased volatility or correlated trades.

- Lock in profits through scaling out and trailing stop-losses to reduce risk and secure gains.

Effective risk management is what transforms a trading plan into a sustainable strategy. These examples demonstrate that by consistently applying risk management principles, you can navigate the markets with confidence, protect your capital, and achieve long-term success. Risk management isn't just a safeguard—it's a competitive edge in the ever-changing landscape of trading.

Conclusion:
The Path to Trading Mastery

SUMMARY OF KEY CONCEPTS

Summary of Key Concepts

As we reach the conclusion of this comprehensive guide, it's important to consolidate the key concepts that form the foundation of successful trading. These principles, when applied consistently and with discipline, can help you navigate the complexities of the financial markets and build a robust, profitable trading practice.

Core Principles of Candlestick and Chart Pattern Trading

1. **Candlestick Patterns:**

   Candlestick patterns provide an immediate visual representation of market sentiment. From single candlesticks like the hammer to more complex formations like the morning star, these patterns reveal critical shifts in buyer and seller dynamics.

2. **Chart Patterns:**

   Chart patterns, such as head and shoulders or triangles, showcase the structure of market trends. Recognizing these patterns within the broader market context enhances the probability of successful trades.

3. **Technical Indicators and Integration:**

   Using indicators like RSI, MACD, and moving averages alongside patterns strengthens trade validation. These tools provide additional layers of analysis, allowing for more precise entries and exits.

Risk Management and Psychology

1. **Risk Management Framework:**

   Protecting capital is paramount. Strategies like position sizing, drawdown control, and adapting to volatility ensure long-term sustainability.

2. **Trading Psychology:**

   Emotional discipline, including managing fear and greed, is the cornerstone of consistent trading performance. Building mental resilience and maintaining confidence are vital to handling market fluctuations.

Practical Application

Conclusion:
The Path to Trading Mastery

1. **Time Frame Relationships:**

    Aligning higher and lower time frames improves trade accuracy, enabling traders to identify the best opportunities while avoiding noise.

2. **Sector and Market Correlation:**

    Recognizing how sectors interact with the broader market provides deeper insights into asset behavior, helping traders align strategies with macroeconomic trends.

3. **Case Studies and Real-World Examples:**

    Practical examples showcase the application of theory in real trading environments, reinforcing the importance of preparation, execution, and adaptation.

By internalizing these concepts and treating trading as a disciplined craft, you are equipped to build a strong foundation for continued growth and mastery. Remember, consistent success in trading doesn't come from a single strategy or tool but from the ability to adapt, learn, and evolve with the markets.

CREATING YOUR TRADING PLAN

A trading plan is your roadmap to navigating the financial markets with clarity, discipline, and consistency. It is the foundation of a successful trading career, outlining your objectives, strategies, risk management rules, and routines. Without a clear plan, traders are more likely to make impulsive decisions driven by emotions, leading to inconsistency and losses.

Why a Trading Plan is Essential

1. **Provides Structure:**

    A plan defines your approach to the market, removing guesswork from decision-making.

2. **Reduces Emotional Trading:**

    Predefined rules minimize the impact of fear and greed on your trades.

3. **Improves Consistency:**

    Following a structured plan ensures that your trading actions align with your overall goals.

4. **Facilitates Evaluation:**

    A written plan allows you to review and refine your strategies, improving performance over time.

Steps to Create Your Trading Plan

1. **Define Your Objectives:**

    - **What do you want to achieve?** Are you trading for supplemental income, wealth generation, or long-term investment?

- Set measurable goals, such as monthly return targets, risk-to-reward ratios, or account growth milestones.

Example Objective: "Achieve a 5% monthly return while maintaining a maximum drawdown of 10%."

2. **Choose Your Market and Instruments:**
   - Decide which markets (stocks, forex, commodities, cryptocurrencies) and instruments (specific pairs, ETFs, or sectors) you will trade.
   - Focus on instruments you understand and that align with your strategy.

Example: "Trade major currency pairs and S&P 500 ETFs due to their liquidity and consistent volatility."

3. **Establish Your Strategy:**

Outline your trading strategies, including the patterns and indicators you will use. Be specific about your entry, exit, and confirmation criteria.

Example:
   - Look for bullish engulfing patterns near support levels.
   - Confirm trades with RSI below 30 and a MACD bullish crossover.
   - Exit when price reaches resistance or RSI exceeds 70.

4. **Define Risk Management Rules:**
   - Determine how much of your account you are willing to risk on each trade and overall.
   - Include rules for position sizing, stop-loss placement, and managing drawdowns.

Example:
   - Risk no more than 1% of capital per trade.
   - Set stop-losses below recent support levels, targeting a 1:3 risk-to-reward ratio.

5. **Set Timeframes and Schedule:**
   - Specify the timeframes you will trade (daily, 4-hour, hourly).
   - Decide your trading schedule based on market hours and your availability.

Example: "Analyze charts during the New York session and review trades daily after market close."

6. **Incorporate Market Analysis:**
   - Include a routine for analyzing broader market trends, sector performance, and news events.
   - Adapt your trading strategy to align with prevailing conditions.

Conclusion:
The Path to Trading Mastery

7. **Create a Trade Journal Template:**
   - Develop a system for recording every trade. Include entry/exit details, rationale, and outcomes.

Sample Trading Plan Framework

Objective:

Achieve consistent monthly account growth of 5% with a maximum drawdown of 10%.

Market and Instruments:

Trade S&P 500 ETFs and EUR/USD during New York trading hours.

Strategy:

- Focus on candlestick patterns like bullish engulfing and hammer formations.
- Confirm trades with RSI and MACD indicators.
- Target a 1:3 risk-to-reward ratio.

Risk Management:

- Risk no more than 1% of account capital per trade.
- Stop-loss placed below key support levels or recent lows.
- Exit trades at predefined profit targets or based on reversal signals.

Daily Routine:

- Morning: Analyze market trends and set alerts for key levels.
- During Session: Monitor setups on hourly and 4-hour charts.
- Evening: Review completed trades and journal observations.

Evaluating and Refining Your Plan

A trading plan is not static; it evolves with your skills and market changes. Regularly review your plan to:

1. Identify areas for improvement based on trade outcomes.
2. Adjust strategies for changing market conditions.
3. Incorporate lessons learned from mistakes or missed opportunities.

Key Takeaways

- A well-defined trading plan is your guide to disciplined and consistent trading.
- Include clear objectives, strategies, risk management rules, and routines.
- Regularly evaluate and refine your plan to stay aligned with market dynamics and personal growth.

By adhering to your trading plan, you establish a solid foundation for achieving long-term success in the financial markets.

FINAL THOUGHTS AND RECOMMENDATIONS

As we conclude this journey through the intricate world of trading, it's important to reflect on the key takeaways and actionable steps that will empower you to navigate the markets with confidence, discipline, and resilience. Trading is not merely about understanding charts and patterns; it is a dynamic, ever-evolving craft that demands a balance of technical expertise, psychological fortitude, and strategic precision.

The Power of Knowledge and Preparation

Knowledge is your greatest ally in the markets. By mastering candlestick patterns, chart analysis, technical indicators, and risk management, you've equipped yourself with the tools necessary for success. However, knowledge alone isn't enough—it's the consistent application of this knowledge through practice and refinement that sets successful traders apart.

- **Embrace Lifelong Learning:** Markets evolve, and so must you. Stay curious and committed to improving your skills.
- **Practice Deliberately:** Use tools like backtesting and demo accounts to test your strategies in a risk-free environment.
- **Stay Informed:** Keep abreast of global market trends, economic data, and sector performance to maintain an edge.

Building Your Edge

Your edge is what separates you from the masses in the market. It's the unique combination of your trading style, strategies, and psychological discipline. To refine your edge:

- **Focus on Your Strengths:** Whether it's pattern recognition, sector analysis, or short-term trades, double down on what you do best.
- **Avoid Overcomplication:** Simplicity often leads to clarity and better decision-making. A concise, well-defined strategy is more effective than one cluttered with conflicting signals.
- **Leverage Technology:** Use modern tools and platforms to enhance your analysis and execution efficiency.

Mindset Matters

Trading success is as much about mindset as it is about mechanics. The emotional highs and lows of the markets can test even the most experienced traders, making psychological resilience a cornerstone of long-term success.

Conclusion:
The Path to Trading Mastery

- **Accept Losses as Part of the Game:** Even the best setups can fail. Learn from losses without letting them erode your confidence.
- **Stay Disciplined:** Stick to your trading plan, even during periods of uncertainty or drawdown. Deviating out of frustration often leads to larger losses.
- **Cultivate Patience:** Success in trading is a marathon, not a sprint. Focus on steady, incremental growth rather than chasing quick wins.

Your Trading Journey

As you move forward, keep in mind that trading is deeply personal. Your journey will be shaped by your unique experiences, goals, and challenges. While this book provides a comprehensive framework, the responsibility of turning knowledge into action lies with you.

- **Set Clear Goals:** Define what success looks like for you—whether it's financial independence, supplemental income, or intellectual challenge.
- **Track Your Progress:** Maintain a detailed trade journal to analyze your performance, identify patterns, and refine your approach.
- **Celebrate Milestones:** Acknowledge your achievements, no matter how small, to stay motivated and confident.

Recommendations for Ongoing Growth

1. **Join a Trading Community:** Engage with other traders to exchange ideas, share insights, and stay motivated.
2. **Expand Your Skillset:** Explore advanced topics like algorithmic trading, intermarket analysis, or options strategies as your expertise grows.
3. **Seek Mentorship:** Learning from experienced traders can accelerate your growth and help you avoid common pitfalls.
4. **Invest in Quality Resources:** Continue to educate yourself with books, courses, and tools that align with your trading goals.

Final Words

Trading is a craft that combines art, science, and discipline. It's a journey filled with challenges but also immense opportunities for personal and financial growth. By mastering the skills outlined in this book, adhering to your trading plan, and maintaining a growth mindset, you are well-equipped to thrive in the financial markets.

Remember, success doesn't come overnight. Be patient with yourself, trust the process, and remain committed to continuous improvement. The markets will reward those who persevere with knowledge, discipline, and an unwavering belief in their ability to succeed.

Now it's your turn. Take what you've learned, apply it with confidence, and forge your own path to trading mastery.